MOTORCYCLE
TOURING & TRAVEL

by Bill Stermer • Second Edition

A HANDBOOK OF TRAVEL BY MOTORCYCLE

A Whirlaway Book
Whitehorse Press
North Conway, New Hampshire

Photography by the author unless otherwise noted.

Cover illustrations by Hector Cademartori

We recognize that some words, model names and designations mentioned herein are the property of the trademark holder. We use them for identification purposes only.

The names Whirlaway and Whitehorse Press are trademarks of Kennedy Associates.

Whitehorse Press books are also available at discounts in bulk quantity for sales and promotional use. For details about special sales or for a catalog of motorcycling books and videos, write to the publisher:

Whitehorse Press
P.O. Box 60
North Conway, New Hampshire 03860-0060

ISBN 1-884313-15-9

5   4   3   2

Printed in the United States

I dedicate this book to Margery, without whose smiling face and love, all the hard work would not have been worth it.

Acknowledgements

Where do you begin, and where do you end, in naming the people who have increased your knowledge of motorcycling and helped to make this book possible? In no particular order I thank: Cook Neilson, Clement Salvadori, Joe Salluzzo, Mark Tuttle Jr., Reg Pridmore, Chad Vick, Scott Hartley, Carl Munter—and my sister Judy, who complains that I never mention her in my articles.

Contents

Introduction

This book is an outgrowth of my previous book, *Motorcycle Touring*, published in 1982 and called by some the definitive work on the subject. But much had changed in the intervening decade when, in 1991, I wrote *Motorcycle Touring and Travel* to take into account the rise of factory dressers and sport-touring machines, the hard-edged sport, and of course many technological advances in tires, oil, clothing, fairings, and just about every other aspect of motorcycle touring and travel. Here we are in 1999 and as we look back, many other changes are evident in our motorcycling world. This second edition of *Motorcycle Touring and Travel* will bring the subject up to date again, if only for a short time.

This book is an attempt to build upon the basic information contained in my earlier books, but to cover the subjects in much more detail while addressing the changes of the last decade. At times, of necessity, the book is repetitive because the same information may be presented in different contexts.

As some things change, others stay the same. A person who has read my earlier books will come across an occasional passage here or there that seems about the same as before; yet, 90 percent of this book is brand new, and the other ten percent rewritten. A few photographs have been re-used where appropriate, but perhaps 70 percent of the photos here are new and as current as publishing allows.

The one thing that does not change is the human desire to travel and to see new things. To all riders I wish that you may have the wind at your back, a song in your heart, and the angel of good fortune riding on your shoulder.

Bill Stermer

1
Motorcycle Touring and Travel

THE WORLD OF TOURING

Motorcycle touring and motorcycle travel are virtually synonymous. I use both terms in this book because, to some people, touring is exclusive to only large motorcycles with fairings, trunks, and saddlebags; however, people travel on many other types and sizes of machines.

Touring is simply travel by motorcycle. Any motorcycle. Anywhere. It is usually differentiated from "day tripping" in that touring involves an overnight stay. Touring is a doctor and his wife riding from Chicago to Pleasant Lake to spend the Memorial Day weekend. It's three good friends from Calgary who follow the Rockies down to Colorado on their lightly loaded sport bikes, camping out for a week in the mountains. Touring is two couples from Alexandria who ride the Blue Ridge Parkway south to catch the spring flowers in bloom.

What else is touring? It's anything you can imagine plus everything in between. It's a grizzled, long-haired drifter who lashes a sleeping bag to his bike's seat and keeps all his worldly possessions in a pair of leather saddlebags. And the young European couple who load huge amounts of luggage to their single-cylinder, dual-sport bike and head off through Africa on their way to Australia, South America, Alaska, and eventually back home. Put one or more people on one or more motorcycles, send them out overnight traveling, and they're touring. I can't put it any more precisely than that.

Why do people tour? Like the mountaineer who saw the peak in the misty half light of morning, because it's there. People like new experiences and love to travel. Let's keep it as simple as that.

Touring has long been linked to the full-dress motorcycle with its fairing, saddlebags and trunk.

Part of the fun of touring is going places with friends, meeting new people and going new places.

Touring is simply travel by motorcycle—any motorcycle.

A sporting machine, such as this BMW K1200RS, becomes an excellent sport-tourer with the addition of hard-sided saddlebags.

Any competent street-legal motorcycle can offer great joy on tour. Yamaha's four-cylinder, 600cc Seca II is essentially a standard motorcycle with an attractive and sporty fairing added. (Photo courtesy of Yamaha Motor Corporation, USA)

Who says you need a big dresser to tour? I met this European couple traveling on a heavily loaded 400cc twin.

The Vetter Windjammer fairing was the touring look of the 1970s. In the 1980s, the look evolved to the integrated factory dresser with color-matched fairing and luggage.

2

Choosing Your Motorcycle

WHICH TYPE IS BEST FOR YOU

In the years since 1982 when I wrote my original book, *Motorcycle Touring,* much has changed. Just two years prior, in 1980, Honda had introduced its new GL1100 Gold Wing Interstate with standard color-matched fairing, saddlebags, and trunk—and created a sensation! Until then, riders (unless they owned certain Harley-Davidson models, or the BMW R100RT introduced in 1979) who wanted to travel by motorcycle had to find, buy, and mount their own accessories to block the wind and to carry their luggage. All of that changed with the GL1100, BMW R100RT, Harley-Davidson FLH dressers and other similar machines.

Following the success of Honda's new fully-dressed Gold Wing, Yamaha introduced its Venture tourers, Suzuki its Cavalcade, and Kawasaki its Voyager series. These bikes, taken in concert with existing Harley-Davidson and BMW models, meant that the dresser revolution was under way.

But, just as dresser models were taking over the touring market, another revolution happened in the 1980s with the advent of sport touring as a separate, identifiable type of riding with its own set of machines and riders. Sport touring really originated years earlier when riders equipped their bikes for this duty by adding smaller saddlebags and cafe fairings, but it wasn't institutionalized until the motorcycle manufacturing companies, also known as the Original Equipment Manufacturers (OEMs), began offering such bikes from the factory.

I define a sport tourer as a sporting oriented motorcycle that comes with a smaller, more sporting fairing and is often equipped with hard-sided, removable saddlebags for touring. BMW started it all with its R90S model in 1974 and added its R100RS twin in 1977. Since then we've seen other sport tourers such as the

Moto Guzzi 1000SP from Italy, and the Japanese have contributed the Kawasaki Concours, the Suzuki Katanas in several sizes, Honda's ST1100, and Yamaha's FJ series. Even Ducati, long known for its sport bikes, has given us a touring version with detachable bags called the ST2. And of course, nearly any BMW model can be equipped with hard-sided, removable bags. Riders also tour on other sport-oriented machines that don't fit this specific definition.

But motorcycle touring has undergone a gradual transformation of late. Today, one of the premier dresser touring machines is Honda's GL1500/6 Gold Wing, a huge, heavy, but extremely competent 1520cc six-cylinder machine that can take two people in luxury anywhere that roads go. And the only other full-

Though small, the agile Kawasaki 250 Ninja can make a competent touring mount if you're willing to accept the fact that long-distance comfort may not be part of the package. (Photo courtesy of Kawasaki Motors Corp., USA)

size dressers are the traditional Kawasaki Voyager XII and the brand-new BMW K1200LT luxury tourer.

I feel it is both significant and regrettable that the engines of premier touring machines have exactly doubled in displacement in the past 20 years. From the first FLH, through the 750s and to the 1500 of today, the implication has increasingly become that in order to go touring you need an ever larger, ever heavier, and ever more complex bike. There is one fact that you need to understand immediately: you do *not* need a big, heavy, complex motorcycle on which to go touring.

What you do need is simply a reliable, street-legal motorcycle that is capable of carrying the required number of persons and luggage. That's all. You can tour, and I guarantee you that people *have* toured, on a 550cc four, a 350cc twin, and a 125cc single. I know, because I have personally owned bikes that fit each of those descriptions, and have taken overnight trips on each—including a passenger on the two larger bikes.

Another dramatic shift in the touring market has occcured in the late 1990s. The movement really began when Harley-Davidson introduced its Road King model in 1994, a successor to its Electra Glide Sport. Here was a hybrid model, one with all the underpinnings of a dresser motorcycle, but without the heavy fairing, trunk and fancy radio and such. All the Road King offered was a windshield and a set of saddlebags, but that was enough. The model was a huge success, as it was equally at home cruising on the boulevard as it was heading for Daytona Beach, Florida, for Bike Week, or any other long-distance destination.

Soon Yamaha was emulating it with the Tour Classic model of its new Royal Star cruiser in 1996, Honda offered its Shadow 1100 Tourer in '97 and the following year Kawasaki added bags and a shield to one of its models to create the Nomad. For 1999 both Honda and Yamaha introduced cruisers with fairings and hard saddlebags. The new Valkyrie Interstate and Royal Star Venture models were based upon engines that just happened to be in the companies' dresser models only a few years earlier. Cruiser touring was gaining momentum.

The beauty of cruiser touring is that its a simpler form of "bedroll" touring. Where dressers are gussied up with radios and tape players and CBs, and all sorts of bells and whistles, cruiser tourers are simpler, more basic and less expensive. And to some this is perhaps more of a means of "getting away from it all" than a dresser.

Considerations in Choosing a Motorcycle

The bike on which most people choose to tour tends to be the one they own at the time. In other words, the bike came before the need arose. I have seen teenagers touring in Michigan's Upper Peninsula on dual-sport (also called dual-purpose) bikes, having the time of their lives. By the way, dual-sports are usually single-cylinder machines that are street-legal, yet are based upon dirt bikes so they can be taken on trails. Adventure Tourers are usually larger machines such as the BMW GS series and Triumph Tiger that can be ridden great distances on rough dirt roads, but aren't intended for serious off-road bashing. And In Europe, I've seen couples in full leathers and helmets touring on relatively tiny 450cc machines with a huge bundle of camping gear lashed to the back. And I've seen a man ride a Vespa motor scooter from Tijuana, Mexico, to Vancouver, British Columbia—a distance of about 1,400 miles—in three days during an international poker run called The Three Flags Classic. Certainly any reliable, street-legal motorcycle can deliver you to and from your destination, but some will be better suited to the task than others. Let's look at some of the basic requirements for a touring bike.

The most basic requirement is reliability—that is, it must be mechanically sound and in good operating condition. Obviously if the machine won't run, you won't get there. Virtually every major brand motorcycle sold in the United States in the past 25 years should, if properly maintained, be capable of running many thousands of miles without fear of major mechanical problems.

Next, while you're riding along you require a reasonable degree of comfort. This means a freedom from intrusive vibration that puts your extremities to sleep. It also means maintaining a seating position that is neither cramped, nor one that holds your feet, hands or body in an extreme position caused by a lack of forethought in the placement of the footpegs, handgrips, or by any aberrations in the seat.

Furthermore, the bike should not intrude upon your thoughts. Rather, it should allow you to observe the countryside and breathe the air freely. Your mind should remain uncluttered by thoughts of, "Ooh, that hurts," or "I just hope this thing holds together until I get there." Like a good child, a touring bike should be seen but not heard.

Third, a touring—or travel—machine should be relatively maintenance free. Sure, many of us like to tinker with our bikes on a Saturday morning with all of our tools laid out, a roof over our heads and another vehicle available should things go wrong. That's when an oil change, chain adjustment, valve check or fork oil change is fun. But these rituals lose their charm when they need to be performed in a backwoods campground without the proper tools, the proper parts and adequate lighting, with billows of dust blowing everywhere and a 500-mile day staring us in the face.

The motorcycle must offer a sufficient Gross Vehicle Weight Rating (GVWR) to carry safely any load you're likely to haul. It must be large enough to enable a rider—or two—to spread out upon it. Fuel capacity and economy should be balanced to provide a reasonable range, say at least 150 miles, between gas stops. In some remote areas, less range is simply not sufficient.

For lack of a better word, the ideal touring bike is "competent." This includes many subjective, but nevertheless discernible, traits. The bike must have adequate power to haul a rider, passenger and luggage up, down, and around anything the route may throw at them. It must feel right when you sit on it or take a turn with it. It must stop with confidence, and its suspension must soak up the bumps while keeping the tires firmly planted on the surface. There should be no kinks in the drive chain, rough spots in the steering, high-speed weave or low-speed shudder. It shouldn't leak from the petcocks or leave an oil slick every time it's parked.

This cheeseburger trike gives a whole new meaning to the term "road food."

Simply, it must work well enough to inspire confidence in the rider and not intrude upon his or her enjoyment of the trip.

Motorcycles have become much larger, heavier and more complex since the 1960s. In that decade, a Triumph 650 was a big, fast bike. When the Honda 450 arrived in mid-decade, it caused a sensation. It was a big bike for a Japanese machine, and it arrived at a time when common engine sizes of Japanese bikes ranged from 50cc to 350cc. In the decades since, we have seen bikes from Japan with three times the engine displacement of the Honda 450, yet people did in fact tour on those little machines—and they had fun on them. You can have fun on them, too, once you understand what effect engine displacement has upon touring suitability, and choose accordingly.

Engine Displacement

How big a bike do you need to tour? One that's big enough to do the job. Engine displacement in motorcycles is generally measured in cubic centimeters, a metric unit that corresponds to 0.061 cubic inches and is abbreviated "cc." One liter is 1,000cc, which corresponds to about 61 cubic inches. Harley-Davidsons, which are manufactured in the United States, measure their big engines in cubic inches (at this writing, they're 88 cubic inches, or 1450cc). Harley's small bike is called the 883 for its cubic-centimeter displacement; it displaces about 54 cubic inches.

Engine displacement refers to the amount of volume displaced by the piston(s) in an engine when they move from the bottom of their stroke to the top. The displacement figure for each piston, multiplied by the number of pistons in the engine (its number of cylinders), gives you the total displacement for the engine.

Each motorcycle is a compromise, with strong and weak points in various areas of use. Here, Isle of Man TT legend Joey Dunlop jumps Ballaugh Bridge on his way to another win. Though a truly exciting ride, his two-stroke Castrol Honda racer would not be suitable for touring use.

Hans and Ursula, from Austria, rode this Honda dual-sport around the world together.

The greater the displacement, the greater the potential for power and performance—though so many variables are involved that there is no direct, linear relationship between displacement and horsepower any longer. For example, some turn-of-the century motorcycles had huge 1000cc engines but, because of the technological limitations of the time, produced only six to eight horsepower. Today, some 600cc sport bikes produce in excess of 100 horsepower, which is more power than that produced by many larger touring bikes. Race tuners have been able to coax about 180 horsepower from only 500cc in a grand prix bike.

As mentioned earlier, the engine size of "big" bikes about doubled in the decades between 1970 and 1990. Horsepower has also increased a great deal. A 750cc bike in 1970 was likely to produce between 55 and 75 horsepower. By 1998, a bike of the same displacement was able to crank out well in excess of 100 horsepower.

To merely admire the horsepower figures that modern engineers have produced is to look in the wrong direction. While increased horsepower is definitely useful and certainly fun, motorcycle touring and travel, unlike motorcycle racing, demands a vastly wider array of attributes than simply raw horsepower. Let's look at some of them, and how these attributes are likely to be sprinkled throughout the various displacement classes.

Fads and fashion in motorcycle size have changed over the years. In the 1960s, riders tended to begin riding bikes of 250cc or smaller and then graduated to a 350, while bikes of 500 to 650cc were considered big and intimidating. Honda's CB750 four-cylinder that was introduced in 1969 was, hands down, the most influential bike on the motorcycling scene in the last 35 years, and its influence has been felt ever since. Consider that it was the first truly modern four-cylinder, the first to offer a disc brake as standard equipment, a wonder of smoothness, and priced at only $1,498. Its sophistication and technical credentials, with its low price, lured many people to abandon their smaller machines and leap right onto a Honda 750.

When Honda's CB750 helped to destroy the traditional step-up approach to engine displacement, riders were now suddenly leaping from 125s and 350s onto much larger bikes. That trend continues today, as riders are likely to start riding midsized or larger machines, and some first-time touring riders leap right onto huge 1000cc or larger machines.

The point to remember about engine displacement in motorcycles is that you can travel on virtually any size of machine that is street legal, as long as you're willing to put up with its limitations. My first long tour, from Michigan to Virginia, was on a Honda CB350 that withstood the 800 miles just fine. My riding buddy on that trip weighed 240 pounds—which outweighed his 160cc Honda. The seat did not suit his rather generous rear porch very well, and he was in some pain, but we had an absolutely wonderful ride!

In addition, some good friends of ours, who are from Austria, toured the world two-up (two people on the motorcycle) on a 600cc dual-sport single designed for on- and off-road use. Hans carried a spare tire on a rack bolted to the fork, and their belongings were piled high on the back of their bike. Before feeling too sorry for them, consider that they had chosen the perfect motorcycle for their trip—as in South America and Alaska they traveled in areas in which the roads were little more than trails. When it rained they sometimes had to physically wrestle the machine out of the mud. A dresser would have bogged down very early into the trip and never would have survived the raft trip they had to take across a wild river. In touring, less can often be more.

Keep in mind that smaller bikes, those below the 750cc class, have many advantages over their larger brethren. Besides being less expensive to buy, they are usually also less expensive to insure, get better fuel mileage, weigh less, require less expensive parts, and are very maneuverable. Finally, riders who are smaller in stature will appreciate their lighter weight. Here are some basics about general displacement classes.

Below 350cc. In the below 350cc category you'll find an array of single- and twin-cylinder machines, usually air-cooled and of rather diminutive proportions. A major criterion for any motorcycle used for travel is that it should be able to maintain the speed limit while carrying its rider and luggage, and have a little more available for hills and passing. By this I mean it should not simply have a top speed of at least 55 to 65 MPH; rather it should be able to travel comfortably at those speeds, with its top speed being somewhat higher.

This consideration virtually rules out machines smaller than about 200cc, and generally a 250cc is considered about the smallest machine you would practically consider for serious on-road touring. Also, some states have minimum size or horsepower requirements regulating which machines can travel their freeways. While it may be possible to ride a 90cc machine across the United States, it may not be possible to do so on the national freeway system. You may love back-road riding, but still, for safety's sake, a bike has to be fast enough at least to get out of its own way. Anything much smaller than 250cc is not recommended for touring unless you're going to travel trails

Engine displacement is a very important consideration in your choice of a motorcycle.

and rough roads. I definitely do *not* recommend a bike as small as a 250 if you're going to travel *two-up*.

Another consideration of touring on smaller bikes is that even though they may be capable of a top speed of 75 to 80 MPH, while traveling at legal freeway speeds their little engines may be turning at 75 to 80 percent of their maximum allowable RPM. This may produce a level of mechanical frenzy that the rider(s) find annoying, and which may intrude upon their enjoyment of their trip.

Also be aware that each machine has a load factor as to the amount of weight it can safely carry. Smaller motorcycles have more diminutive tires, wheels, frame

A 250cc machine, like this Honda Nighthawk, is about the smallest bike you should consider for highway use or serious travel. (Photo courtesy of American Honda Motor Co., Inc.)

A 500cc twin, like this Kawasaki Ninja 500, would be fine for middleweight travel if the rider and passenger were not too physically large. (Photo courtesy of Kawasaki Motors Corp., USA)

Sporting bikes, like this Honda VFR750, can easily be put to touring use with the addition of soft luggage. The author comfortably rode this bike to Colorado, covering more than 1,200 miles in two days. There he toured the Rockies for a week and then rode back to California again in two days.

and suspension components, and thus have a lower "Gross Vehicle Weight Rating" (GVWR) than larger machines. This factor refers to the maximum amount of weight a particular motorcycle should carry; the amount is listed on a plate usually attached to the steering stem, but it could be elsewhere on the frame. Don't think that just because you can't afford a 500cc bike, you'll get a 250 and load it with the same amount of weight. Things simply don't work that way. I'll cover this point in more detail later in this chapter.

Finally, smaller bikes have smaller seats and fuel tanks, and are proportioned smaller overall, leaving less room on which to mount a tank bag, saddlebags, or other luggage. The physical limitations of the machines may limit what you can carry on them. Because they aren't considered seriously for touring, accessory manufacturers do not offer as many accessories such as fairings, windscreens, luggage racks, etc., for them.

400–499cc.

Many of the machines in the 400–499cc class are twin-cylinder, freeway-legal models that are adequate for comfortable solo touring, and will carry a passenger. They're ideal for the budget-minded rider who wants adequacy in terms of power and size, and a realistic expectation of getting 60 miles per gallon on the road.

In general, these smaller bikes have less sophisticated suspensions and engines—they may not be liquid cooled, though some are. They usually do not offer a driveshaft, which is a disadvantage because a shaft increases reliability and requires little maintenance.

Even considering such drawbacks, some of my most enjoyable rides have been on such smaller machines—further evidence that the reason why we tour resides in the heart and guts rather than in the machinery.

Especially for solo riders, bikes in this class are adequate for weekending and week-at-a-time tours. For two-up tourers, they're not likely to offer sufficient load capacity for all you may want to take. For longer rides their cramped quarters and busy engines make them less than satisfying.

500–659cc.

Chances are that motorcyclists who live by the golden mean, "Everything in moderation—nothing to excess," ride bikes in the 500 to 659cc class. On a pound-for-pound basis, middleweights are extremely competent motorcycles. They're proportioned adequately so that the average-sized rider can be comfortable aboard them for hours at a time. I could say they provide adequate power, but that's like saying a grizzly bear has adequate power to rip open a plastic garbage sack. Some sport bikes in this category produce more than 100 horsepower!

On the other hand, bikes in this class have an identity problem. We live in a society that indulges itself in wretched excess, and these machines don't play that game. Too many riders automatically think of touring as requiring a huge amount of size and power, and don't believe these bikes can deliver. They're wrong. The realities of a conservative national speed limit, nonrenewable natural resources, and the usual financial burdens make these bikes a sensible alternative.

Sidestand Sense

What to do when over she goes

In Japan, before they can get their motorcycle licenses, riders must demonstrate the ability to pick up a 500cc motorcycle once it has been set on its side. Apparently, the Japanese don't want their roadways clogged with downed bikes blocking traffic or leaking their various vital fluids onto the roadway.

You and I, as riders, have our own reasons for wanting to get our bikes aright as soon as possible—it's downright embarrassing to have that big hunka metal on the ground, and in an isolated campground where you've camped alone, you may not be able to leave unless you can get your bike aright yourself. It's food for thought.

In the Western Hemisphere, being able to right your downed bike is not a common requirement, but it's good to be able to do so when the need arises. In the '60s, bell-bottom pants were a common cause of falls as the generous cuffs would catch on a peg or other protruding piece when the rider tried to put his foot down. The most common reason people drop their bikes today is footing problems involving oil, wetness, gravel or pavement irregularities. The lesson here is to look before you pull to a halt, especially if your bike is heavy enough to be a handful under normal riding conditions.

The second most common reason bikes fall over is careless use of the sidestand. Under the influence of a hot sun, asphalt can turn to the consistency of tapioca pudding, a fact first noticed by the part of the motorcycle bearing the greatest weight per square inch. Plop. Some riders carry a thin piece of tin for use under their sidestand in these situations. An aluminum can, crushed flat, will also do in a pinch.

Okay, let's say all else fails and you still suffer the ignominy of dropping your bike. How do you set it back on its wheels? Well, you're talking to a guy who is still proud of the fact that, 20 years ago, he righted an enormous Kawasaki KZ1300 six—alone. I was in the desert, the day

was quite hot, and I had stepped into some oil in a parking lot. Also, I weigh about 155 pounds.

Step One: If it's going to be a struggle, pull off everything easily removable including the tank bag and other luggage including removable saddlebags.

Step Two: The handlebar is really the only suitable handhold for a solo rider to use in righting a downed bike. If you have help, have them get on the low side of the bike and push up on something solid such as a frame rail, fixed saddlebag or lifting handle. Avoid putting your weight against something that could give way, such as a seat, fender, rack or backrest.

I knew I couldn't dead lift the Kawi, do I did the next best thing. I knelt beside the bike, wrestled the handlebar inches off the pavement, and wedged my knee under it. Slowly, by lifting and wedging my leg further and further up the bar, I was able then to begin wedging my other leg under the tank. Eventually, I was able to raise the bike to a position from which I could stand it upright. If you're faced with this situation, keep in mind that rocks or logs can be rolled under the bike as need be, though they can make a mess of your paint.

The big Kawasaki weighed perhaps 700 pounds, and I have since dropped a fully dressed Gold Wing in a field while photographing it alone. At the time I soon learned that because a dresser carries its weight higher and has considerably more of it, I was unable to right it myself. Luckily, a friendly motorist stopped by and gave me a hand.

Since then, I have learned another key to righting dressers. As the personnel at Honda have demonstrated, the key to lifting a GL1500 Gold Wing alone (once you have emptied the bags, of course) is to back up to the bike and grasp a handlebar grip with one hand, and some other solid handhold with the other. Now, facing away from the bike, straighten your legs and pick it up. Easy for me to say, but I've seen it done by an average-size person.

■

Suzuki's Katana is a good all-around sporting tourer. It is not as heavy or expensive as traditional sport tourers, yet provides the added dimension of sportiness without an extreme riding position.

One of today's premiere all-around sporting machines is Honda's CBR1100XX. At a test track, the author was clocked at 165 mph on this machine by a radar gun, then installed soft luggage and went for a memorable tour.

They're large enough to tour upon for weeks at a time, as long as you and your partner are not the size or heft of NFL linemen. On the highway their engines are less frenzied than the 400s, yet they boast miles-per-gallon figures from the mid-40s to the mid-50s. Insurance and maintenance costs are lower than those of larger bikes, and many accessories fit midsizers perfectly.

Finally, midsizers deliver a level of performance that, in 1980, was possible only with bike of approximately 900–1000cc. For people who want competence without overkill, midsizers are the golden mean.

700-999cc. Bikes in the 700–999cc class are some of the quickest, fastest and best handling machines in the world. Engine technology has advanced to the point that the absolute biggest engines are no longer considered necessary to deliver top performance. Incredible size means a corresponding amount of weight, and weight is the enemy of good handling. Presently, most of the best sport bikes are in the 600–1000cc class. There is no need to go any larger, as these bikes are cranking out plenty of horsepower to keep the talented, experienced rider well entertained. Many bikes in this class are aimed toward sporting and sport touring riding.

Bikes of 700–999cc are for serious riders who feel their bikes must be as passionately devoted to the sport as they are themselves. Here's enough dragstrip performance to blow away any stock four-wheeler, enough power for a load, sufficient room for two-up touring and a seemingly endless list of accessories. Many bikes in this class offer virtually every innovation known to

motorcycling such as four-valve heads, triple disc brakes, multiadjustable suspension systems, V- or Z-rated radial tires and lightweight aluminum-alloy perimeter frames for great rigidity.

Bikes in this class are excellent for two-up touring, especially sport touring, if their riding positions are not so extreme as to be uncomfortable long-term. If your riding is more passion than pastime, and if you prefer superlatives to mere adequacy, this is *your* class!

1000cc and up. The 1000cc and above range includes bikes that are a continuation of the very quick sport machines from the previous class, and this is the playground of the dressers. (In motorcycling, a *full dresser* is a machine dressed up with a fairing, saddlebags, and often a trunk.) Some folks delight in owning the biggest, fastest or most expensive vehicle, regardless of the practicalities or the speed limits; there's a certain comfort in knowing you can't be outgunned.

In this group we have the epitome of both dresser touring and sport-touring machines. Under most conceivable riding situations, bikes in this class are yawningly understressed. They can take you across the continent quickly, comfortably, and competently. With proper care, any of them should last for years and many thousands of miles. In fact, I know several riders who have put in excess of 100,000 miles on 1000cc or larger machines, and these people don't necessarily ride like the little old lady who just rides to church and back.

Bikes in this class tend to be complex and sophisticated, powerful but heavy, utterly tractable, and smooth. They'll haul two-up in comfort, carry all kinds of accessories, pull a trailer or sidecar—or both—and cross the continent at any speed you'd care to dial in. Yet, these land yachts will deliver fuel mileage figures in the 40s when ridden sanely, or in the 30s when you have to get somewhere far away by nightfall.

Engine size and other considerations. As engine size increases, other components of the motorcycle also must increase in size and weight in order to compensate. For example, a 1000cc machine will usually be equipped with much larger brakes, wheels, tires, frame, suspension components, seats—and even instruments—than a 500cc bike. After all, a Mack truck is more than just a pickup with a big engine.

The extra power of a 1000cc machine offers several benefits, some obvious and some not. We all expect the power to show its usefulness in passing situations and when hauling heavy loads uphill. But these larger engines also tend to produce their power at relatively low engine speeds; therefore, they can be geared to turn fewer RPM at a given road speed in high gear. For example, a Honda GL1500 Gold Wing turns a very conservative 2,600 RPM at 60 MPH in top gear. By contrast, a Honda VFR750 sport machine turns a much busier 4,360 RPM at the same speed and a 500cc machine may turn around 5,000 RPM. The point is that higher revolutions can result in an engine that buzzes more and is therefore less relaxing than the rumble of a larger, slower-turning machine.

Big, slower-turning engines usually require less-frequent maintenance. They also generally last longer than smaller, higher-revving machines. The reason for this is partly explained by doing the math. If you ride your 500cc bike 2,000 miles in high gear, and it turns 5,000 revolutions per mile, by the end of the trip it would have turned 10,000,000 revolutions. On the same trip, a 1500cc machine turning 2,600 revolutions per mile would have turned 5,200,000 revolutions. Fewer revolutions mean fewer openings and closings of valves, sparking of plugs, and spins of the transmission's many shafts and gears. Granted, each of the big engine's yanks is stronger than the little one's, but bigger engines are built with appropriately sized bearings, gears, and other components.

There is not necessarily a direct proportional relationship between smaller and larger engines and maintenance and longevity; however variables in design, construction, care, and use more often will affect a bike's longevity. Still, it has been my experience that bigger engines generally require less frequent

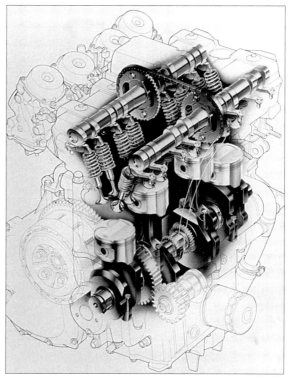

Today's motorcycle engines are high-tech, sophisticated devices that deliver abundant power while requiring relatively little maintenance. (Photo courtesy American Honda)

maintenance and that they last longer than smaller engines. Bikes with larger engines, such as 1200cc BMWs, 1340cc Harley-Davidsons, and 1520cc Honda Gold Wings can be expected to run 100,000 miles and longer without a rebuild, provided they're ridden sanely and given proper care and regular maintenance.

Before you decide to rush out and buy your next motorcycle strictly based upon engine displacement and weight, keep in mind that there are certain disadvantages to owning such a big bike. The first is the usually higher initial price. Insurance costs are higher, and parts cost more. Tires on big road burners may wear out more quickly, and because of their size, they are expensive. Their high degree of complexity can also mean that they're more difficult to work on, resulting in more expensive tuneups and repairs.

Big dresser motorcycles that are ready to roll can weigh from 700 to 900 pounds fully gassed but without luggage. Once underway some of that great weight seems to evaporate, as the bikes are usually well balanced. However, when they have to be muscled out of a garage or around a parking lot, you'll feel much of their weight. Hoisting a big bike that's loaded with luggage onto its centerstand can be a real chore, although some are much easier to deal with than others. Honda's six-cylinder GL1500 crushes the scales at over 900

Shorter riders often, of necessity, must ride smaller bikes that sit lower to the ground, such a this Kawasaki EX500.

pounds, yet its stand is so well designed that the bike can easily be lifted onto it.

Large-displacement, heavy motorcycles are physically large; thus, riders with shorter inseams may have difficulty reaching the ground from the seat. Without secure footing, the operator of a big bike can be intimidated, and in an awkward situation the bike is more likely to get away and tip over.

A small, but sometimes significant, amount of control can be gained for shorter persons by making any or all of the following modifications: 1) add thicker soles to your boots, 2) remove some padding from the seat to place you closer to the ground, or remove it from the front edges of the seat to allow you to get your legs down more easily, 3) remove one or perhaps two coils from each of the coil springs in the suspension (you must remove the same number of coils from each suspension unit at the front or rear of the motorcycle), or 4) slide the front triple-clamp down the fork tubes an inch or two. WARNING: Each of the last two modifications will decrease ground clearance. The suspended parts of the motorcycle will sit closer to the pavement, and will begin to drag sooner when the bike is leaned over in a turn. This can prevent the motorcycle from turning properly, and cause it to run wide in the turn. Grounding out could also lever the tires right off the pavement, causing a loss of control and possibly a crash resulting in injury or death. For these reasons, do

NOT attempt these modifications yourself. Consult a competent mechanic and proceed with extreme caution; if these modifications are performed, relearn the cornering limits of your motorcycle.

Frankly, if you don't feel comfortable with a larger motorcycle, and the situation cannot be easily remedied, shop for a smaller bike.

In Japan, in order to obtain a license for a particular motorcycle, the rider must demonstrate the ability to set it back upright should it tip over. If such a law existed in the United States, sales of dresser models would likely plummet. One final disadvantage of large motorcycles is that should one fall over in a parking lot or on a gravel campground driveway, it is very difficult for one person to stand it upright. I once rode a dresser into a field of flowers to photograph it, and then tipped it over when I hit a plowed rut. The result was a long hike back to the road, and the embarrassment of having to flag down a driver who was willing to help me right the machine.

If you're looking for a small, inexpensive, uncomplicated machine for solo touring, the minimum to consider would be a freeway-legal machine of 250–450cc. Consider a midsizer of 450–500cc as the minimum for traveling two-up comfortably for long distances. Anything else is gravy.

Engine Cylinder Numbers

Not only do motorcycles come in many sizes, types, and weights, but they also vary in the number of cylinders in their engines. Every reciprocating piston engine offers a certain number of cylinders. In simplified terms, the controlled burning of the fuel and air mixture within these cylinders forces the piston(s) down which, through leverage applied via the connecting rods, causes the crankshaft to rotate. This rotating power is fed through the transmission (or gearbox) and eventually finds its way to the rear wheel, which drives the motorcycle.

The number of cylinders in the motorcycle engine offers certain power characteristics of which you should be aware. First, all modern motorcycles are powered by engines having either one, two, three, four, or six cylinders. A V-8 has been tried a few times, but for the foreseeable future it's unlikely we'll ever see eight-cylinder engines in mainstream motorcycles. The arrangement of these cylinders (which I'll talk about in the next section) may be in the inline, vee, or opposed configuration arranged in a number of ways relative to the frame. Let's consider some general characteristics of each cylinder number.

Singles. You can't get much simpler than a single-cylinder engine, which is most commonly used in smaller motorcycles, especially dirt bikes. The single's advantages are low weight, simplicity, and relatively low expense and maintenance.

The single's main problem is that the single piston, slogging up and down inside the cylinder, can create an imbalance which the rider feels as a vibration. The larger the piston, the more likely it is to vibrate as that one cylinder fires once every two crankshaft revolutions in a four-stroke engine. Some manufacturers smooth them with contra-rotating bob weights called *balancers* or *counterbalancers.*

Singles are associated with machines of 600cc and smaller, and often are designed to deliver low-RPM torque rather than high-RPM horsepower; this low-RPM torque gives rise to their nickname "thumpers." The single's unique characteristics make it especially suitable for situations, such as dirt riding, in which low-RPM power is required instantaneously. For touring, however, engine smoothness is valued more highly—which is not the single's forte. While some singles are used for adventure touring on- and off-road, and some notable exceptions do exist such as the old Yamaha SR500 and SR600, singles are not generally considered desirable for pavement touring.

Twins. Two-cylinder engines (twins) are available in a variety of configurations from the transverse inline to the vee and to the opposed. Twins cost a little more to manufacture than singles, but the payoff is that they provide twice as many power pulses per crankshaft revolution as singles. This doubling of power pulses enables twins to run noticeably smoother (if all other factors are equal). Still, some configurations of twins suffer from inbred imbalances, causing many of the more sophisticated twins to utilize counterbalancers for smoothness, or to employ rubber mounts to isolate the vibration from the rider. Horizontally opposed twins and 90-degree V-twins are inherently smoother than other configurations.

Despite having only two cylinders, some of the very largest motorcycle engines made are twins. Current leaders include the Kawasaki 1500 Vulcan, the 1500 Suzuki Intruder, the 1450cc Harley-Davidson Big-Twins and the 92-inch Polaris V92 Victory.

Don't believe that all singles are bare-bones simple. This Kawasaki KLR650 offers a liquid-cooled, four-valve engine. (Photo courtesy of Kawasaki Motors Corp., USA)

Twins can come in any of a number of configurations. Here's a sporting Suzuki TL1000S that carries a longitudinal V-twin. (Photo courtesy of US Suzuki Motor Corporation)

The new Triumph motorcycle company offers its machines primarily as 885cc, liquid-cooled triples in the United States. They are big, long, tall machine, which offer plenty of torque and power. Note the custom bodywork on this machine—it was once featured in a magazine.

One of only two six-cylinder motorcycles offered today (the other is the Gold Wing), the Honda Valkyrie is a performance cruiser that features a hotted-up version of the Wing's flat six. The company also offers touring versions of the same machine. (Photo courtesy of American Honda Motor Co.)

Triples. By positioning the crankshaft throws at 120 degrees apart, triples can offer excellent smoothness with respectable power. Three may sound like an odd number, and it is not a common cylinder count in motorcycling, but some very notable machines have been triples. Remember that the Triumph Trident and BSA 750 Rocket 3 triples were the quickest machines in their day when they were introduced in the late 1960s. The Japanese manufacturers had a love affair with high-powered, lightning-quick two-stroke triples from the early to the middle 1970s, with bikes such as the Kawasaki Mach 1 and Mach 2, and Suzuki's LeMans 500. The Italian company Laverda offered some very torquey, sporting triples in the 1000–1200cc range in the 1970s and into the 1980s. The 750 and 850cc Yamaha triples offered in the same era were notable touring machines. BMW offered very competent 750cc inline flat triples that were renowned for their smoothness and reliability in the '80s and '90s as touring, sport, and basic machines. And Triumph continues to offer 900 triples with wonderful engines.

Fours. Modern, four-cylinder, air-cooled motorcycles were popularized by Honda with its CB750 Four introduced in 1969. The bike was quick, fast, and incredibly smooth. The CB750 Four also introduced the first mass-produced disc brake in motorcycling. The four-cylinder concept had been tried previously, by Henderson and Ace back in the early part of the century, by Indian in the 1940s, and by the exotic Ariel Square Four in the 1950s. Unfortunately, the relatively unsophisticated state of metallurgy of the times led to cooling problems with the early fours, but Honda was the first to mount the engine transversely (across the frame) and the first to do it right.

Four-cylinder engines proliferated following the introduction of the CB750, as every Japanese manufacturer came to offer one or more inline models in the 1970s and '80s. In 1975 Honda introduced its wildly successful opposed four, the GL1000 Gold Wing, which really revolutionized touring in the United States. V-fours were offered by Honda, Yamaha, and Suzuki in touring machines, while BMW's K-series fours are the only flat, inline fours on the market.

Fours offer a great deal of smoothness and reliability with an acceptable level of complication. There's a great deal of performance in the fours, also. Each of the quickest, fastest machines in motorcycling for the last 20 years, and the majority of touring models, have been fours.

Sixes. Because they're so exotic and complex to build, you can count the number of standard-production, six-cylinder motorcycles on the fingers of one hand. Benelli introduced a 750cc six, appropriately called the *Sei* (Six), in the 1970s, followed by a 900. In 1978, Honda caused a stir by introducing the sporting, air-cooled CBX six-cylinder that displaced 1047cc. At the time it was the quickest and fastest motorcycle available. The following year, Kawasaki countered with a touring six, the KZ1300, which offered liquid cooling and a driveshaft.

The only sixes currently sold in the United States are from Honda. Their GL1500/6 Gold Wing made its debut in 1988, and is still considered by many to be the premier dresser machine available. Honda's other six is the Valkyrie, a cruiser-style machine powered by a hotted-up Gold Wing engine. Unlike previous sixes, which carried their engines in a transverse, inline configuration, the GL1500 is a flat, opposed six with liquid cooling and driveshaft.

The benefit of a six is silky smoothness and abundant power. All contemporary sixes have been big, luxurious flagship machines whose power delivery has been tuned for a wide torque band. Because there are so few six-cylinder motorcycles, it would be more valuable for the reader to consider each six on its own merits rather than for me to make generalizations about them.

Engine Configuration

Engine configuration refers to the arrangement of the engine's cylinders. Single-cylinder engines tend to be arranged upright, but engines having two or more cylinders may be arranged in inline, vee, or opposed configurations. Let's look at the advantages and disadvantages of each type.

Inline. Inline engines are configured with all cylinders arranged side by side in a straight line. The advantage to this configuration is that these engines are relatively inexpensive to manufacture as the entire head and the block can each be cast as a single piece. Early examples of air-cooled, inline fours (such as the Ace, Henderson, and Indian) were arranged with the engine sitting front to back (longitudinally) in the frame, which led to cooling problems with the rear cylinders. Modern inline fours tend to be arranged transversely, that is, across the frame, left to right. The exhaust valve is always faced forward to take advantage of the cooling airflow. The major exception to these two arrangements are BMW K-series machines, in which their three- and four-cylinder engines are configured longitudinally, laid on their sides, and liquid-cooled.

The disadvantage of inline engines, particularly fours and sixes arranged transversely, is that they are long and result in very wide motorcycles; to provide adequate ground clearance these engines must be set relatively high in their frames, and weight carried high makes a motorcycle relatively less responsive in turns. In the late 1970s and early 1980s, before standard suspension systems became adequate, it was common to see Japanese four-cylinder motorcycles with gouges and scratch marks on their points and alternator covers from where they had dragged on the pavement in turns.

Vees. Motorcycling has seen V-twins and V-fours, but not a V-six. All Harley-Davidson twins are air-cooled vees arranged with the vee running longitudinally, along the frame. All four Japanese manufacturers have made V-twins since the 1980s. All V-fours to date have been liquid-cooled machines, and we have seen such bikes from Honda, Yamaha, and Suzuki. Most were arranged with the crankshaft running transversely, but the Honda ST1100 (introduced in 1990 as a 1991 model) was the first with its crankshaft running longitudinally.

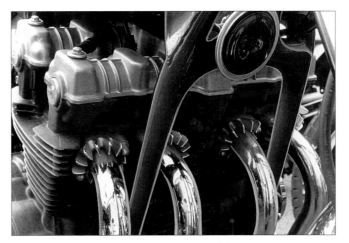

The 1970s and early 1980s were the heyday of the transverse, air-cooled Japanese four such as this Honda.

Another vee configuration is to arrange the two cylinders transversely, across the front of the machine. The Italian company Moto Guzzi has done this for the past several decades; Honda CX and GL models of 500 and 650cc sizes were also arranged in this manner.

The advantage of vee engines is that they can be relatively narrow, which is a real plus in ground clearance. V-twins arranged transversely, such as those by Moto Guzzi, have the added advantage that both cylinders protrude into the cooling air stream. Longitudinal air-cooled vees, such as Harley-Davidsons, can experience difficulties in cooling the rear cylinder; however,

A vee engine can be arranged either longitudinally as with this Harley-Davidson, or transversely as with Moto Guzzi twins. (Photo courtesy of Harley-Davidson Motor Company)

In a world that seemingly was going for multi-cylinder engines or V-twins, Suzuki continued to offer its proven air-cooled GS500. The bike offers sophistication in terms of its dual overhead cams, four valves per cylinder and six-speed transmission.

BMW's K1200 series bikes are powered by longitudinal, inline engines laid on their sides. They're fuel injected and liquid cooled. (Photo courtesy of BMW of North America)

later Harleys have not had this problem. Over the years this Milwaukee, Wisconsin-based company has engineered itself through its problems. The Evolution engine, which first appeared in 1984 and featured aluminum heads, no longer suffers from maladies related to the overheating of the rear cylinder nor does its new generation Twin Cam 88.

One disadvantage of the vee configuration is that these engines are relatively expensive to build, as each cylinder (or bank of cylinders) must be cast separately. Also, such engines are not the smoothest-running bikes around. The general exception to this is when the two cylinders are arranged 90 degrees to each other, resulting in perfect primary balance. However, a 90-degree spread is extreme, explaining why few V-twins (such as Ducatis) are configured as such. Rather, modern V-twin designs tend to be configured more conventionally, and utilize contra-rotating balancers to engineer in smoothness.

Harley-Davidson has been making motorcycles since 1903, and V-twins since 1909. The distinctive sound and feel of its V-twins is a result of its uniquely

staggered firing order. Traditionalists swear by them, claiming that they speak to the soul in voices of power and thunder. Nonbelievers may refer to these pulses as "vibration," but the cognoscenti revel in the feel of a throbbing V-twin. In order to assuage those less in love with the vibes, Harley-Davidson has rubber mounted the engines of selected models so that its riders can have it either way.

Another factor in vibration is whether the engine has staggered or joined crankpins. Honda's 1,099cc, liquid-cooled, 45-degree V-twin Shadow 1100 cruiser has been around since 1985 in several incarnations. The original was designed with smoothness in mind and carried a staggered-crankpin engine. For the 1995 model year Honda introduced a version called the American Classic Edition (A.C.E. for short) that carried a joined-crankpin engine intended to sound and shake more like something out of Milwaukee.

To best explain the difference between the two types of engines, imagine yourself pedaling a bicycle. Each pedal represents a crankpin on a staggered- (or dual-) crankpin engine, 180 degrees of rotation apart. Pedaling in this manner is smooth and even, as the bicyclist gets in two good pushes with each rotation.

Now imagine that the rider hops sidesaddle off the bike and, through a great contortionist effort, places both feet on the same pedal and attempts to ride. This crude illustration represents a joined-crankpin arrangement, and the result is much greater roughness and less power. Of course the analogy is far from perfect as our legs are not arranged in a 45-degree vee, and the offset on a staggered-crankpin engine will often be about 45 degrees, but you get the idea. It is that joined crankpin that helps give a Harley-Davidson its unmistakable sound and feel, and which Honda was attempting to emulate with its A.C.E.

Opposed Engines. In an opposed engine, the cylinders are arranged opposite each other and the pistons on each side (or each bank in a multi) both move in and out in unison. Honda has made its Gold Wings in both four- and six-cylinder opposed configurations, and BMW has continually offered its legendary opposed two-cylinder, air-cooled boxer engine that it began producing in 1923.

The "boxer" motor (the opposed twin) got its name from the way boxers rhythmically move their arms in and out across their bodies as they prepare to give and take blows, a motion which mimics the pistons in an opposed twin.

The advantages of the opposed engine include a great deal of smoothness, as an equal number and weight of pistons moving in and out in unison cancel out the movement of each other's mass. They're naturals for use with a driveshaft, as the crankshaft rotates on the same plane as the driveshaft. An opposed transverse twin, such as the BMW, sticks both its cylinders out into the airstream for optimum cooling. Opposed engines of four or more cylinders tend to be liquid cooled, because the forward cylinders block airflow to those in the rear.

The major disadvantage of opposed engines is their extreme width; they must be set relatively high in the frame to provide adequate ground clearance. Old-style air-cooled BMW twins that are ridden very hard, especially those without upgraded suspension components, often sport scrapes and gouges on the undersides of their valve covers from their being dragged on the pavement in high-speed turns. Such situations result from extreme lean angles that most riders do not encounter. For those who *do* sometimes drag valve covers on their old BMWs, longer, stiffer fork springs with a good aftermarket rear suspension will usually improve ground clearance to the point that the problem disappears. On the newer R1100 twins (which are air/oil cooled, the engines are set up high enough in the frames that ground clearance is not a problem.

A few final words about engine configuration. First, the advent of liquid cooling for most large motorcycles

BMW has long been known for its legendary flat twins, like that on this R1100S. The latest version features four valves per cylinder, air/oil cooling and electronic fuel injection. (Photo courtesy of BMW North America)

Honda's older Gold Wings, including the GL1000, GL1100 and GL1200, used opposed four-cylinder engines. Later GL1500s are powered by six cylinders.

(with the exception of Harley-Davidsons) means that many other types of engine configurations are now possible, as airflow over the cooling fins is no longer a major consideration. The classic Ariel Square Four was a beautiful machine, and was manufactured for a number of years before various problems brought about by overheating caused its demise. Two to three decades later, however, many grand prix racing machines (which generate incredible amounts of power and heat) were able to successfully use the same configuration, thanks to liquid cooling.

Second, whether the bike will transfer power to the rear wheel through a driveshaft or a chain is also a

Kawasaki's Voyager XII is a full-dress machine that is powered by a modern, liquid-cooled engine with this well integrated radiator.

consideration when deciding upon engine configuration. Let's find out why.

Imagine you're looking at the left side of a motorcycle (left and right are designated from the rider's position, therefore left would be toward the left hand of a rider sitting astride a bike facing forward). As the bike rolled forward (to the left as you're viewing it), the wheels would rotate counterclockwise. Now wouldn't it make good sense if the crankshaft and gearbox also rotated on the same plane as the countershaft and drive sprockets, and the rear wheel? If it didn't, the direction of rotation would have to be turned, usually with bevel gears. Each time the direction of rotation is turned 90 degrees, such as to align a transverse, inline engine with a driveshaft, several percent of the engine's power is sacrificed through friction losses. Engines that are compatible with chain or belt final drive include transverse, inline engines and longitudinal V-twins.

Now consider a bike with a driveshaft view head-on from the front. Looking toward the rear, the shaft rotates either clockwise or counterclockwise, depending upon which side of the bike the rear hub is located. The crankshaft of opposed engines (BMW twins, Honda Gold Wings), transverse vees (Moto Guzzis, Honda's old CX and GL500s and 650s), and BMW's inline, pancake K-bikes all spin in this same plane, which is why these configurations are more compatible with a driveshaft.

Liquid cooling versus air cooling. Most engines are cooled by air or liquid, so let's explain the advantages of each system. When internal-combustion engines were first developed, they were simple affairs that used simple systems. Cooling by airflow is stone-axe simple, and nearly all motorcycles until the mid-1970s had air-cooled engines. In air-cooled systems, a series of ridges called cooling fins are cast into the block and head of an engine; their purpose is to increase the surface area available for giving off heat. In the presence of adequate airflow for low-powered engines, air cooling is perfectly adequate. Also, it is less expensive to manufacture, and its simplicity means never having to stop because of a broken water pump or a leaking radiator.

The first modern liquid-cooled motorcycle was the Suzuki GT750 LeMans that initially appeared in the early 1970s. It was affectionately known as the "water buffalo" and was soon followed by the Honda GL1000 Gold Wing, the rotary-engined Suzuki RE-5, Kawasaki KZ1300, and a veritable flood of machines in all shapes and sizes throughout the 1980s.

Liquid cooling offers many advantages. As engines run through their operating cycles they are first stone cold after a night sitting idle, then begin to warm when they're started, and finally reach operating temperature. If that were the total picture of engine operations, air cooling could be perfectly adequate. However, engines are subject to a variety of loads and temperatures ranging from a solo rider cruising a big motorcycle on a flat freeway at 55 MPH during a day when the temperature is 45 degrees, to a couple hauling (as quickly as they can) a trailer, sidecar, and all of their luggage up Pike's Peak during a 90-degree day. Guess who needs liquid cooling most!

A liquid-cooling system is a temperature-controlled environment utilizing a radiator, water jackets, thermostat, and a coolant medium. Within these components lies its strength. The liquid-cooled engine can be built with tighter internal clearances than an air-cooled unit because it operates within a more controlled temperature range, which reduces the degree of internal expansion and contraction of its parts. This contributes to longer engine life, greater service and oil-change intervals, and quieter operation.

You'll notice that I refer to these engines as liquid-cooled rather than water-cooled. While these engines do utilize water for cooling, they also use ethelyne glycol (to control freezing), rust inhibitors, cleaners, etc., which means that there's much more in the mix than merely water.

Engines today produce much more power than they did a decade ago. In 1980, a typical 750cc four was producing about 70–75 horsepower. Today, a typical sporting 750 may crank out well over 100 horsepower from the same amount of displacement. With more horses available these sports are ridden harder, and that produces more heat. Emissions standards required by the Environmental Protection Agency (EPA) mean that engines may have to run leaner than optimum, a condition that further contributes to hotter running, but liquid cooling can handle these conditions effectively. Also, surrounding an engine with blanketing water jackets, rather than with cooling fins that radiate a ringing sound, helps them to meet noise emission standards. Finally, if all motorcycle engines had to be configured today to allow for proper cooling airflow, our choices would be severely limited. We would see fewer V-twins and V-fours. Opposed flat fours would be difficult, and sixes virtually impossible except for the transverse variety.

The only downside to having liquid cooling is the added weight and complexity of the radiator, hoses, pump, and coolant, yet today's sporting motorcycles are not that much heavier than their air-cooled brethren of a decade past. Maintenance is minimal and involves merely checking the coolant level regularly, topping it off when needed, and replacing it every year or so.

Liquid cooling is a more modern, functional means of keeping a motorcycle in good shape for many years of hard use. For safeguarding your engine from heat, liquid cooling is much preferred to air.

Air/Oil Cooling. A third type of cooling is a compromise between the above types, and involves circulating quantities of oil through the engine via special cooling jackets. Engines that are air/oil cooled will have cooling fins, yet will also circulate oil through passages in the heads. Increased oil capacity and a large oil cooler will be evident, and benefits include less weight and complication than liquid cooling. Bikes that utilize this type of cooling include BMW's R1100 series, early Suzuki's GSX-R sportbikes and the Polaris Victory line.

Turbocharging. Turbocharging is a means of force feeding the fuel and air mixture to an engine by pressurizing that mixture. Pressure is built up by a tiny impeller that is located in the exhaust tract and spun by

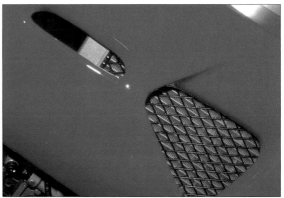

Honda's liquid-cooled VFR800 carries its twin radiators beside its engine for improved mass centralization. Keeping the mass centralized allows the bike to turn more effectively.

exhaust gases. The turbo is in effect self-actuating; the quicker the engine revs the more pressure it builds in the engine and, in turn, the harder it can rev.

In the early 1980s, the Japanese motorcycle manufacturers all jumped on the turbo bandwagon within a few years of each other and produced some very quick machines. However, by the middle 1980s turbocharging was a red herring, a dead issue.

The flaw in the system is that there is a delay, or lag, between the time the impeller begins to build up boost, and the moment that it begins to cause the engine to produce that strong, hard pull. The short pause was acceptable for the auto driver pulling out to pass on a straight highway, but motorcyclists aren't accustomed to riding that way. Riders instead prefer the thrill of cornering on a canyon or mountain road where throttle response has to be both precise and instantaneous. On a tight road, by the time a turbo had gathered itself up for some serious poke, it was already time to shut down for the next corner.

Turbocharged bikes came and went quickly in the early 1980s. (Honda CX500 Turbo photo courtesy American Honda)

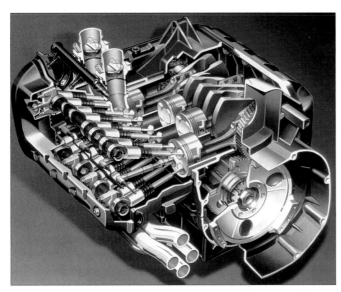

The four valves in the head, and dual overhead camshafts are readily visible in this shot of a BMW K1200LT's internals. (Photo courtesy BMW of North America)

The seemingly obvious advantage of a four-valve head is that twice as many of a good thing must be better, but it's a bit more complex than that. The individual valves in a four-valve engine are smaller than those utilized in a similar size of two-valve engine. Flow is superior in a four-valve engine because when the valves lift, the gases rush in or out along the circumference of the valves—and two small valves can have a significantly greater circumference than one large valve.

Second, the smaller valves can be significantly lighter, which cuts down on the amount of reciprocating mass that eats up horsepower. Third, the spark plug can be more centrally located in a four-valve engine; this promotes cleaner, more complete burning. Four-valvers do put out more horsepower on the top end, but more importantly they're also stronger in the midrange—where most of us do the great majority of our riding. Combine these factors, and an engine with four valves per cylinder is a real performance plus for anyone, including the touring rider.

Dual-overhead cams. Motorcycle engines use various methods to actuate their valves, including pushrods, chains and belts, single-overhead camshafts, and dual-overhead camshafts, the latter of which are often abbreviated as DOHC. On a pushrod engine, the camshaft is located near the crankshaft, and the cam's movement is transferred to the overhead valve via the pushrod. Sporting purists consider pushrods, probably correctly so, to be low technology. However, all Harley-Davidson's V-twins and BMW's old line of twin-cylinder engines had pushrod-actuated valves, and are known for longevity and reliability.

Dual-overhead-cam engines with shim-adjusted valves usually can be run for much longer intervals before requiring valve adjustments. For example, an old BMW air-cooled twin with conventional pushrods called for a valve check every 5,000 miles. The liquid-cooled, four-cylinder K100 had a 15,000-mile valve adjustment interval.

On most DOHC engines, valve clearance is set by placing the proper thickness of shim in the tappet between the camshaft lobe and valve stem. This efficient system rarely requires adjustment, but when it does it's not a job for the tinkerer. Changing shims often requires special tools and removal of the camshaft. The shims are precision-ground, hardened-steel items of very precise thickness. In short, there's no free lunch.

In addition, all the turbo bikes offered by the Japanese manufacturers ranged from 500cc to 750cc, for fear that the uninitiated would have problems controlling larger turbocharged bikes. Riders found that for the price of a 650 turbo they could buy a normally-aspirated 1100 sport that weighed about the same, produced as much acceleration instantaneously, and didn't possess such complex apparatus in which potential problems could lurk. Simply, motorcycles could generate incredible acceleration without the complexity, weight, and expense of turbos, and they quietly went away.

Valve considerations. A four-valve head is a cheap, easy way to get more power from a given size of engine. The fuel and air mixture is introduced into the engine through its intake valve(s), and spent gases exit through exhaust valve(s). An internal-combustion engine is essentially an air pump, and the greater the volume that can be pumped in and out, the greater the power that engine can potentially deliver.

Four-valve engines began appearing in the late 1970s in such bikes as the Suzuki GS750 and GS1000, and the Honda CBX six-cylinder. Today, four-valve heads have proliferated to all serious sport bikes, to most big road-burners, and even BMW's lineup. In fact, some Yamaha sport models even used a *five-valve* head!

A DOHC engine with shim-over-bucket valves will not require a valve adjustment often, but when it does it's really a job for the dealer's mechanic.

Types of Touring and Traveling Motorcycles

Much has changed in motorcycling since the 1970s. Until that era, motorcycles were motorcycles, and they came in different displacement sizes. That was about it. A young man (or woman) could buy a standard motorcycle, such as a Honda CB750, and add accessories to make it fit his or her specific needs. If he wanted to ride fast and hard he'd add an aftermarket exhaust system, stickier brake pads, and aftermarket suspension units. If he wanted to cruise he'd extend the front end, add a stepped seat, and shorty exhausts. For touring he'd add a fairing and saddlebags. One motorcycle could be tailored to a variety of different uses.

The decade of the 1980s became the age of specialization. The OEMs noted this trend and realized that they could design specialized motorcycles better than their customers could. Throughout the 1980s various commpanies began offering very specialized motorcycles that were in truth better sports, cruisers, or tourers than riders could build themselves. For sport riding, bikes came with such names as Interceptor, Hurricane, GPz, Ninja, GSX-R, FZR, or FJ. Each Japanese company offered very fine cruising bikes with V-twin engines; some models were called Shadow, Vulcan, Intruder, and Virago. Their full-dress tourers such as the Gold Wing, Voyager, Cavalcade, Venture, FLH, FLT, RT, and LT carried fairings and luggage.

These motorcycles were very capable and worked very well, but in carrying all the equipment the enthusiast used to add himself, their prices increased. Along with higher prices came decreased creativity—now that riders no longer had to outfit their bikes themselves, their machines tended to remain as they had come from the factory, and a great sameness settled upon the motorcycling landscape.

Over the decade, for many and complex reasons, new motorcycle sales dropped by about half. As the 1990s began, the OEMs tried to counter the drop in sales by offering, once again, "standard" motorcycles that provided lower levels of performance and technology, cost less, and could be accessorized just the way the rider wanted. Other machines filled in the spaces between existing bikes to create real niche markets

The Harley-Davidson Electra Glide Classic is a fine example of a dresser motorcycle with its prominent fairing, hard saddlebags and trunk.

such as sport tourers and adventure tourers and, for many other complex reasons, motorcycle sales recovered during the 1990s. Let's take a look at the suitability of these various types of motorcycles for touring so that you can identify them, and how they may fit your needs.

Dresser Tourers

The name dresser tourer says it all. The term means that the bike is "dressed" for touring with a fairing and windshield, plus saddlebags and perhaps a trunk. These bikes excel in comfort, and usually are powered by big, slow-turning, under-stressed engines designed for smoothness and long life. Most use a driveshaft to transfer power to the rear wheel, although Harley-Davidsons use a drive belt. Examples of dressers include the BMW RT and LT models, Honda Gold Wing, Harley-Davidson FLH and FLT variations, the Kawasaki Voyager, and Yamaha Venture. The Suzuki Cavalcade is no longer in production.

Dressers are designed to carry huge amounts of gear in their standard luggage systems, and they're available with all sorts of features such as sound systems, intercoms, adjustable windshields, adjustable headlights, additional storage areas in their fairings, cushy saddles, and much more. Co-riders (passengers) love them because they're usually equipped with a backrest to lean against.

The downside of luxury dressers is that they're the biggest, heaviest, and often the most expensive

A Ducati, such as this 900 FE, is a joy on a winding road. (Photo courtesy of Ducati North America, Inc.)

machines available. Some models start at $12,000, while others cost much more. They often weigh in the range of 800–900 pounds, fully gassed and ready to go. Allow one to tip over, and it's a strain for the typical riding couple to set aright.

For long-distance touring on good roads, especially for two persons, the dresser tourer is king. They're unsurpassed in terms of comfort, features, and luggage capacity. Their fairings offer a level of protection usually greater than that offered by lighter motorcycles, especially for touring two-up. Dressers are the tops in luxury.

Sport Tourers

Sporting motorcycles are great fun to ride at speed, and even to tour upon if your riding is oriented toward the high end of the intensity scale. They're often higher-performance bikes than the "standard" type motorcycles, but stop short of being street-legal racers.

The good things about sport tourers are their fun factor on a winding road and their ability to cover great distances in a short span of time if the road allows it and the rider is willing. Usually they're equipped with a sporting type of fairing that blocks some of the wind from the rider's chest but stops well short of the type of protection the dresser fairings provide. Examples of sport tourers include the BMW K1200RS and R1100RS; Ducati's ST2; Honda's CBR1000 and ST1100; Kawasaki's Concours and Ninjas; the Suzuki

Katanas; Triumph's Trophy models and Yamaha used to offer the FJ1100 and FJ1200.

In order to maintain their sportier intent, sport tourers may not offer quite the luggage capacity of a dresser. Still, some are equipped with hard, lockable saddlebags, although they may be optional on some. Often, soft luggage is considered *de rigueur* on them. The sporting riding position, leaning forward, is actually much more comfortable than it looks because the wind helps support the rider's weight. Some sports set the footpegs relatively high to provide extra ground clearance, and the degree of knee bend dictated by this position may limit comfort over the miles. Sport-tourer fairings usually leave the rider's shoulders, head, and hands out in the windstream where they can be buffeted and chilled. Passenger accommodations on sport tourers usually are not nearly as luxurious as those on dressers, and the co-rider would definitely appreciate the addition of a backrest for touring.

Sport suspensions tend to be oriented toward the stiff, well-controlled end of the spectrum, necessary for precise control at higher speeds. Riders more used to the plushness of dressers may not like this tautness, though the adjustability range of these suspension systems may well provide them with some more agreeable settings.

The choice between a dresser or a sport tourer is really a matter of personal taste. Aggressive riders who like to go fast in the turns while traveling light and solo prefer sport tourers. Those who travel two-up and loaded at a more leisurely pace, and who like comfort, prefer dresser. Yet there's a lot of leeway in between.

Adventure Tourers

Adventure tourers are the people you see exploring to the far reaches of Alaska, the back roads of Mexico, the Andes of Peru or the wilds of the African continent by motorcycle. I met an Austrian couple who flew with their Honda XL600 single to Miami, Florida, rode it up to above the Arctic Circle in Alaska, then down to the tip of South America. Hans and Ursula then shipped the bike to Australia and crossed that huge continent before they ran low on funds and flew back to Austria.

This type of touring has been common for years, especially among Europeans. The popularity of the demanding Paris-to-Dakar Races in the 1980s, and extensive coverage given in the media there, spawned a new generation of motorcycles loosely based upon the bikes raced in these events, and also called adventure tourers. BMW won the first three such races, and then Honda successfully became involved. These racing bikes are designed to compete not only on highways, but on gravel roads and even trackless desert sand dunes. With only one, two or possibly three cylinders, extremely long-travel suspension systems, and huge fuel tanks, these machines are hybrids between full-on dirt bikes and extremely rugged, simple street bikes.

Examples of adventure tourers include the BMW R1100GS models, including one aptly named PD, or Paris-Dakar, and Triumph offers the Tiger. Other recent adventure tourers no longer sold in the United States include Honda's Transalp, the Yamaha Ténéré, Cagiva Elefant, and Kawasaki Tengai. Other basic single-cylinder dual-sports, like the one used by my Austrian friends, are commonly used by tourers who just keep going when the roads stop.

Now let's clarify a few points. Adventure touring involves using street-legal machines to travel both on and off roads. The motorcycles are referred to as dual-purpose (or dual-sport) machines. When the term adventure tourer is applied to a specific motorcycle, it usually means one that is designed to travel on poor roads, and even trails, and is usually based upon a dual-sport bike. The difference between an adventure tourer and a dual-sport is that adventurers tend to be larger (650–1100cc), while dual-sports top out at about 650cc. Also, adventure bikes tend to have extremely large fuel tanks, and are designed around the purpose of travel. Dual-sports, on the other hand, are intended primarily as budget transportation and recreation. Splitting hairs about definitions becomes moot after a time—both types of bikes can be used for serious adventure touring.

Now here's some information you're going to have to promise to keep to yourself. Despite their dirt-bike looks, adventure tourers and dual-sports are incredibly competent street bikes. With their torquey power, unlimited ground clearance, low weight, nimble handling and dirt-capable suspensions they can embarrass riders of larger sport bikes on tight, twisty roads. Once the roads open up, however, the more powerful sports are gone in a puff of smoke.

Though their tires are compromises, and they are biased for street use over dirt, adventure tourers and dual-sports keep going when the road stops. They're

Perphaps the best known adventure tourer is BMW's GS series. Shown is the R100GS P/D, with a 9.2-gallon tank. (Photo courtesy of BMW North America)

much too heavy and too compromised for true dirt riding, especially when loaded with luggage, but when ridden within their capabilities they are very capable on trails and for exploring to such places as the Yucatan, North Africa, India, and the interior of Australia. Or Michigan, Arizona, and Georgia.

The main advantages of adventure tourers are their low weight, simplicity, good fuel mileage, great suspension systems, and versatility. These attributes make them not only great for their intended purpose, but also for commuting, touring, and all-around riding. About the only drawbacks I could think of for these machines is that of necessity for ground clearance they sit very high, and shorter riders will not feel confident on them. Also, their semi-knobby tires must be fairly fresh to perform well on both the street and dirt. When they wear down a bit, which happens in a relatively short number of miles, they lose much of their abilities in the dirt.

Another drawback is that these bikes (with the exception of BMW's landmark R80GS, R100GS and R1100GS machines, including the Paris-Dakar models) don't offer suitable luggage-carrying ability for the world traveler. BMW's machines, on the other hand, offer hard, removable saddlebags specifically designed for these bikes, plus sturdy racks and high-capacity fuel tanks; the R100GS Paris-Dakar (no longer available) carried 9.2 gallons of fuel. Also, BMW's GS models are the only adventure tourers equipped with a driveshaft. On other dual-sports and adventure

Cruisers can make suitable tourers, especially when fitted with leather saddlebags.

bikes, the rider will either have to use less rugged soft luggage, or attach aftermarket hard bags to the bikes.

In conclusion, adventure touring bikes are great all-around machines, although they aren't for everyone. If I could have just one bike, especially if I lived where there were rural trails and back unpaved roads, and I also wanted to tour, I would happily have an adventure tourer.

Cruisers

The cruiser bike is a modern adaptation of the old chopper, which was an adaptation of the standard Harley-Davidson of the 1930s and 1940s. Choppers had their heyday in the rebellious 1960s and 1970s. Riders fell in love with their style despite the choppers' obvious drawbacks in comfort and handling. In the middle 1970s, the Japanese motorcycle makers began bolting cruiser styling items onto some of their standard bikes by adding peanut-styled tanks, stepped seats, high handlebars, shorty mufflers and 16-inch rear wheels with fat tires.

Cruising took another giant step forward in the early 1980s when the Japanese OEMs decided that mere styling was not enough, and created new cruiser motorcycles with V-twin engines in emulation of the Harley-Davidson. With names like Shadow, Vulcan, Virago, and Intruder these bikes sold well, although purists still said they were incapable of encapsulating the Harley mystique. Meanwhile, Harley-Davidson staged a

massive comeback in the 1980s, propelled by its wildly successful new aluminum Evolution V-twin engine. With Harley's new ascendance and price competitiveness for its 883 Sportster model, sales of Japanese cruisers suddenly fell.

The suitability of cruisers as touring machines depends upon the particular cruiser. Real home-built Harley-Davidson choppers, despite the romantic image portrayed in the film *Easy Rider,* are primarily exercises in style. Their high handlebars, tiny tanks, narrow stepped seats, hard-tail rear ends and extended forks are a real challenge to ride great distances. Modern customs, however, tend to be much more functional, and those of the late 1990s have become the new face of touring.

The early Japanese cruiser bikes, the ones based upon standard four-cylinder and other engines, were likewise styling exercises. They frequently suffered from strange handlebar bends and grip placements, and they forced riders into a nearly bolt upright seating position. This position sent every road jolt right up his spine while he had to keep a constant pull on the handlebar to hold himself upright into the wind blast. On bikes so configured, such a riding position quickly became tiring, and sometimes painful.

The Japanese learned from their experiences with their first-generation cruisers and incorporated meaningful changes into their V-twins. The bikes offered real engine smoothness, additional fuel capacity, and more comfortable seats and riding positions. Still, these machines were designed with an eye toward styling first, and touring function somewhere down the list of priorities.

What can you say about Harley-Davidsons that has not been said elsewhere in volumes? The company, which was literally hours from bankruptcy and was laboring under "vibrate and leak oil" jokes about its engineering and quality control, was purchased by its top executives at the 11th hour and brought back from the brink. The Evolution engine solved all the old problems, and the company launched an aggressive and innovative program to return to profitability.

The company has made a happy comeback offering dresser and cruiser-style bikes for both the heavy-duty rider and the more casual enthusiast. Their huge 80-cubic-inch (1340cc) V-twin Evolution engines shake a bit, but many models offer rubber mounting that very effectively prevents the shakes from reaching the rider.

Evolution Harleys are very high-quality, respected machines from a company whose comeback represents a true American success story. For 1999, Harley-Davidson introduced its new Twin Cam 88 engine on Dyna and touring models, which offers more power and greater smoothness.

As for the suitability of their cruisers for touring, tens of thousands ride them millions of miles to such major annual events as Daytona Bike Week in Florida each spring and the Black Hills Motor Classic in Sturgis, South Dakota, each August. The bikes are big and smooth in the rubber-mounted configuration and are easy to love. Harley-Davidson has a liberal demonstration ride program, so if you think you'd like to own a Harley, go try one.

In the late 1990s, with the development of dressers bikes at a seeming standstill, the OEMs have turned their attention toward making cruisers the new touring bikes. Rather than all the bells and whistles of full fairings, sound systems, lights and the rest the cruiser represents a more laid-back style that one motorcycle company executive referred to as "bedroll touring." He meant that rather than couples taking along huge amounts of luggage as they do on their dressers, the cruiser tourers wanted a simpler approach like the true nomad of a generation ago who threw a bedroll on the back and took off for weeks at a time. Today, a touring cruiser tends to have a set of saddlebags and windshield, with possibly a backrest and that's it. However, some models now offer fairings, and are coming full circle as touring bikes.

Cruisers for touring include the Harley-Davidson Road King, Dyna Convertible, and Heritage Softail Classic; the Honda Shadow 1100 Tourer, Kawasaki Vulcan 1500 Nomad; and several models of the Yamaha Royal Star including the Tour Classic, Tour Classic II, Tour Deluxe, and Tour Deluxe and Tour Deluxe Solitaire. With a fairing, the dressiest Royal Star is the Venture.

Standards

A standard motorcycle is just a basic machine that is more defined by what it is not than by what it is. It's a bike that does not fit into any of the above categories. It may have a windshield, but no fairing or luggage. It can have any size engine, but its orientation does not make any kind of statement such as "I'm fast," "I cruise," or "I tour."

The standard motorcycle, such as this Suzuki 1200 Bandit, has again become available in the 1990s. Though reasonably priced, standards have never really staged a comeback as the public seems to prefer bikes that are more specialized. (Photo courtesy of American Suzuki Motor Corporation)

Throughout the 1970s, all motorcycles were pretty much standard machines. Then bikes became compartmentalized into specialized dressers, sports, cruisers and adventure machines and the all-around, do-everything motorcycle generally fell behind in the race for increasing technical improvement.

Standard bikes usually cost less than other types because they don't have expensive fairings, luggage, or exotic engines and suspension systems. They're designed to be more basic machines, and simplicity can be its own reward. Like the original Honda CB750, the standard motorcycle can be accessorized any of these ways, or it can be left alone as is and simply enjoyed. Some standard bikes include the BMW R1100R and R850R, Ducati Monster, Honda 750 Nighthawk, Suzuki Bandits, Kawasaki Zephyrs and the Suzuki GS500E. The Zephyrs are no longer available.

Other Considerations

When choosing a motorcycle you don't have a choice as to the type of features it offers. However, it helps to understand these features, and what they may mean to you. Let's look over several other considerations in choosing your motorcycle.

Gross Vehicle Weight Rating. Gross Vehicle Weight Rating is abbreviated as GVWR, and it refers to the amount of weight your motorcycle should be able to safely support, including its own weight. The limiting factors center around its suspension, and the tires with which it was supplied. Let's take an example of a cou-

The GVWR Plate, such as this from a Suzuki, contains valuable information regarding loading, tires and other facts.

ple of GVWR figures and determine what they mean to you as a rider.

A six-cylinder Honda GL1500/6 Gold Wing SE has a GVWR of 1,274 pounds—the highest recommended weight the designers say this bike should carry. When fully gassed, the SE has a curb weight of 914 pounds, which eats up nearly three-quarters of the GVWR figure. Subtracting the bike's road-ready weight from its GVWR leaves a figure of 360 pounds that the bike can carry in riders and luggage.

Now consider that a male rider weighs 180 pounds, and his wife weighs 110. Keep in mind that people weigh themselves in the buff, but they don't ride that way. Each person will wear up to eight pounds in clothing and helmet. Add their two weights (180 + 110) plus their clothing (8 + 8) and the total is 306. Subtract that figure from the 360-pound carrying capacity, and you'll find that this couple can carry 54 pounds of luggage before they exceed the theoretical design capacities of the bike. That is a reasonable figure, but by no means a comfortable margin, especially if our couple carries camping and cooking gear.

What does GVWR actually mean? Well, let me assure you that if you load 360 pounds onto this bike and then pick up a pound of hamburger, it is not going to crack in half or self destruct. More than any other factor, GVWR reflects the ability of the tires to handle loads at particular inflation pressures. As more weight is piled onto the tires, the more the tires deflect and build up heat. In extreme cases, the heat can build to the point the tire blows out with sometimes disastrous results. Increasing air pressure reduces tire deflection, which helps stave off problems.

If you find that your bike is nearing its GVWR figure, lighten your load. Second, check for the maximum air pressure allowed in each tire (this figure is also listed on each tire's sidewall). Inflate them to their recommended maximum pressures. Always check air pressure when the tires are cold, such as in the morning before the bike is ridden. Also note that once the machine is loaded beyond its GVWR figure, it will probably not meet its performance specifications as listed in the owner's manual, so take it easy.

Brake Basics

Most motorcycles today are equipped with single or dual front disc brakes, and either a disc or a drum brake on the rear wheel. The more powerful brake is attached to the front wheel because 75–90 percent of the stopping force is generated by the front brake(s). As the brakes are utilized, weight transfers forward, compressing the front suspension and weighting the front tire. The forward weight transfer unweights the rear tire; it becomes very easy to lock the rear wheel if that brake is overused.

If the brakes are used very hard over a short period of time they can "fade," causing their stopping ability to deteriorate rapidly and dramatically. Fading is a result of excessive heat buildup in the braking system that can boil the brake fluid in a disc system, or cause the brake pads or shoes to lose their rigidity. The control begins to feel uncertain, mushy, and pedal or lever travel increases noticeably. When you notice these conditions, pull over and stop at the first safe opportunity, because your brakes will not offer a significant amount of stopping power until they cool again. This could take 10 minutes or longer, but the cool-down period is absolutely necessary. Then, as soon as possible, have your braking system inspected. Check the hydraulic fluid level, pad wear, and be certain that the disc rotors have not warped.

Disc brakes versus drum brakes. In general, disc brakes are superior to drum brakes. Discs offer a very progressive feel—as you squeeze the brake lever or depress the rear pedal, the braking force is directly proportional to the amount the rider squeezes the controls. A skilled rider can gauge his braking safety margin by lever feedback and tire howl.

Drum brakes, on the other hand, become self-actuating at extreme application pressures. As the brake lining is forced against the drum and approaches lockup, the shoe will be pressed so hard against the drum that it will want to follow it and jam against it; this will lock the brake, skid the tire and cause a loss of control.

Disc brakes run out in the airstream where they are easily cooled, while drums are shut up in their casings, which retain the heat. Drum brakes are often actuated by cables, which can stretch and diminish their effectiveness; discs are almost always controlled by hydraulic systems, therefore there's no mechanical linkage to bind, stretch, or break. Because disc brakes are hydraulic, they need no adjustment as long as the fluid level is maintained; drum brakes must be adjusted periodically in order to compensate for brake lining wear and cable stretch. When disc pads wear out, it's a simple five-minute job to replace them. When brake linings wear out in drum brakes, the wheel must be removed from the motorcycle, the drum opened, and a dirty operation undertaken. The only maintenance required with discs is to drain and replace the hydraulic fluid at specified intervals.

Most motorcycles offer disc front brakes, and some offer drums in the rear. With the minimal braking demands made upon the rear wheel, that's exactly where a drum brake belongs if you're going to have one. For superior stopping power plus the many advantages mentioned above, a disc brake is vastly superior to a drum brake.

Integrated braking systems. Instead of the common braking systems in which front and rear brakes are totally independent, an integrated braking system links the front and rear brakes together to compensate for people who do not know how to properly use their braking systems. In a common integrated system, operating the front brake lever operates only one of the two front disc brakes. Pressing the rear brake pedal applies both the other front disc brake, and the rear brake. Proportioning valves in the system apportion the correct amount of stopping force to each brake caliper.

A few motorcycles, such as the Honda GL1500 Gold Wing, Yamaha Venture, and some Hondas such as the CBR1100XX and VFR800 Interceptor, have integrated braking systems. Studies have shown that too many inexperienced riders, especially in panic situations, tend to overutilize the rear brake and underuse the front. As I pointed out earlier, the front braking

Here's a peek inside a rear drum brake housing. When it is actuated, the shoes (top and bottom) are pushed outward against the brake drum and friction causes the bike to slow. The springs retract the shoes

Dual front disc brakes offer improved braking modulation, though not necessarily shorter stopping distances.

system is the most powerful, and overusing the rear brake can lead to wheel lockup and a loss of control.

For inexperienced riders, and even for the experienced who may panic and jump too hard on the rear pedal, integrated systems are a blessing. For the

Here is how a modern motorcycle anti-lock brake system works. Actuating the lever or pedal applies the appropriate brake(s) and causes the sensors to "read" signals from the wheels. When the system senses impending lockup, it sends a signal to the modulator (center, right) to release hydraulic braking pressure momentarily and re-apply it several times per second. The rider feels only a slight pulse in the controls. (Illustration courtesy of BMW of North America)

experienced or serious sport bike rider they're less useful. Under conditions of uncertain traction, such as when riding down a steep dirt road in a campground, a rider may wish to control speed by dragging the rear brake—an accidental rear brake lockup is much less serious than locking the front. On a twisty road a rider may prefer to adjust speed slightly in a turn by using the rear brake, which also steadies the bike. With an integrated system the front brake compresses the fork, changes the steering angle and reduces ground clearance slightly. In a slow-speed turn in a parking lot the rider may wish to drag the rear brake to help keep the bike more upright, and doesn't want the front brake to actuate. Finally, a serious sport rider uses the front brake very hard, and the rear little or not at all. In the above situations, integrated braking systems are not as useful for the experienced rider as standard, separate braking systems.

Keep in mind that there was nothing wrong with the integrated braking systems I have tested. They have worked well and have never gotten me into trouble; also, probably other riders have experienced the same.

My feelings against them are for the same reason I do not like a camera that does not allow me to manually change its settings for special situations. I just don't like giving up that degree of control.

Anti-lock braking systems. Motorcycle anti-lock braking systems prevent brakes from locking by causing the braking action to pulse rather than grab, and to release rather than lock. Anti-lock braking systems (ABS) is available on many BMW models, the Honda ST1100, Suzuki 1200 Bandit and a few others. These systems are very high-tech, involving a microprocessor; in simplified terms, the computer oversees a pair of pressure modulators that regulate braking pressure on the front and rear discs.

The system electronically monitors the status of each wheel, and when either approaches lockup it releases braking pressure on that wheel, then restores it at a rate of up to more than 30 pulses per second. The system effectively allows normal braking action when traction conditions are good and prevents lockup when they're not. I have tested these systems on many occasions and have found that they work very well. Yes, these systems tend to be expensive, but if they prevent the rider from falling once in the lifetime of the motorcycle, they could well pay for themselves many times over at that one moment. I would caution you not to allow yourself to become lazy and substitute the ABS system for developing your own braking skills.

Types of Power Transfer

All motorcycles use either a chain, shaft, or belt system to transfer power from the gearbox to the rear wheel. Some motorcyclists feel that chain drive is archaic, while others wouldn't own a shaft, and few seem to understand belt drive at all. Each has its strong and weak points.

First, think back to what I said in the section about engine configuration, and how certain of them hooked up better with shaft or chain final drive. Basically anytime you have to turn the direction of power 90 degrees to its previous axis of rotation, you'll lose a small (2 to 3) percentage of that power because of the weight of additional parts turned and the friction generated. When coupled with a transverse-mounted engine, the power train of a chain-drive bike is aligned. The crankshaft, transmission gears and sprockets all spin on parallel axes.

Mate that same transverse engine to a shaft, and you must turn the power 90 degrees to hook the gearbox to a shaft. Of course, all driveshaft systems must turn the power 90 degrees when mating the shaft's pinion gear to the ring gear in the rear hub. Because driveshaft systems weigh more than chain-drive systems, and eat up power, they are not considered optimum for use in sport bikes. Engines with crankshafts located longitudinally in the frame, whether opposed, vee, or flat, are more compatible with driveshafts as they eliminate that first 90-degree turn in the direction of power.

Chain drive. There's something elegantly simple about a chain-drive system. There's also something awfully suspicious about trusting your well-being to the chain's weakest link. In this system, power is fed through the gearbox to a countershaft output sprocket. A roller chain then connects that sprocket with the drive sprocket on the rear wheel, which then transfers power and makes the motorcycle move forward.

Chain-drive systems offer many advantages including their lower weight. In addition, they don't have to shunt the power through one or two direction changes; therefore, all else being equal, more power reaches the ground with a chain-drive bike than one equipped with a driveshaft.

Another advantage of chain-drive systems is that it's possible to change gear ratios easily by changing to sprockets that have more or fewer teeth. This makes it possible to raise or lower engine RPM in relation to road speed for either more acceleration or easier cruising at road speeds. Also, because the countershaft sprocket usually runs in a tight-fitting housing, it's often more practical to change the rear sprocket. A general rule is to not change the rear sprocket by more than two teeth larger or smaller. A better rule is figuring that correct sprocket sizes is a job for experts; get the advice of your dealer or another knowledgeable person before attempting it.

The chain-drive system also has several disadvantages. The chain must be regularly adjusted and maintained. See your owners manual for the adjustment procedure. It must be cleaned and lubricated regularly, although the advent of the O-ring chain has taken some of the bother out of these tasks.

With the standard roller chain, lubricant must be applied to the side plates often, so that some of it will work its way into the rollers for lubrication. With an O-ring chain, however, lubricant is injected into the

Avoid Rear Brake Lockup

Here's a braking tip to help avoid rear-wheel lockup. One of the most common loss-of-control situations is when the rider locks the rear wheel on a motorcycle in a hard stop. This usually occurs when the rider overreacts to a situation, pulls in the clutch lever and uses both brakes hard simultaneously. Once the clutch is pulled in and the rear wheel disconnected from the engine, it is very easy to lock. The solution is to discipline yourself to not pull in the clutch lever during hard braking unless you're also shifting, or are about to come to a stop. A rear wheel that is still spinning with the engine is being influenced by many horsepower. To lock the wheel you also have to bring the engine to a stop, which is a much more difficult task. ∎

rollers when the chain is manufactured, then sealed with a rubber O-ring at each side of the roller. Not only does this keep the lubricant inside, but also helps to keep moisture and dirt out.

O-ring chains tend to last longer than common roller chains because of this sealed-in lubrication. While it is impossible, because of the many variables involved, to accurately predict drive-chain life, let me leave you with a rule of thumb. A properly cared for roller chain may last 10,000 miles, while an O-ring chain may last twice that long. Be aware that when you replace a worn-out chain, it's also a good idea to replace both sprockets as well, because these components tend to wear into each other. It's a false economy to replace only the drive chain; the old, worn-in sprockets will wear out a new chain long before its time.

Drive chains are also noisy in operation, creating a sizzling, whirring sound as the bike moves along. It's possible to hear when a chain is worn out or in need of lubrication. Set the bike on its centerstand, place the gearbox in neutral with the engine off, and spin the rear wheel in the direction of travel. A good, well-lubricated chain will whir. From one that's in less than

A drive chain is a fairly reliable means of power transfer, but it demands frequent adjustment, lubrication, and eventual replacement.

An O-ring chain utilizes O-shaped rubber rings to seal in lubrication (Note O-rings between sideplates). O-rings should be lubricated to keep them supple.

good shape you'll hear grinding, squeaking and gnashing sounds, and you may observe that certain links have bound and kinked, and will not conform easily to the sprockets. Note which rollers must be freed up, clean the whole chain, and then lubricate it thoroughly. If the grinding and gnashing sounds just won't go away with careful cleaning and lubing, it's time to retire the chain and replace it and its sprockets.

To clean a drive chain, place the bike on its centerstand with the engine off and the gearbox in neutral. Spray a rag with a degreasing agent such as WD-40. Do not spray the cleaner directly onto the chain, as you do not want it to run down in between the rollers and remove the lubricant that is already present. Place the rag around the bottom run of the chain, hold the rear wheel tightly to keep it from spinning, and wipe the grit and grime off a section of chain. As each section is completed, turn the wheel to expose a new section of chain. Do not spin the wheel as you hold the rag, because it's *very* easy to catch the rag or a finger in a sprocket this way.

Lubricate the chain with a good brand of commercial motorcycle chain lubricant (rather than some substitute such as WD-40, motor oil, or light machine oil). A drive chain has very special needs. Most chain lubes use a light solvent carrier that seeps inside the rollers,

bringing with it a good load-bearing molybdenum grease. Once inside, the solvent evaporates, leaving the moly behind. The best time to lube the chain is just after riding the bike, when it is still warm from running, and the lubricant will be free to flow. Spray the lubricant along each edge of the chain between the plates, on the inside surface. When the bike is run, centrifugal force will work the lubricant into the chain. The rollers themselves need only a minimal amount of lubricant; enough lubricant should spill over from the spraying that it's not necessary to spray the rollers directly.

It's not true that O-ring chains do not need lubrications. The rubber O-rings should be lubricated periodically, as the lubricant preserves the life of the rubber. The more fastidious will take care to wipe the chain down after lubing, as this will prevent excess lubricant from being thrown all over the rear wheel and rider's clothing. Drive chains are not clean systems.

Never perform the above operations by running the engine, putting the bike in gear, and then letting out the clutch to spin the chain. That's an excellent way to lose a finger or catch an article of clothing in the machinery. Indoors, this invites the buildup of deadly carbon monoxide. Finally, were the bike to tip off the stand while it's running and in gear, it could embark upon an unexpected, unwelcome trip. Even with the engine off, keep your fingers and the rag away when spinning the rear wheel and chain.

Belt drive. All of the advantages of drive chains—the good power transfer and relative lightness of operation—also apply to the belt drive. The best news is that none of the disadvantages really apply. A belt system never needs lubrication, and may require perhaps only three adjustments during its entire lifetime. A belt is very quiet. Belts have proven to be strong, and Harley-Davidson has used belts on its Big Twins for years now with good results. It is common for a belt final drive to go 100,000 miles between replacements.

Still, belts aren't for every application. They are not as strong as chains and must be wider to handle a given amount of horsepower, which makes them less desirable on high-horsepower machines. Also, there is a strong trend with custom Harley-Davidsons to mount very wide rear tires, and the belt width makes mounting the very widest tires problematical.

Shaft drive. On a motorcycle, a driveshaft is simply a shaft that attaches to the gearbox output shaft at one end, and its pinion gear meshes with the ring gear at the other. The shaft's pinion gear runs in an oil bath. A driveshaft's main advantages are reliability, quietness, and ease of maintenance. Most automobiles use driveshafts, and they last the life of the car with little or no maintenance required.

Unlike a chain that requires lubrication and adjustment periodically, a shaft requires only that the lubricant in its oil bath be changed perhaps once a year, or about every 10,000 to 20,000 miles, whichever comes first. Inspection and topping up fluid levels are not usually required between annual changes.

It's also a good idea to lubricate the splines of the rear wheel that mesh with the splines on the rear hub; this job is routinely performed when rear tire is changed and the wheel has to be pulled anyway. That's it. That's how easy it is to live with a driveshaft.

Because there are no external moving parts, the shaft runs more quietly than a chain, and its sealed innards aren't subject to contamination by dirt or water. As for reliability, think of the massive shaft and gear teeth in comparison with the relative lightness of a chain's individual links.

The shaft's disadvantages are that they're heavy, and require force to turn, which eats up some horsepower. They're also more expensive to manufacture than chain-drive systems, and there is no simple way to

A belt-drive system, such as that on this Harley-Davidson, offers the benefits of a chain-drive system without the drawbacks.

The driveshaft rotates in the horizontal housing at left. Its pinion gear mates with the ring gear in the rear hub to power the rear wheel. (Photo courtesy of Yamaha Motor Corporation, USA)

change gear ratios as there is with a chain-drive system.

The shaft system's major shortcoming is the tendency of the shaft-drive-equipped machine's rear end to rise when the throttle is opened and to fall when the throttle is closed. This quirk is controlled more in some machines than in others by the damping effect of the suspension components. It is of no real concern in most cases, but in high-powered bikes with worn-out suspension systems the bike can rise and fall several inches when the throttle is opened and closed hard in the lower gears. In a bike that sits low, this falling action can restrict ground clearance in a turn and possibly cause the mufflers, stands, or frame to drag on the pavement. In extreme cases, the bike can drop so hard onto its undercarriage that the rear tire will be levered completely off the pavement, causing the motorcycle to slide out of control. This is a worst-case situation and not one to worry about unless your shaft-drive bike often drags its unyielding parts in turns.

In conclusion, your choice of power transfer depends upon your riding style and the types of bikes available to match that style. For their extreme reliability and ease of maintenance, a driveshaft is preferred by most touring riders, and most large touring bikes are equipped with them as standard equipment. They are very desirable for long-distance touring. Late-model BMWs use the Paralever, a driveshaft that is jointed at both ends and effectively cancels out the up/down motions of the conventional shaft. The sport rider will usually prefer a chain drive because it robs less power, weighs less, and the up-and-down motion of a shaft would be disconcerting. As for a belt, currently your only choice is Harley-Davidson—which really isn't such a bad choice if Harleys fit your riding style.

Wheelbase

The motorcycle's wheelbase is the distance measured from its front axle center to its rear axle center—and this figure is a rough approximation of its size. The wheelbase is an actual base upon which the motorcycle sits, and it influences many factors.

Ever wonder why a dirt bike can pop wheelies so easily, but your street bike may not even be able to get the front wheel off the ground? The reasons have to do with factors such as torque, weight distribution, and gear ratios, but part of the reason is that dirt bikes have relatively short wheelbases. The dirt-bike rider sits almost over the rear axle, so when he cracks the throttle and pulls back on the handlebar, he has more effective leverage on the front wheel. On a street bike, however, you're sitting between the axles, which greatly reduces your leverage.

Bikes with very short wheelbases, all else being equal, tend to turn more quickly than bikes with longer wheelbases. The tradeoff is that longer-wheelbase bikes tend to track better in a straight line at speed. Dirt

bikes, which need to make instant steering corrections to avoid rocks and other obstacles, need relatively short wheelbases. Street and touring bikes, which require stability on the highway, need longer ones.

Wheelbase is a general indication of size, as I've said. The bigger the bike, generally the longer the wheelbase. Here are some actual wheelbase specifications for several bikes of various engine displacements.

Table 2.1 Wheelbase Specifications for Various Engine Displacements	
Displacement (cc)	Wheelbase (inches)
250	53.9
450	54.5
600	57.9
750	58.8
1000	59.7
1100	60.6
1340	62.5
1500	66.9

These are actual figures; some bikes in each class may have a longer wheelbase, some are shorter. The chart is intended merely to illustrate the general relationship between displacement size and wheelbase.

The wheelbase is important to the tourer because it indicates the amount of room available for riders and accessories. Table 2.1 shows a difference of 4.3 inches between the 450 and the 750, which translates into that much more room on the seat for the riders. There's a whopping nine inches of difference between the 600 and the 1500—the difference between a cramped ride as opposed to being able to stretch out.

Also, because wheelbase is the base upon which the motorcycle rides, its load should be carried between its axles. Any weight carried a significant distance behind the rear axle—a travel trunk on a long luggage rack, for example—uses the rear axle as a fulcrum to lever the weight off the front wheel. Hang too much weight off the rear and the front end will feel light, causing the bike to understeer. In other words, it will not turn as sharply as the rider expects it should. This can lead to a dangerous situation.

Wheelbase also correlates to general stability. Envision a skateboard, a bicycle, and a big touring bike. Consider the relative quickness with which each can change direction. Now envision the first two being towed down a highway at 60 MPH, with the touring bike riding along behind. Which do you feel would be most stable? Which do you feel would be most controllable at this speed? Isn't this an easy quiz?

Suspension Systems

The suspension system literally suspends the motorcycle, more or less in a state of equilibrium as it travels. Its job is to minimize the amount of energy from bumps and other impacts reaching the motorcycle and rider, while allowing the rider to maintain control. Many newer motorcycles have multiadjustable suspensions, and it's important that you understand them so that you can best utilize them for comfort and control.

Let's begin by imagining a motorcycle without a suspension system. You can consider a bicycle if you wish, though a non-suspended motorcycle would weigh much more and travel at much higher speeds. As the bike travels, the bumps and holes it encounters in the road transfer some of its motion forward into up-and-down motion.

Some of that transferred energy is dissipated through tire and frame flex, but the majority of it is fed into the frame and to the rider. Feed enough energy into the motorcycle and not only does it become uncomfortable for the rider, but also the tires can be bounced right off the pavement. Think of a bicycle jouncing over a series of bumps. Tires that are not in contact with the pavement cannot act to influence acceleration, braking, or steering. The vehicle can only loosely be considered to be under control.

The suspension system's job, therefore, is to not only suspend the weight of the motorcycle and rider, but also to damp out the excess energy fed into it by the road. With a perfect suspension system, the tires would always remain in contact with the road, the suspension would damp out the excess energy, and the suspended bike and rider would remain level to the pavement at all times. In essence, the suspension is there for comfort and to keep the tires nailed down. Let's answer some basic questions about how suspensions work, and about their parts, before we consider how the rider can adjust these systems.

The motorcycle has a front and rear suspension system. On most bikes the front is contained within the fork tubes, and the rear within a single or twin shock

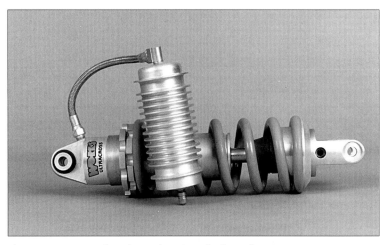

This competition-quality aftermarket monoshock employs a screw-type spring preload adjuster, and a nitrogen-charged reservoir. (Photo courtesy Works Performance)

absorbers. In simplified terms, the systems use one or more coil springs to support the weight of the motorcycle, and a hydraulic system to damp out the energy from road irregularities. Some systems use air pressure as a spring. With some suspension systems the rider can adjust the spring preload and/or damping rates, but on others there are no such adjustments. Let's look at each of these features in turn.

Springs. Motorcycle suspensions utilize coil springs inside their fork legs, and wrapped around their shock absorbers, to support the weight of bike and rider(s). Standard coil springs compress at a linear rate. If a force of, say, 40 pounds will compress a fork spring one inch, then a force of 80 pounds will compress it two inches. It does not matter if the fork springs have already been partially compressed; a constant-rate spring will always compress at the same rate when a specific weight is applied.

Let's take the example of a street motorcycle that has a suspension system with six inches of travel. Travel is the distance the fork or shock will move from full extension till it bottoms (the springs become coil bound or the system reaches its rubber stops). Commonly, the weight of the parked motorcycle at rest will use up a couple inches of suspension travel, and when the rider climbs aboard the springs will sag another inch. To deal with the road and load environment, that leaves only three inches of usable suspension travel, which is not a lot. One response had been to replace the standard springs with those of a heavier rate. True, this

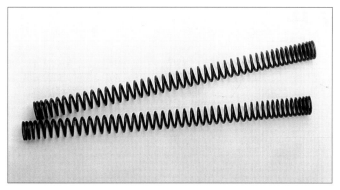

Quality aftermarket fork springs will usually improve a motorcycle's ride and handling. This system uses dual-rate springs. (Photo courtesy of Progressive Suspension, Inc.)

will make it more difficult to bottom the suspension, but now the ride will be more firm, which may not be as comfortable. Is there any means of having both plushness on the highway, with firm control on back roads? Yes! What we need is a progressive-rate (or multi-rate) spring, one that provides progressively more resistance to compression the further it is compressed.

To provide the benefits of a rising-rate suspension, many motorcycle companies now equip their suspension systems with progressive-rate springs. You can identify these springs by the fact that they are progressively wound—their coils are wound more tightly at one end, progressing to a more open spacing at the other. Another approach is to use several separate individual springs having different spring rates. Using progressive- or multi-rate springs creates a rising-rate suspension system; it offers a softer, plusher ride on smooth roads, but also progressively resists bottoming over larger bumps or holes.

Another way to design a rising-rate suspension is by arranging a linkage system on the shock absorber. Most modern sport bikes and motocrossers are suspended in the rear by a centrally located single shock absorber. Look at the bottom of this shock and chances are you'll see a complex lever system. It is designed to work with the spring and damping rates to create a suspension that is plush at the beginning of its travel, and becomes progressively more resistant to movement as it compresses.

Most motorcycles offer spring preload adjustments in the form of a ramped collar on their shock absorbers, usually providing the rider anywhere from about three to six settings. If your bike has constant-rate shock springs, pre-compressing them will help the bike maintain ride height, but it will not "stiffen" the ride. If your bike has progressive springs, however, pre-compressing them will use up the softer rate first, increasing the overall spring rate and stiffening the ride. If a bike has ground clearance problems, dialing in more spring preload will provide a little more clearance.

Motorcycles with preload adjustments on their fork springs tend to be high-performance bikes fitted with progressive springs. As with the rear progressive springs, pre-compressing progressive-rate fork springs will help the bike maintain ride height, and will increase overall spring rate.

Here's a tip to consider if your bike's fork springing is too limp for your tastes. Put the bike on its center stand and place a block under the motor (if necessary) to lift the front tire off the ground. Remove the fork caps, being wary that they will be under some spring tension, and will extend suddenly with several pounds of force when the caps are released.

Slide the fork springs out and measure them, then consult a shop manual to determine if they are still within factory specifications. If they are not, they should be replaced. If they're within spec but too soft for your liking, you can replace them with an aftermarket progressive spring available from companies such as Works Performance Products in Van Nuys, California, or Progressive Suspension, Inc. in Hesperia, California.

Another option is to preload the fork springs, whether they be constant rate or progressive. Usually, just one to two inches of spring preload will make a dramatic difference in the front end, lessening dive under braking, maintaining ground clearance and causing the bike to feel more controlled at speed. The easiest way to preload fork springs is to find the largest size of PVC pipe, such as that used for sprinkler systems, that will fit inside your fork tubes. Cut two equal lengths of pipe, from one to two inches long, and use them as spacers above the fork springs with an appropriately sized washer between the spacers and springs. It will take a bit more force now to push the spacers into the fork tubes against the additional spring compression, but the results should be worth it. It may take a bit of experimenting with different lengths of spacers to get the effect you want.

Fork oil. It's unusual for a rider to replace his entire fork, as to do so is very expensive and raises compatibility problems with other components. Though most riders choose to live with the forks provided on their motorcycles, they can set up their forks to their own particular needs. I've already discussed changing fork springs and adjusting spring preload. Another option is to change the viscosity, or the "weight," of fork oil.

As with motor oil, fork oil is available in various viscosities. Viscosity is a measure of the oil's ability to flow. Fork oil is usually available in viscosity indexes ranging from five to 15 or 20 weight. Lower viscosities flow more freely, while the upper viscosities would increase damping rates.

If you've adjusted your fork springs satisfactorily, but your fork still feels underdamped, ask your dealer or mechanic for advice about experimenting with fork oil. If you get the go-ahead, consult your owner's manual for the recommended fork oil viscosity. I suggest that you confine your experimentation to an increase of no more than a doubling of recommended viscosity—if the bike manufacturer calls for five weight fork oil, don't go any higher than 10 weight unless you have consulted a mechanic to make certain that the fork is working properly.

Note that you can mix various weights of fork oil, so long as they are of the same brand and type, to custom blend your own viscosity. For example, I have determined that my fork is too mushy when I use the standard five-weight fork oil, but too harsh with 10 weight. So I custom blend my fork oil to eight weight by mixing the proper amounts of the same brands of five weight with 10 weight. Stick to factory recommendations for the amount of fork oil in each leg, and consult your owner's manual for the recommended procedure for changing fork oil.

Air suspension. "Riding on air" becomes more than a cliché with some heavyweight and high-performance motorcycles, including motocross bikes. The air suspension system is another approach to what I talked about earlier: an attempt to provide a progressive-rate suspension system.

Air is a gas, and with gases there is a direct relationship between pressure and volume. Compress a given amount of air in a sealed chamber by half, and its pressure will double. Now relate this fact to a sealed air-suspension system. Consider a street motorcycle with six inches of travel available in its air-assisted fork. As

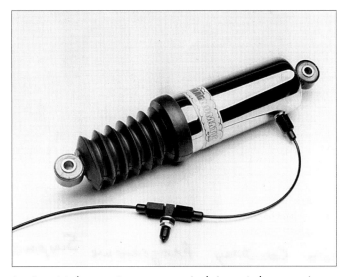

An air-assisted suspension uses pressurized air as a truly progressive spring. (Photo courtesy of Progressive Suspension, Inc.)

an illustration, let's say that 50 pounds of pressure is needed to compress the fork the first three inches, at which point pressure in the fork now doubles. Assuming the fork remains at a constant temperature (air pressure is affected by temperature—pressure rises when temperature rises), the next 50 pounds of force will compress the fork only an additional 1.5 inches. To compress the fork that final 1.5 inches will require 100 additional pounds of force. Here, again, we have a rising-rate suspension.

But air suspension is not perfect. While it works well at the plush end, pressure rises dramatically as a small-volume air suspension compresses; this can cause a harsh ride when the road gets rough. The answer is to provide additional air volume, which Harley-Davidson formerly did on some models by directing pressure to the chromed safety bar or handlebar and using it as an air reservoir. In most air-suspension systems, coil springs are left in place to handle part of the suspending duties, and as a backup, should the system lose air pressure.

Damping adjustments. While the springs are supporting the weight of the motorcycle, the damping system is at work removing the energy that is fed into it. Because it's much less expensive to make springs than it is to build a quality damping system, many motorcycles arrive from the factory oversprung and underdamped. This means that on a rough road the bike feels

A modern fork, such as that on this Suzuki TL1000S, offers multi adjustability for spring preload and damping so that it can be tuned specifically to rider weight and type of riding.

bouncy, as its damping system is not able to adequately control suspension movement.

Suspension systems are damped by a mechanism that forces internal fluids through a series of orifices. Some systems offer damping adjustments; by turning a circular control on the shock or fork leg, any of several different orifices can be rotated into place.

Another damping system is the DeCarbon type damper, which also provides several orifices of various sizes, but is not adjustable from the outside. With the DeCarbon type, each orifice is capped by a valve that is controlled by a spring. As the bike strikes varying sizes of bumps, some (but perhaps not all) of the orifices will come into play. By matching orifice size with the proper spring rate, the DeCarbon damping unit can provide a very progressive rate of damping, and can work very well.

The quality of stock OEM suspension units varies, but those on sport bikes are often of very high quality while cruisers often receive marginal dampers. It has been my experience that aftermarket performance shock absorbers (dampers) are usually superior to OEM units, plus they can be custom tailored by the manufacturer to your particular bike, weight and riding

habits if you provide that information when you order them.

When a motorcycle is ridden hard, its suspension fluid can become overheated, and can aerate. Liquid is what damps a suspension system, not air bubbles; when damping fluid aerates, damping action degrades. We call this condition "suspension fade." Higher-quality shock absorbers will be nitrogen charged—a pressurized nitrogen gas reservoir is built into the shock, and separated from the shock oil by a flexible membrane. The pressure from the nitrogen lessens the possibility of aeration; such shocks will often also be equipped with a remote nitrogen reservoir to encourage cooling and to increase the volume of nitrogen.

Suspension setup. No suspension system can work as well as it should if it's not properly set up by the rider. I've already discussed such subjects as fork oil viscosity and spring preload. Here are some tips on how to adjust your suspension settings to your needs.

First, consider that your suspension needs change depending upon the amount of weight you carry, the type of riding you're doing and the roads you're traveling. You would set your suspension adjustments much differently for cruising the freeway solo at 55 MPH than you would if you were carrying a passenger and luggage through winding mountain roads at speed.

Setting (or "dialing in") sophisticated suspension systems is a process. To familiarize yourself with your suspension system, experiment with it. First, set the spring preload properly according to your owners manual. The process usually goes something like this. Stand beside the bike and hold it upright as a friend takes a measurement between two fixed points, one suspended and one not. Suspended parts could be any part of the seat or upper frame. An unsuspended point would be on the swingarm. Now sit on the bike wearing your riding gear, and have your friend take a second measurement at the same two points. Because your weight has compressed the suspension, this second measurement should be shorter and is called "sack." Your owners manual or aftermarket shock manual should list a recommended figure for spring sack — it is often about 1.5 to 2.0 inches. If sack is greater than recommended, you should increase spring preload. If less, decrease spring preload.

With spring preload now properly adjusted, set damping adjusters to their minimum (Number One) position. Ride a familiar loop of road, paying attention

The blue piece protruding from this fork cap is a pre-load adjuster. Turning it down into the fork will increase load on the fork spring (preload it) for greater ground clearance. If the fork springs are progressively wound, increasing preload will also deliver a more firm ride. Backing the spring adjusters out will lessen preload. Spring preload can also help the fork deal with loads. (Photo courtesy of Yamaha Motor Corporation, USA)

These gauge-mounted pumps are designed for precise adjustment of air-suspension systems. This one is made by Progressive Suspension.

to how the bike feels as you ride. Do not try to ride at speed, as minimum settings will provide minimum ground clearance.

NOTE: *Always* adjust like fork and like shock controls (if you have twin shock absorbers) to the same setting. For example, both fork legs should be adjusted to the same amount of spring preload, air pressure and damping. If you have twin shocks, each shock should be adjusted to the same preload, pressure and damping setting as the other. To do otherwise would cause side-to-side imbalances in the suspension system. Note that many air-suspension systems utilize crossover tubes that link both fork legs and both shocks; with these, one setting will equalize both components.

Once you complete your loop, adjust damping settings to the maximum recommended and ride again at the same speeds. Try to hit the same bumps and notice how things have changed. Now you will have an idea of how certain adjustments affect your machine. Before your third loop, adjust your damping to what you believe would be ideal settings for this stretch of roadway. If the settings are not satisfactory, find a safe place to pull off and adjust them again. Repeat the process until you're satisfied that, for this section of road, these particular settings are ideal. Now you can use

these settings as a frame of reference for other types of roads and loads.

To summarize the process: first, set your spring preload (or air pressure) for the weight you will be carrying. This is done by turning the ramped preload collar on the shock absorbers (on some shocks, preload is set by turning a screw-in collar, then locking the setting with a second threaded collar). Then, set air pressure by using a pump to add pressure to the various air fittings, or by bleeding pressure from them. Progressive Suspension offers a hand-held pump, complete with low-pressure air gauge, that is specifically designed for adjusting air suspension systems. Finally, set your damping to control your suspension's movement. Keep in mind that no one setting will suffice for all situations, but if you understand what each setting does you'll be able to set up your suspension system properly.

Fuel Capacity and Mileage

If you tour extensively, you know that on certain stretches of roadway in remote areas, gas stations can be few and far between. In areas such as this, especially late or early in the day when stations may not be open, it's a real advantage to have a motorcycle that offers substantial mileage range.

The author's old 1976 BMW R75/6 has been fitted with a European sport-touring fairing and eight-gallon Heinrich tank. The bike now offers a useful range approaching 350 miles.

Range. Range is the distance a motorcycle can realistically travel on a tank of gas. Figure your range by multiplying your bike's average miles per gallon times its fuel capacity. A motorcycle with a 4.5-gallon tank, for example, that averages 52 miles per gallon, can run approximately 234 miles before it runs out of gas. Another bike that averages 47 miles per gallon, and has a 6.3-gallon tank, can expect to run about 296 miles before it hits empty. Obviously, a greater range is preferable to a lesser one—a fact appreciated by anyone who has ever hiked down a lonely, deserted road looking for a gas station.

Your bike's trip odometer will help prevent you from running out of gas. Reset it to zero each time you fill up. Note at what mileage your bike tends to hit reserve, or the red zone on your fuel gauge. Once you become acquainted with your bike's touring range, a glance at the miles elapsed on your trip odometer will give you a fair idea of how soon you should refill.

Also, be sure to understand the idiosyncrasies of your bike's fuel system. It's common for a motorcycle to hold slightly less fuel than the specifications chart says it should. Often that figure is arrived at mathematically and does not take into account the realities such as air pockets that develop at the top of the tank. With

their anti-pollution systems, some tanks cannot or should not be filled to the very top.

Fuel gauges are notoriously unreliable, usually indicating full for the first 50–75 miles, and empty long before the last drop slides into the carburetors. There is method to the madness here, as the motorcycle companies would like to help prevent you from having to take that long, lonely walk. To develop a more realistic sense of your bike's capacity and range, mentally note the number of miles into a tank that the fuel gauge normally reads empty, and fill up. Compare the volume of gas it takes with the tank capacity listed on the specifications page. If at some time you run the tank down to virtually empty, note how much gas the tank will accept. How much more is this than the tank accepts when the gas gauge reads empty? Knowledge of these various figures will help you plan your gas stops.

Until the early 1980s, nearly all motorcycles offered a petcock arrangement that provided for RUN, RESERVE, and OFF positions. Rather than a separate reserve tank, each petcock includes a short metal tube that sticks up several inches into the tank from the bottom. With the valve set to ON or RUN, fuel is drawn from an orifice in the top of this tube. When the fuel level drops below this orifice, the engine begins sputtering and the rider switches the petcock valve to the RESERVE position. Now fuel is drawn from an orifice near the bottom of the tank. The amount of fuel available in this reserve setting varies from bike to bike, but usually is between 0.5 to 1.2 gallons.

Motorcyclists lament the passing of the petcock in favor of the fuel gauge, as the petcock gave them a very distinctive sign—that could not be ignored—as to when the fuel level reached a certain point. One reason the petcock may eventually disappear is because the engine suddenly runs out of gas and loses power when the fuel drops below the top orifice. It's just not what you want to have happen when you've pulled out to pass a couple of cars on a tight road.

Brands of Motorcycles

About a dozen companies currently offer street-legal motorcycles in the United States. Each company offers several models in various sizes. Despite what you may believe, the machines offered by some motorcycle companies actually do have distinct personalities—strong points and weak points. Let's take a quick, and perhaps opinionated, look at each of these companies.

Motorcycle dashboards have become much more complete of late. In addition to the usual speedometer and tachometer, this one also includes a fuel gauge (at upper right) and coolant temperature gauge. Keep in mind that because of the often convoluted shapes of their fuel tanks, motorcycle fuel gauges usually don't provide a true linear indication of the fuel level.

The fuel petcock usually offers a choice of ON, OFF, or RESERVE. Once you have turned to RESERVE and topped off, be certain to turn the petcock back to ON (or RUN) again.

BMW. BMW, a German company, originally built aircraft; the company logo showing white and blue areas alternating in a circle is a stylized rendition of a spinning propeller. The company decided to jump into the lucrative motorcycle business in 1923, and the story goes that BMW's chief engineer was not interested in designing a motorcycle. However, his office was cold in the winter, and the company made him an offer he could not refuse. If he would design a motorcycle for them, they would put a fine, new stove in his office.

The motorcycle he designed was a 500cc opposed, air-cooled twin with a driveshaft. Ever since, BMW has offered opposed, air-cooled twins with shafts, and an air-cooled single of about 250cc for a number of years. A line of 980cc fours, known as the K100, appeared in 1985, followed soon after by the K75 750cc triple. Today, BMW offers its line of new R1100 and R1200 air/oil-cooled twins, and several 1100 and 1200cc fours. Other than the F650 air-cooled singles with chain drive, all BMW models are equipped with a driveshaft.

BMWs are sportier machines known for their reliability, classiness, smoothness and driveshaft. The air-cooled twins are no longer in production, but used models are still readily available. They are relatively low in weight and light in power, but are among the most satisfying machines available. I have personally put well over 160,000 miles on the venerable old twins.

K-series fours have been produced in 1,000cc, 1100cc and 1200cc versions, and are known to be very long lived. They are liquid-cooled, fuel injected, longitudinal machines that offer an abundance of midrange grunt, and develop respectable power. Dresser (RT and LT) models, sport touring (RS), and sport (S) versions are available in the various series. The K1200RS and LT both offer the Paralever and Telelever.

BMW is known for long-distance, sporty, shaft-driven machines. Shown here is the K1200LT luxury tourer with electrically operated windscreen, great luggage capacity, anti-lock brakes, optional CD changer, and heated grips and seats.

A relatively recent addition to the motorcycle world, the sporty Buell is owned by Harley-Davidson. Its machines are powered by hotted-up 1,200cc Harley Sportster engines. The company's sport-touring models include the S3 Thunderbolt with removable saddlebags. (Photo courtesy of Buell Motor Co.)

Ducatis are sporty V-twins that are very technically advanced. The ST (pictured) is its most touring oriented with higher handlebars and hard-shelled, removable saddlebags. (Photo courtesy of Ducati North America, Inc.)

The R1100 series, introduced for the 1994 model year, is an air/oil-cooled twin with four-valve heads, fuel injection and a stressed-member frame. A unique suspension feature is the Paralever driveshaft, which utilizes a U-joint at each end that cancels out the up/down motion typical of most shaft-driven motorcycles. At the front, its Telelever fork is attached via an A-arm to the engine; the system is very well braced, does not flex appreciably and offers plush suspension with little dive under braking.

K75 triples are no longer in production, but many used machines are still around. They are very smooth, but offer somewhat less power and perhaps five percent less weight than K100s. Hard-shell, removable saddlebags are available with all new BMWs, and these bikes are all biased toward sporting travel. The company was the first to offer anti-lock braking systems for motorcycles.

Finally, the F650 is a light single-cylinder machine that is simple, fun and made by Rotax for BMW. It sports a four-valve head, and is the only BMW ever to come with a chain final drive.

Buell. Buell, which began in the 1980s, is a relative newcomer to the motorcycle market. The company was formed by former Superbike racer Erik Buell, and is now owned by Harley-Davidson. Think of Buell as the sporting division of H-D as these sport bikes with their lightweight frames and belt final drive are powered by 1200cc Sportster engines that have been muscled up for some serious power. Buell Thunderbolts are

serious sport tourers that offer hard-sided, removable luggage.

Ducati. Ducati, an Italian company, offers marvelous, closely focused sport bikes powered by 90-degree, longitudinal, V-twin engines. Some are liquid-cooled engines, and others are air-cooled; some are injected and others carbureted. They're relatively smooth, light, and powerful, but demand a sporting riding position. Handling is excellent, and most models have multi-adjustable suspensions. The ST2 handles well, and with its integral saddlebags is designed for sport touring.

This marque has become famous for its desmodromic valve trains, which open and close the valves with mechanical fingers rather than the usual rocker and spring assembly. The exotic valve actuation system is very positive, but does not offer any particular performance advantage. It is also much more difficult to adjust the valves on a desmodromic system.

Ducatis are fine sport tourers when mounted with suitable luggage, so long as the rider is amenable to the sporting riding position.

Harley-Davidson. There is little to say about Harleys that has not been said before in a number of ways. Founded in 1903 in Milwaukee, Wisconsin, the company built its first V-twin in 1909. Ever since, Milwaukee iron has been synonymous with throbbing, low-RPM power.

Let's be frank. Through the early 1980s, Harley-Davidsons earned a less-than-enviable reputation for

Powered by its venerable air-cooled, 45-degree V-twins, Harley-Davidsons have been relentlessly updated and improved. Shown is its fuel-injected Road Glide model. (Photo courtesy of Harley-Davidson Motor Co.)

Honda's flagship is the six-cylinder Gold Wing Special Edition, a very sophisticated tourer that has been improved over the years and is laden with features. (Photo courtesy of American Honda Motor Co., Inc.)

reliability. The machines vibrated and leaked oil, and were technically archaic when compared with machines from other countries. Then came the big buyout when several of the company's top executives purchased it from American Machine and Foundry (AMF), its parent company. The new executives implemented significant changes, engineered the new "Evolution" engine with aluminum heads, paid attention to every component of the bikes, and offered additional models with rubber-mounted engines. The new bikes were much more reliable and worked much better than former models, and suddenly authors were writing books about the company's dramatic turnaround. Show-business celebrities embraced these big, heavy, mechanical bikes as a means of expression, and suddenly it was cool again to have a Harley.

Harley-Davidsons are much better machines than they ever have been before, and within their particular fields of cruising and touring can be counted among the best motorcycles in their class. They're still air cooled, some models offer fuel injection and all now have belt final drive. They're big, heavy and classy, and nothing quite sounds or feels like one of those big, joined-crankpin V-twins. If you're buying a used Harley, I recommend you stay with Evolution or later models only: these 80-cubic-inch (1340cc) machines first began to appear in 1984, and the smaller Evolution Sportsters of 883cc first appeared in 1986. The updated Twin Cam 88 first appeared in 1999.

Honda. Honda started the motorcycle revolution in the early 1960s and at one time made one of every two motorcycles sold in the United States. It led the market with engineering innovations and, since the beginning, has offered four-stroke engines when no other Japanese company did. But times have changed, and rather than trying to be Everyman's inexpensive mode of travel, Honda began a shift to making more well-rounded, rather than specialized, machines based upon higher quality of fit, finish, and operation. Honda makes some marvelous motorcycles for sport, touring, sport touring, and cruising.

Honda's liquid-cooled, 1520cc six-cylinder Gold Wing is synonymous with dresser touring, and the V-four ST1100 is one of the best sport-touring machines on the market. For a sporting mount that will allow you to travel in relative comfort, I must mention its hyper-fast CBR1100XX. This machine sticks in my mind because in 1996 I was clocked by a radar gun on one at 165.1 mph on a Honda test track. Its 750 Nighthawk is an excellent standard machine for those on a budget, and the VFR800 is one of the best all-around machines made. Finally, Honda offers a variety of cruisers called the Shadow and the Magna.

Kawasaki. In the 1960s and into the 1970s, Kawasaki, a Japanese company, made its name with high-powered two-strokes, then four-strokes, that were always at or near the top of the quarter-mile dragstrip wars. Kawasaki has continued to be a performance-oriented company, though its machines have certainly grown in sophistication.

In its sporting line, its Ninjas are certainly capable sport tourers, and Kawasaki offers its Voyager liquid-

In production for a decade and nearly unchanged, Kawasaki's Voyager XII is a four-cylinder dresser that may lack the technical sophistication of some other models, but offers a lot of value for the money. (Photo courtesy of Kawasaki Motors Corp., USA)

The Italian company Moto Guzzi has offered small numbers of its funky, transverse, air-cooled V-twins to the world market for years. (Photo courtesy of Moto America, Inc.)

Suzuki offers big V-twin cruisers such as this Intruder 1500; its sport-tourers are called the Katanas. (Photo courtesy of American Suzuki Motor Corp.)

cooled touring bike with driveshafts that is low on technology, but high on value. Its cruisers are the V-twin Vulcans.

The Concours, a sport tourer based upon the Ninja, is a good handling machine with big power and decent luggage capacity. For high-speed travel, the ZX1100 is smooth, fast and will travel well into triple digits.

Moto Guzzi. Moto Guzzi's transverse, air-cooled V-twins enjoyed a heyday in the 1960s and 1970s when they were considered one of the premier touring motorcycles in the world, but then were nearly buried by the onslaught of liquid-cooled machines from Japan. The dealer network for these Italian machines has come and gone a few times in the ensuing decades, and the bikes came to be dismissed to what I call "The Home for the Terminally Funky."

Through the 1980s, Moto Guzzi has tried to shed its work-horse image by offering sportier machines such as the LeMans and SP, which are in fact fine sport tourers, although known for benign quirkiness. Today they offer such bikes as the Sport 1100i, an injected model that handles well and is a real kick to ride. "Gooses" are considered reliable, quick enough, and their engines are very understressed, which again contributes to reliability. They're marvelous machines for those who prefer to go their own way, but your biggest challenge will often be simply to locate a dealer near you.

Suzuki. Suzuki, a Japanese company, offers a number of fine machines in diverse families, as do the other three companies from the Orient. At one time it offered a dresser touring machine called the Cavalcade, but has dropped it. Its GSX-R machines are excellent sports that do well in club and supersport racing, and its Katanas are sport tourers that are slightly tamed versions of these hyper sports. Its standard machines are called the Bandits, and its cruisers are the V-twin Intruders.

Triumph. This British company made wonderful air-cooled singles, twins, and triples through the 1970s, including the Bonnevilles, but they were finally swept away by the onslaught of less expensive, more technically sophisticated machines from Japan. The company stopped making motorcycles early in the 1980s, but each passing year seemed to bring yet another promise that Triumph would rise again, followed by yet another disappointment.

Then a British real estate magnate named John Bloor purchased the Triumph name, hired a staff of engineers and revived the Triumph name with a line of 750 and 900cc triples, and 1200cc fours in 1991, and the marque was back with a vengeance. Now, Triumph is well proven, with wonderful engines and chassis. Its sport tourers are the Trophy models with hard-sided, removable luggage. The company also offers performance models and all-around standards.

Victory.   The Victory is made by Polaris, which has made top-line snowmobiles for more than 30 years, plus ATVs and personal watercraft. However, Polaris introduced a brand-new motorcycle called the Victory in 1998. Based upon a 92-inch air/oil-cooled V-twin, this first machine was a big fuel-injected cruiser with four-valve heads and a belt final drive.

As Polaris builds up its dealer base in the future, new models of the Victory will be introduced in sporting, touring and standard versions. Here's a made-in-America effort to watch closely in the future.

Yamaha.   The last of the "big four" Japanese motorcycle companies in the alphabet, Yamaha has paralleled the development of bikes from Honda, Kawasaki, and Suzuki since the 1960s. The company made good, reliable two-strokes until it joined the move to four-strokes in the late 1970s.

During the past two decades Yamaha has, like the other Japanese companies, filled all the gaps including V-twin cruisers, sports, sport tourers, dressers, and the rest. It dropped its big dresser, the V-four Venture, early in the '90s. In its place, a few years later, it introduced the Royal Star, a huge cruiser based upon the Venture's 1300cc engine (except the counterbalancer was left out to induce some shake or "character"), and it was tuned more for low-end power. For 1999 the Venture came back as a dresser version of the Royal Star.

Yamaha also makes V-twin cruisers called the Viragos, and its YZF sportbikes are leading-edge. For all-around use its Seca II is an excellent machine.

Triumph, which went out of business in the early 1980s, has come back strong under new ownership with a line of powerful triples and fours. Shown is its sport-touring Trophy model with comfortable seating and hard-sided, removable bags.

The Victory was first released as a 1998 model, and is powered by a high-tech, 92-cubic-inch, air/oil-cooled V-twin engine with four valves per cylinder and fuel injection. Its parent company is Polaris, which has manufactured snowmobiles for more than 30 years. (Photo courtesy of Polaris Industries)

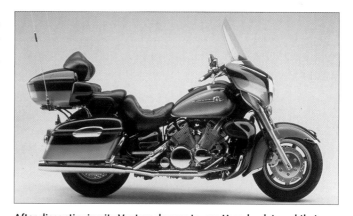

After discontinuing its Venture dresser tourer, Yamaha detuned that bike's V4 engine, put it into a new frame and fashioned a high-end cruiser called the Royal Star. Now they have come full circle by attaching a dresser-style fairing and trunk to their touring Royal Star and calling the new model the Venture. (Photo courtesy of Yamaha Motor Corporation, USA)

3
Accessories

MAKE THE MOTORCYCLE YOURS

Your basic motorcycle is just the starting point on the way to turning it into a well-equipped touring machine that expressly fits your personal travel needs. Even the top-rated, best-equipped machine from the manufacturer cannot begin to answer all the little needs you, as an individual rider (and perhaps also your co-rider), have for comfort, competence and safety on the road. True, some of the items listed here may already be part of the standard equipment on your bike, but in most cases there's much more to making the bike yours than in simply handing the dealer a check and riding away. Let's look at some of these accessory items—some basic, some not—that are so vital to enjoyable travel by motorcycle.

Accessories can make an everyday machine into YOUR machine. This light show award winner carries not only an array of lights, but also numerous other accessories.

Wind Protection

Part of the joy of riding a motorcycle is in being among the elements as you ride; part of the discomfort of motorcycling is in being among the elements as you ride. We may all like the wind in our face, but over the course of a long tour the wind can be tiring, cold, wet, and relentless. While I have no quarrel with those who feel they do not need wind protection, I certainly agree with those who feel they do.

Frame-Mounted Fairings

A fairing is a plastic, fiberglass, or acrylic shaped form that is attached to the front of a motorcycle and designed to push the wind aside. Some fairings attach to the handlebar, and others to the frame. A major benefit to frame mounting is that the loads from wind gusts are imparted to the frame rather than the handlebar; therefore, the fairing can be made relatively large and heavy. This means better protection and the opportunity to carry more weight. Secondly, you do not want to have loads fed into the handlebar for obvious reasons.

Through the 1970s, most motorcycles came from the factory with no wind protection. A few BMW and Harley-Davidson models offered fairings, but most riders bought and installed their own wind cheaters from companies such as Vetter, Pacifico, Bates, Wixom, Calafia, Luftmeister, and others. Each of the above companies offered frame-mounted fairings, and to install them you bolted a subframe to the motorcycle's frame. Then the fairing was bolted to that. The wiring was grafted in, the headlight installed, and the rider was ready to roll in comfort.

Vetter's Windjammer was the most popular aftermarket frame-mounted fairing in the 1970s and early '80s. Since then, most touring and sport-touring bikes have come standard with their own fairings, and few companies offer such aftermarket items any longer.

A few companies still offer handlebar-mounted fairings for standard-style bikes. Here is a Parabellum mounted on a BMW twin. (Photo courtesy of Parabellum)

A sea change in motorcycling occurred when Honda introduced its GL1100 Gold Wing Interstate in 1980. To a degree far surpassing anything that had come before, the bike came fully dressed from the factory with saddlebags, a fairing, and a trunk, all installed and color coordinated. It was an instant success. Soon, dressers followed from the other manufacturers: Kawasaki had its KZ1300 Voyager, Yamaha its 1100 Venture, and Suzuki its 1200 Cavalcade. Harley-Davidson already offered several dressers, and BMW had introduced its RT touring series in 1979. As a result, the aftermarket frame-mounted fairing died a lingering death in the 1980s.

Frame-mounted fairings offer the best protection from the wind, but tend to be heavy (often 25–30 pounds) and expensive. Most were constructed of inner and outer shells, with storage areas between them. Usually, an access door was located on each side of the fairing, covered by either a soft snap-on cover, or a hard lockable one. It has become very difficult to find frame-mounted fairings any longer, but sometimes they are found among a dealer's used or unsold stock, or come attached to older used machines.

Handlebar-Mounted Fairings

Long before the frame-mounted fairing was developed, riders found that they could attach a lightweight framework to their handlebars and spread canvas across it. By adding a clear piece of plastic to the top as a windshield, the handlebar-mounted fairing was born. In the 1960s and early 1970s, fiberglass fairings were developed and became a touring standard until the frame-mounted fairing came to dominate the market in the late 1970s.

Late in the 1970s, numerous companies developed clear acrylic or Lexan plastic fairings that were essentially more elaborate windshields. They were either clear or tinted, and differed from windshields in that they had a lower portion that splayed out to shield the legs. A few riders painted the lower portion of their clear fairings to match their bikes, but stone chips soon took their toll and the fairings looked terrible. Here's a tip: anytime you wish to paint clear plastic, such as a fairing or windshield, paint only the inner surface rather than the outer. The color shows through just as vibrantly, only there's no chance for stones to chip it, and the clear plastic lends the appearance of a deep sheen.

Handlebar-mounted fairings are lighter and less expensive than the frame-mounted variety, as well they should be. Because they're mounted to the handlebar, they can feed inputs from the wind into the bar, thus affecting steering control. Keep in mind that under most foreseeable circumstances, handlebar-mounted fairings

Clear handlebar-mounted fairings offer more lower protection than simple windshields, yet are easy to attach.

Windshields are relatively flat, but are available in different sizes and tints. (Photo courtesy Slipstreamer)

are quite acceptable, but be aware that in strong side-wind conditions they can affect steering.

Clear fairings are very light and have the least affect upon the appearance of the bike. They're also usually the least expensive wind protection you can buy for a bare bike. Their disadvantage is that in an accident they can split and break, and are not repairable. Also, those broken pieces can have sharp, nasty edges and they can be hazardous to the rider. Although fiberglass fairings can be repaired, their windshields are also made of the same plastics as clear fairings, and they can present a problem when broken. Replacement windshields are readily available.

Whenever cleaning a plastic windshield or helmet face shield, take care. First, rinse off grit and wipe the wet shield with your bare hand to dislodge bugs and other hard objects. Your hand can feel grit; an unfeeling rag would just grind that grit into the shield. Once you're sure the grit is gone, wash the shield with mild soap (only necessary if it's really dirty) and dry with a clean, soft towel. Paper towels are made from wood fibers and are more abrasive than cloth towels. However, most quality windshields are made of a grade of plastic (or of coated Lexan) that is sufficient to withstand them.

Windshields

What's the difference between a clear fairing and a windshield? The windshield utilizes a simply curved shape, while the clear fairing often has a convoluted lower section that hangs downward to protect the legs. The windshield can stand alone, attached to the handlebar, or it can be part of a fairing.

Be aware that many full-dress motorcycles offer several optional windshield lengths, and chances are that if the windshield on your bike isn't quite right for you, there's a replacement size that is. They're often available in short, standard, and tall sizes, usually in increments of one to two inches. If your windshield's height doesn't suit you, chances are your motorcycle dealer or accessory store can find you one that will.

The ideal height for a windshield is low enough that the rider can look over it for an unobstructed view, yet high enough that it can deflect the majority of the wind blast over the helmet's face shield, thus keeping it clear of bugs and grime. Some riders prefer a very tall shield that they can look through, but I don't recommend this. When the sun hits a windshield at a certain angle, it can "white out," making it very difficult for the rider to see through. The same effect can be caused by headlights at night, or by rain. I recommend arranging your windshield so that you can look over it rather than through it. And keep in mind that having a windshield may well be noisier than riding without one, as a shield may create a buffeting around your head.

Café Fairings

In the high Alps, European riders like to sprint from café to café, stopping only for gas and a cup of coffee, espresso, or cappuccino. Rather than big, wind-parting fairings, the café racers (as they came to be called) simply wanted to keep the wind off their chests. What resulted was a genre of wind cheaters known as café fairings.

Usually handlebar mounted, café fairings (sometimes called "bikini fairings" for obvious reasons) have come standard on a few bikes such as the BMW R90S and R100S, the Kawasaki Z1, various Ducatis, and the Moto Guzzi LeMans. They were also available occasionally as aftermarket items that could be mounted on bare bikes. The café fairing usually consists of only a fiberglass shell that encircles the headlight with a vestigial windshield above. It shunts the wind away from the chest, but usually provides little leg protection and none for the hands.

By the late 1990s so many bikes now come standard with fairings that that there are few opportunities to add one to a bike. If you ride an unfaired bike and want it to appear sportier while providing a minimal amount of wind protection, add a café fairing. Frame-mounted fairings are recommended for touring, and clear fairings for commuting or lighter-duty work.

Sport Fairings

If you ride a bike such as a Ninja or ZX Kawasaki, Hurricane or CBR from Honda, Suzuki GSX-R, an FZR or YZF from Yamaha, your bike is equipped with a plastic sport fairing and related, full-coverage bodywork. Sport fairings evolved from café fairings, then to half fairings on bikes such as the Suzuki GS series and Kawasaki turbos in the middle 1980s, to the full enclosing bodywork of the bikes mentioned above.

There is little possibility that a rider could outfit his bare bike with a full-coverage sport fairing. The logistics of fitting the shape and making suitable mounting brackets would take a prohibitive amount of time and money. Instead, let's concentrate on what a sport fairing does and does not do, and how you can help care for one.

Sport fairings not only lend a very racy appearance to the motorcycle but also add some degree of aerodynamics to help it pass more easily through the air at elevated speeds. Despite the breathtaking cost of replacing full sport fairings, they do save money in

The fairings on today's sportbikes are all enclosing, which is an aid to styling, streamlining and ease of cleaning. Hidden components don't need to be so nicely finished, saving costs, but these bright fairings can be expensive to replace if damaged. (Photo of GSX-R750 courtesy of American Suzuki Motor Corp.)

another way. It is very costly to finish all the bits and pieces of hardware on an exposed motorcycle engine. By hiding it all away under a sport fairing, the manufacturers can keep costs in line by not having to finish and plate all those bits and pieces.

Tip a sport bike over in a parking lot, or drop one at speed, and the repair bill on the fairing and bodywork could make your hair stand on end. Before tossing away the mangled pieces and calling your banker, be aware that it is now possible to fix body parts with a process called plastic welding. The operation requires use of a special heat gun and the skill to operate it, but sport-oriented dealers often can provide this service—or know where to find it. Once the plastic is repaired it can be painted and new decals applied. Overall, the job should cost about half as much as new body panels.

Luggage Systems

Travel means packing, and the lack of packing space on a motorcycle can mean either a headache to the traveler who never has enough room, or a blessing to the one who wants to unburden himself of life's residue of stuff. Motorcyclists, who are an ingenious lot to begin with, have devised many methods of carrying their luggage. In a product sense, these methods can be divided into two basic luggage types—hard or soft. Let's take a brief look at each.

Hard, removable saddlebags can be left at home when you're not traveling, and make a lot of sense for sporty touring. Some brands hold a great deal, and are waterproof. (Photo courtesy of Yamaha Motor Corporation, USA)

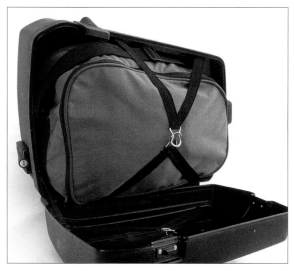

Removable saddlebag liners, such as these by RKA, are sized to fit into particular hard bags and lift out for easy transportation.

Hard Luggage

The two basic types of enclosed carriers on a motorcycle are saddlebags (also called pannier cases by the British), and a tail trunk—which is also referred to as a tour box, TourPak (a Harley-Davidson trademark), or Scoot Boot (also a trademarked name). By "hard" I'm referring to rigid saddlebags made usually of fiberglass or plastic.

Saddlebags are the basic luggage carriers, ranking right behind a duffel bag strapped behind the seat. They fit along the sides of the bike in an area that is otherwise wasted space. They keep the weight between the axles where it belongs, and in toward the center of the bike.

Hard luggage has many advantages. It's lockable and not easily cut as soft luggage can be, so your gear is more secure. In rainy weather it won't soak through as soft luggage can, and provided there's a good seal where they open, hard bags will keep your luggage dry. Hard bags can help keep the bike off the ground in a tip-over, absorbing some of the damage that otherwise would have been inflicted on the expensive motorcycle. They will last for many years and, if damaged, they can be repaired. Finally, they won't fade if coated with a quality paint.

Fixed Luggage

Fixed luggage refers to luggage that is permanently mounted to the motorcycle and is not designed to be removed. On dresser motorcycles with integrated luggage systems, the luggage is usually color matched to the bike, providing an integrated, impressive appearance. Be certain to adequately fasten your bags shut each time you ride or you could lose a lid or some luggage.

Fixed bags usually hold a great deal of luggage, and may have light bars (guards that incorporate additional lighting) built in for added style and visibility. Bumpers or guards on the outside prevent scrapes in the parking lot or if the bike tips over.

Disadvantages? Well, this is not a perfect world and hard bags are not the answer for everyone. For one thing they're quite heavy in comparison with other styles of luggage, which means more wear and tear on the motorcycle and less performance overall. Even when you're just going to work and not even in need of luggage capacity, the bags are always there, weighing upon your bike and slowing you down.

Saddlebag Liners

Now consider how inconvenient it would be if, after throwing dozens of loose items into your saddlebags, you had to frog around inside each one to retrieve those items and carry them up to your motel room on the second floor. To add to the bags' convenience, most manufacturers offer standard lightweight nylon liner bags that are shaped to the inner contours of the saddlebags. The riders pack these removable liners at home, then simply drop them into their saddlebags. This solved one major drawback for hard, nonremovable bags.

On some dressers one or both of the saddlebags must be removed, along with their bracketry, in order to change a rear tire. Unsuspecting riders may go in for a tire change, then find that they owe for several additional hours of shop work to remove and reinstall the saddlebags. As for fixing a rear flat on the road, it's going to take some time and a considerable effort.

Removable Saddlebags

On motorcycles such as most BMWs, the Kawasaki Concours, Triumph Trophy and Honda ST1100, the hard saddlebags can be unlocked and removed from the bike with the turn of a key. With the handles provided they can be carried into a tent or motel room, increasing their convenience dramatically. Some also offer liner bags as mentioned above, so it's not even necessary to remove the saddlebags themselves.

Removable hard saddlebags tend to be lighter than the nonremovable types. When you don't need them, they can stay in the garage out of harm's way, where they can't hinder the motorcycle's progress either. On some brands, the brackets can also be removed for unencumbered riding. On more recent bikes that come from the factory with removable bags, more is also being done with styling so that the bikes look good whether the bags are on or off.

The down side to removable bags is that, if they can remove on purpose, there's the chance they can remove accidentally. Brackets, hardware, and locks should be inspected regularly to be certain that everything is in secure working order. It's one of life's major disappointments to see one of your saddlebags cartwheeling down the road after you—spewing your camera, souvenir glasswear, shoes, wardrobe, and dirty underwear.

Travel Trunks

In case saddlebags do not hold enough for you, consider adding a travel trunk that is located behind the rear seat on a luggage rack. Trunk capacity often rivals that of either saddlebag, and there's no arguing with the convenience when it's arranged horizontally and has a

A trunk on a motorcycle, such as this one on a Honda GL1500 Gold Wing, is a great place for carrying less bulky items to which you'll need immediate access.

lift-up lid. On dresser bikes, the trunk often is equipped with taillights and/or brake lights. They're usually color-coordinated to the rest of the bike, and lockable.

Trunks are convenient; however, their large size contributes to their major drawback. People are tempted to overload them, and often do, which can induce handling irregularities. Consider this: put your bike up on its centerstand, then go behind it and push down on the trunk or the rear of the seat. You'll notice that by using the trunk or seat as a lever, it's possible to

I can guarantee that if it's loaded heavily, this radically rearset trunk will adversely affect this motorcycle's handling.

Some more complex soft saddlebags offer the option of separating your gear into multiple compartments. These Wolfman bags include main, side and top compartments, in addition to anchor points for additional gear. Note how they're cut away to clear a passenger's heels.

A tank bag is your most convenient luggage item, and is an ideal location in which to carry spare gloves, a sweater and shield cleaner. Note top map pouch and rear pocket. The side pockets on this RKA unit detach and become belt carriers, and the bag expands.

move the rear end up and down to some extent, depending upon the bike you have, how it's balanced on the centerstand, and how hard you're pushing.

Now look at your bike from the side, noting the location of the trunk in relation to the rear axle. Unless your bike is very unusual, the luggage rack and trunk will be located high and behind the rear axle. What happens is that the weight in the trunk uses its distance from the rear axle as a lever, and the axle itself as a fulcrum, to reduce the weighting of the front wheel. In a practical sense this means that, if you go for a ride with a very heavy load in your trunk, your motorcycle will suddenly not want to turn very readily. It will run wider in the turns than you're used to, because there is now less weight pushing down on the front wheel.

Keep this fact in mind, and make it a point to load accordingly. Use the trunk for less dense items you'll need quick access to such as a rain suit, cold-weather gear, a purse, camera, etc.

Soft Luggage

As its name implies, soft luggage is that which is made of pliable materials such as nylon or leather. Many individual types of carriers are available, and we'll look at each in turn.

Soft luggage is much lighter than hard luggage, although it usually does not offer as much capacity. Hard bags often hold in the neighborhood of 2,000 cubic inches; soft bags average between 1,000 and 1,500. But soft bags are also much less expensive and usually very easy to mount. Most soft luggage is made of Cordura nylon or similar fabrics, although leather bags have become popular for cruisers. Nylon bags can be offered in colors from the factory; however, black is still the overwhelming color of choice for most riders.

But soft luggage cannot be effectively locked closed, or even locked to the bike. An impatient thief could even cut the bags open, or cut them off the bike. If they come in contact with a hot engine part or the exhaust system, the nylon can melt through. Although sheet nylon is usually treated so that it's virtually waterproof, rain nevertheless can sneak in past the zipper teeth, and likewise through the stitch holes. Premium tank bags, soft saddlebags, and tail packs often come equipped with rain bonnets.

Tank Bags

For many years, European riders have known that the best place to carry a light load is in a luggage bag strapped to the fuel tank. The weight is placed centrally between the axles, and in a location that's easy to monitor. If your saddlebag accidentally opens, you may not notice it until you're 20 miles down the road and your underwear is long gone. If a tank bag gets loose, you'll know it immediately.

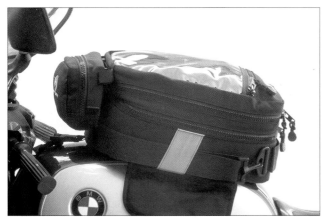

This Marsee Magnetic Tank Bag expands. Note that it tethers to the handlebar in case the magnets lose their grip. It features a removable front pouch, reflective striping, and side lacing that adjusts the bag to its load.

Tank bags are usually made of heavy nylon, although some are made of vinyl and old-line European bags are made of leather. Look at the top of a tank bag—it's flat and could be put to some use. Most tank bags offer a clear plastic pouch on the top that will hold a map open right under your snoot where you want it.

Be aware that the tank bag will be the first thing you'll come in contact with in the event of a frontal accident; it's wise to carry only soft objects there. Tool kits, engine parts, and boat anchors should be carried elsewhere.

What do you put in a tank bag? I've taken solo weekend jaunts during which all I needed—a change of clothes and toiletries—was carried in a tank bag. Traveling light is one of life's pleasures. Tank bags vary in size, but they can hold a great deal. Think of a tanker as your bike's purse. On a day trip my tank bag carries a spare sweater and rain suit, heavier gloves, map, small camera, water bottle, candy bar, shield cleaner and a rag, small flashlight, plus other little odds and ends.

The only disadvantage to a tank bag is that, if not properly fastened, it can shift its position and possibly scuff your tank. I recommend using a tank cover in conjunction with a tank bag, if one is available to fit your machine. They're usually easy to find for BMWs, but seldom available for other brands. Wash and wax your tank well (and see the section on tank covers in this chapter) before installing such a cover.

If you can't find a tank cover, minimize the possibility of damage to your paint by washing and waxing it well before attaching the tank bag. Inspect the bottom of the bag to be certain it hasn't picked up any dirt that can do a power sander routine on your tank. Snug the bag down well, as it's the movement set up by relentless, repeated vibration that causes the scuffing.

I prefer tank bags on which the pad is separate from the body. On these, the pad stays attached to the bike, but the bag can be detached. If the pad is integral with the bag, there's the very real possibility it will be set down in the dirt, and then grind that dirt into your paint.

Soft Saddlebags

In the late 1970s, when touring suddenly became very popular, numerous manufacturers began producing soft saddlebags. Most bikes did not come standard with luggage, and there was not a wide array of hard luggage to fit them. Soft bags vary in size, but few will carry as much as either a fixed or removable hard saddlebag. They're usually attached together by two straps that fit over the rear portion of the seat, and their leading edges buckle to receptors that are attached to the motorcycle down by its passenger footpegs. This helps keep the bags from flapping in the wind when lightly loaded, and away from the rear tire. Once, a duffel bag that I had improperly attached to the seat came loose, swung down, and was caught by the rear wheel. It jammed between the tire and the swingarm, locked up the rear wheel immediately, and threw me into a skid. I'm fortunate that I didn't go down or collide with something. You *must* be certain to secure any luggage items well, as should such an item come loose and catch in a wheel it could cause injury and possibly death.

On a cruiser, the only way to go seems to be leather saddlebags. These bags, by S&S, are shown on a Harley-Davidson.

Look for good, solid zippers and solid attachments in soft saddlebags. Because rain and grimy road spray can reduce your bags to a filthy mess in a short time, I highly recommend nylon rain bonnets, which are included with the better bags and optional on most others. Some brands offer inner liners that also keep your luggage dry, but do nothing for the outside of your bags.

As a matter of comfort if you carry a passenger, check that the overseat straps are relatively wide and thin. It's one thing to sit on a strap, but buckles are definitely not appreciated. It may be possible to remove your bike's seat and re-install it over the bag straps. This will prevent someone from having to sit on the straps, and will also make the bags more secure to the bike. Be certain that they're not hanging so low now that they may contact the hot exhaust system.

Check the integrity and adjustment of your bag straps often. Nylon is a wonderful material, but soft saddlebags will melt if they accidentally slip down onto the mufflers. Not only will this destroy the bags, but their contents may also be damaged.

Finally, as with other types of soft luggage, soft saddlebags are susceptible to theft. Certainly, so also are hard bags, but at least their hard shell and locks are a deterrent to theft. There is no practical way to lock soft bags to a motorcycle, or to seal their zippers. Your only hope here is to park in conspicuous places and to use common sense. In my 35 years of riding the only thing I've lost from a motorcycle is one bungee cord, but I'm not naive enough to believe that all is goodness and light, either. See Chapter 10 on touring security.

Duffel Bags

When I first began touring, the ubiquitous army duffel was my luggage system of choice. Tough and capacious, the army duffel can be locked, and it offers the most capacity for the money. Sure, it's difficult to pack well, and it also looks cobby on the back of a shiny motorcycle, but in a practical sense you can't beat it.

As the years passed and touring grew more sophisticated, I outgrew the army duffel, which is not to say that I outgrew the duffel bag entirely. Duffels in all colors and sizes are still readily available on the market, often at a good price.

Modern duffels are more configured and sized for motorcycle use, often with attaching points. Look for features on good duffels such as a heavier grade of material, high-quality zippers, and several extra pockets that are so handy for those little things that would be impossible to find in the main compartment. Look for a sturdy carrying handle for when you remove it from the bike, and possibly a rain bonnet.

Tail Packs

Tail packs are those sporty little packs (also called "sport bags") that fit on the passenger portion of the seat, and are particularly popular with sport-bike riders. Although similar to duffels, tail packs are smaller (they'll hold perhaps a helmet, but little more). Most offer built-in attaching straps or bungee cords, as most sport bikes offer some sort of fixed or flip-out hooks for their attachment.

Along with a tank bag, a tail pack usually offers sufficient capacity for the solo person traveling light on a weekend ride. They come in all sorts of attractive colors, often have external pockets and are also relatively inexpensive.

Fanny Packs

You've probably figured out from its name that the fanny pack attaches around the waist with a belt, and is usually worn at the back. They offer the least capacity of any of the luggage items but are excellent for the rider who just needs that little extra pair of gloves or snack on the ride. Dirt riders wear them religiously as they stay attached but don't get in the way.

Because they're attached near the rider's spine, it's important that you pack only soft articles in a fanny pack. I cringe every time I see a rider carrying a camera back there, as falling on such an item could cause serious injury.

Day Packs

Day packs are smaller versions of a backpack and are worn by school children, hikers, and sometimes by motorcycle riders. They hold considerably more than a fanny pack, and can be either simple or complex.

Because they're worn on the back, once again, don't carry anything in them that represents a potential threat to your safety should you fall. In addition, the weight of the pack is carried on the shoulders and back, which can become very tiring by the end of a long day. Add to that the wind buffeting factor and you've got the potential for some serious discomfort. Day packs are fine for short trips, but they really aren't a great idea for long-distance motorcycling.

Backpacks

Backpacks are designed for backpackers, and they distribute the weight to the hips as a person is hiking. On a motorcycle, they have the same drawbacks as daypacks, only they're larger. Frankly, backpacks are fine for their design purpose, but not for motorcycling, especially if the rider attempts to wear the pack. You also have to add in the wind-resistance factor because the pack is usually taller and wider than the rider.

If you absolutely have to use a backpack to carry your gear on a motorcycle trip, at least lay it flat on the rear portion of the seat and fasten it securely. Then ride over to your dealership and price some soft saddlebags.

Luggage Nets

The traditional means of carrying loose items on a motorcycle has been to secure them with several bungee cords. But of course, things can work loose over time and miles, and fall off. Then some clever inventor decided to combine the best features of bungee cords by weaving shock cords into a net with hooks liberally sprinkled about the edges. With this system, a separate sleeping bag, duffel, air mattress, or whatever can be carried beneath the all-encompassing net. They're very handy, and are an excellent means of carrying many loose items.

This tail bag by Roadgear (many other companies also offer them) can hold a helmet, or when teamed with a tank bag can provide plenty of luggage capacity for a solo weekend ride.

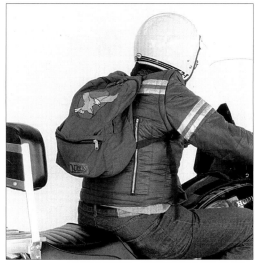

A day pack is useful for commuting, but having to carry it may tire a touring rider on an extended trip.

A backpack? On a motorcycle? It's really bulky—there are better ways to carry luggage.

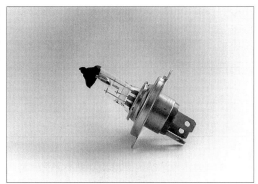

High-wattage headlight bulbs can really light up the night.

The headlight modulator pulses the light several times per second to make the rider more visible. (Photo courtesy Nady Systems)

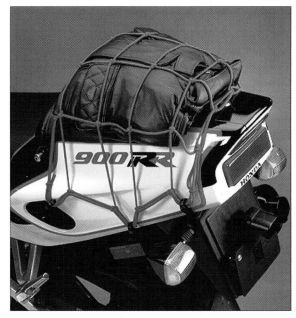

For carrying several items, a net carrier offers more security than several bungee cords can.

Lights

Accessory lighting is divided lighting into two categories here: functional lighting that helps the rider see and be seen, and decorative lighting meant to entertain as much as it is meant to seriously illuminate.

Functional Lighting

First under the category of functional lighting are additional driving lights, usually twin individual units mounted to a fairing or safety bars. Their purpose is usually to illuminate the road closer to, rather than farther from, the motorcycle. Because of this, they tend to be mounted low to the ground, sometimes even in the fairing lowers, and are designed with a wide beam to splash light upon the road. They're especially helpful on winding roads where they can illuminate oncoming corners that far-focused headlights cannot.

High-powered headlights are an alternative to some driving lights. In this situation, rather than the extra weight, expense, and complication of auxiliary lights, all the rider buys is a replacement H4 halogen headlight bulb with increased wattage. A standard headlight bulb is usually rated at 65 watts on high beam and 55 on low. High-powered alternatives may be 80/55, 100/55, or even 100/80.

I have used the 100/55-watt variety and have found it very effective for high-beam use out on remote roads. Check your local laws, as in many localities such high-powered lights are approved for off-road use only. Officials fear that inconsiderate drivers will annoy or momentarily blind other drivers by using their high beams inappropriately. Please be considerate of oncoming drivers. Still, when you've got a lot of miles to cover on a remote, little-traveled road at night, these lights are your distant early warning system.

Additional tail lights add a margin of safety when the bike is viewed from the side or behind. Most motorcycles have only a single tail light, which can be hard to see under certain conditions. Several manufacturers offer smaller outboard auxiliary tail lights for that added margin of visibility. Whenever you mount extra luggage on the back, be certain that nothing hangs down far enough to obscure your tail light.

Some accessory tail lights pulse when the brake is applied, which provides an extra bit of notice to trailing drivers. However, check your local laws, as pulsing tail lights are not legal everywhere.

Headlight modulators are devices that cause the headlight to pulse at a rate of about four times per second. Why? The majority of motorcycle accidents occur at intersections when another vehicle pulls out in front of the hapless rider. The usual reaction by the other motorist is, "Gee, I didn't see him." I have little tolerance for this attempted cop-out. Motorcycles aren't invisible; the reason the other person didn't see the motorcycle coming is because he didn't look.

Headlight modulators cause the light to pulse, or flash, which draws a great deal of attention to the motorcycle—even if another motorist is not paying much attention. They're relatively inexpensive, and very effective at attracting attention. For nighttime use, the rider throws a switch to restore the light to standard, non-pulsing operation. Check your local laws, as headlight modulators are not legal everywhere.

Decorative Lighting

Decorative lighting started among the truckers of the Southwest, hard-driving guys who mounted clearance lights all over their rigs for safety and for show. When they got into touring, especially aboard Honda Gold Wings, they began adorning their bikes with all sorts of decorative lighting, too. These lights are often located in chromed light bars that encircle the luggage system, in strip lights on the fairing, or in individual lights on the fork. They differ from functional lighting in that decorative lights are intended more as decorations to delight rather than used to illuminate.

One caution about decorative lighting systems is that you must take care not to overload your motorcycle's electrical system. The amount of wattage your bike's alternator puts out may be listed in your owner's manual, or in information your dealer can provide. A typical figure will range from 380 to more than 700 watts, but only at higher rev ranges. Once you know how many watts your system is putting out, your dealer may be able to give you approximate figures for how many watts your bike draws. Typically, the headlight will use 65 watts on high beam, other lights 25 watts, the ignition system 40 watts, and other electrical equipment another 100 watts for a total general figure of approximately 250 watts. Using an electric vest? Better

You say you like chromed goodies on a bike? This will test your sense of taste!

add in another 60 watts, and double it if your passenger is staying warm, too. It's best to design a lighting system that will not draw more electricity than your bike's alternator can produce, as the battery could become discharged over time. The alternative is to simply limit the amount of time you use your nonessential lighting.

Chromed Goodies

One of the joys of owning a dresser or cruiser motorcycle is that there's plenty of room to hang things. The major specialty accessory companies offer hundreds of chromed items for them that will dress them up and make each bike distinctive, and the OEMs now offer their own lines of chromed accessories. What's the sense of having a motorcycle if you don't personalize it?

There are more chromed items than I could possibly list here, and they range from such things as headlight shields, horn grillwork, and turn signal trim to rails around the luggage, eagle figurines, and safety bars. Some people speak disparagingly of chrome-accented bikes—but one person's work of art is another's "garbage barge." My best advice is that if it makes you feel good, *do* it!

Motorcycle sound systems have become increasingly complex. This one, on a Honda GL1500 Gold Wing, includes AM/FM sound, plus tape player, headphone jacks and CB capabilities.

Horns

Because motorcycles are physically small, it's more difficult for other motorists (who often aren't looking for them) to see them. When they don't see the motorcycle, and begin changing lanes into its space, it's time for the rider to take effective defensive action, and also to sound a warning if appropriate. I've avoided several near collisions with snoozing vehicle drivers by blasting them back into consciousness with the strong set of electric horns my motorcycle carries.

Unfortunately, most motorcycles carry rather weak hooters that are barely audible at any great distance. Add to that factor a driver with his windows rolled up and the radio on, and it's difficult for the rider to get his important message across. I recommend that, if your motorcycle is not equipped with a proper set of LOUD horns, so equip it. Contact your dealer or accessory shop for these items, and have them mounted where they will face outward and toward the front. Sometimes, sound waves can move metal.

Sound and Communications Systems

Some people still consider sound systems for motorcycles a rather silly idea, but if cars can have them, why not bikes? Some riders just like to have music, talk shows, tapes, or the big game accompany them as they ride, and who's to say they're wrong?

The basic problem with sound on bikes is that the acoustics are lousy because of the wind and ambient noises. Sound reception is usually much better on these systems when they're used on bikes with fairings or

windshields that block the wind, and don't generate additional wind noise reaching the rider and co-rider. Second, the sun, wind, rain, and vibration play havoc with a sensitive sound system, and make it imperative that your system be well sealed from the elements. For this reason, be certain to use high-quality systems specifically designed for motorcycles.

Sound systems for motorcycles take many forms, so let's consider the various types.

AM/FM Radio

The AM/FM radio is the most basic type of sound system, but the disadvantage is you're at the mercy of the quality of reception, and what happens to be on the air at the time. With any radio you'll need a good antenna, so don't neglect this necessary item.

Cassette Players

Stereo cassette players solve the problem of hearing what you want to hear, *when* you want to hear it. However, some riders insist upon inserting and removing cassettes while they're moving down the road, which diverts their attention from the important task at hand. It's best to not do any such thing while you're riding, but if you must, use the utmost care so as to not allow your attention to wander.

Also keep in mind that tape cassettes function best in a clean environment and are susceptible to dirt and wear. Handle and store them with care, and keep your system as clean as possible.

Compact Discs (CDs)

Compact discs have become the standard for home and automotive use. Discs are essentially tiny records played by a laser beam rather than a needle, and they can skip if the vehicle is used on a bumpy road or under aggressive conditions. Because only a beam of light touches the disc's surface, it will not be harmed by a minimal amount of bouncing. The greater problem is that the delicate internal workings may not do well in an environment that involves intense temperature changes, dirt, and vibration. At this time, only the BMW K1200LT offers a CD player.

Citizens Band Radios

Usually referred to as the CB radio, this device became popular in the late 1970s by constant use and several low-budget movies that featured the colorful language

An intercom system, such as this one by J & M Corporation, allows rider and passenger to talk with each other and enjoy the sound system. (Photo courtesy *Rider* magazine)

and lives of over-the-road truckers. The CB is a small radio with a range of several miles that allows the operator to both talk and listen, commenting upon road conditions, fuel availability, the weather, traffic conditions, the location of the closest police radar surveillance or patrol car, and where the best food is in town. CBs are now being used during guided motorcycle tours at rallies as the tour guide offers a running commentary about the scenery and historic sights.

CB radios are offered both as standard and optional equipment on some dresser motorcycles, and as accessories available through motorcycle dealers. It's important to use a CB specifically designed for motorcycle use, as these units provide better weather and vibration proofing than non-motorcycle units. Also, they tend to be designed more in keeping with the rider's safety—with hands-free operation.

Helmet Speakers

Wind and other ambient noise is always a problem when riding a motorcycle, and one method of countering it is to mount tiny speakers within your helmet. They often mount with Velcro-type hook-and-loop fasteners, and weigh a minimal amount. The microphone attaches either inside the chinbar of a full-face helmet, or outside on a stalk on an open-face. Ads in the motorcycle magazines will lead you to companies that offer such speakers.

Intercoms

These systems allow the rider and passenger to speak directly to each other via microphones and speakers. They are hard-wired and speakers fit inside the helmets. For any rider and co-rider who have ever tried to shout to each other above the wind, misunderstanding each other half of the time, they're a real blessing.

Some of these systems are a part of the motorcycle, while others are independent and are powered by a separate flashlight-type battery and may have separate volume controls for rider and passenger. Usually they work well, especially on a bike equipped with a large fairing or windshield that keeps wind, and the resultant wind noise, from interfering with clear hearing. The only drawback to these systems is that they must be unplugged each time the riders dismount, so check that they have sturdy plugs and that the wires are not susceptible to tangling when they're put away.

Bike-to-Bike Systems

Other bike-to-bike systems are similar to CB radios but operate on the 49-megahertz frequency, the same as baby monitors and garage-door openers. They are powered by AA batteries, and their effective range is about 2/10 of a mile in line-of-sight only. They're designed for two or more bikes traveling together and riding within a few hundred feet of each other. Depending upon bike, helmets and wind conditions the 49-MHz systems tend to be overwhelmed by wind noise at between 45 to 55 mph.

Family Radios: Motorola has introduced a line of sport hand-held, walkie-talkie-type radios that, because of their broad range of usage for hunting, fishing,

The round thumb wheel on this front brake lever allows the rider to adjust the distance between the lever and the handgrip to any of four positions for greater comfort. Such thumb wheel adjustments are also becoming common on clutch levers. (Photo courtesy of Yamaha Motor Corporation, USA)

Footboards, as opposed to pegs, provide the rider with a longer perch so that he can move his feet around. They're popular on cruiser bikes, and are often rubber mounted for comfort.

hiking, skiing, etc., have come to be known as "family" radios. When teamed with the proper helmet speakers and push-to-talk equipment to adapt them to motorcycle use, in my experience they offer a minimum range of two miles over rough terrain. And when the ride is over, they can be unplugged and used as hand-helds.

As you'll note from the accompanying sidebar, you should check local laws regarding the legality of using speakers inside your helmet.

Miscellaneous Accessories

Heated Grips

Heated grips are a true luxury, and a wonderful necessary device. The cold is a thief. It steals not only your comfort, but your attention and ability to control your machine as well. Your hands are the primary controllers of your motorcycle, and without their precise control, you're going to be in trouble.

BMW offers heated grips on some models as standard equipment, and also sells kits to retrofit other models. Also, aftermarket companies offer kits to fit most any bike. Snowmobile dealers may have them if your motorcycle dealer does not. They install inside the grips and heat them electrically; some kits offer two-position switches for high or low heat.

The primary benefit of heated grips is that you don't have to use big, heavy gloves as soon as you would otherwise, and you can continue riding in lighter, more comfortable gloves with a better feel. If your bike lacks wind protection for the hands, and/or if you often ride in cooler weather, I highly recommend heated grips. Like electrically heated garments, you won't realize what you're missing until you try them.

Safety Bars and Engine Guards

Safety bars and engine guards are chromed tubular or rectangular steel bars designed for protection. Safety bars, often referred to (shudder) as "crash bars," were a common accessory in the 1970s that attached to the front down tube(s) of the frame and protruded out to the sides. The idea here was that if the motorcycle went down, the bars would hold the front end up off the pavement and perhaps save the rider some injury to the lower extremities. However, a comprehensive motorcycle accident study known as "The Hurt Report" noted that the use of such bars merely moved the location of the injury from the rider's ankle area to farther up the leg.

Another safety factor was that when a bike fell at speed, the impact would be transferred through the safety bar to the frame. Riders of BMW twins often mounted these bars to protect their protruding valve covers from damage. Then the joke became, "I protected my $35 valve cover by bending my $1,000 frame." Sometimes you just can't win.

Finally, safety bars are a good place on which to mount additional accessories such as radar detectors, highway pegs (see following section), and driving lights.

Engine guards are usually tubular or rectangular-tube steel brackets that fit around engine cases and take the brunt of the impact should the bike fall over. A pair will usually be less expensive than replacing one engine case cover and certainly more convenient. Be certain, however, that your engine guards do not hang so low that they limit ground clearance when the bike is leaned over into a curve.

Safety bars are designed to protect the motorcycle if it falls over, but offer little protection to the rider.

Case guards protect the engine cases from damage caused by a tipover. Be certain they don't limit your ground clearance in turns.

Hiway pegs, such as these, offer the rider the opportunity to stretch out while riding, but often at the expense of moving the feet away from the controls.

In parking lots and in gravel driveways motorcycle riders may lose their footing and go toppling over, much to their embarrassment and sometimes minor injury. The bike will often sustain some minor cosmetic damage, especially if it has plastic or fiberglass bodywork, but usually not anything that would prevent its being ridden away. Oops, that's *usually*.

Sometimes in a tip-over, depending upon how the bike falls, the shift lever on the left—or the brake lever on the right side—will be driven into the engine case, holing it. In this situation the bike should not be ridden until the extent of damage can be determined and the case can be repaired or replaced and made oil tight again.

Highway Pegs

Highway pegs are accessory footpegs that mount at some additional location away from the standard pegs. The idea is that highway pegs allow the rider to stretch his legs and be more comfortable on the highway. The problem is that highway pegs bring the feet away from the rear brake pedal (which also operates one front brake disc on an integrated braking system) and shift lever, both of which could be of critical importance in an emergency. For this reason, I do not recommend highway pegs.

Custom Seats and Seat Covers

Let's face it, some motorcycle seats are simply not comfortable for long-distance rides. On dresser touring bikes of the 1970s and early 1980s, it was common to replace the stock seat with an aftermarket unit that offered much better padding and support. By the late 1980s, the manufacturers were offering much better standard seats on their dressers, and custom seats were becoming much less of a necessity. Still, they offer a custom look and often a superior ride to the stock seat.

Some aftermarket companies ask the rider to send his seat pan in so that they can use it as a base to build

Custom seats are available for most bikes. They usually offer more padding and better materials. (Photo courtesy Mike Corbin)

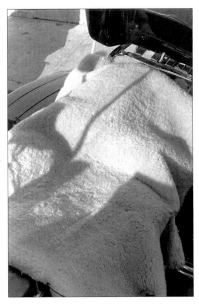

The sheepskin was very popular in the 1980s, but its popularity has since waned. Whether it's a natural product or man-made such as this item, it will be warmer in cool weather and cooler when it's hot. Be certain to secure it well so that it cannot flap and become entangled in the rear wheel.

A passenger backrest is a real blessing as it lends a great sense of security, and the co-rider no longer has to maintain muscle tension to sit upright. Some racks incorporate an integral backrest.

the new seat upon. This is not desirable, however, as it forces the rider to be without a seat, any seat, for several weeks. In some cases, they'll send you the new seat first, and you send in your old seat pan. Most seat companies today will build a seat for you if you simply tell them the brand and model bike you have. Now, most dresser machines no longer require a better seat immediately, but many other bikes do. Cruiser riders often mount an aftermarket seat for that custom look.

If your seat feels hard after an hour or two in the saddle, a custom seat will probably add to your comfort and ability to stay on the road longer. Just keep in mind that many custom seats provide more padding, which means that if you're already having a problem reaching the ground from your present seat, a custom job is likely to make the reach to the ground even longer. Custom thicknesses and shapes are available, and if you specify that you're having trouble reaching the ground, a custom seat maker may be able to help with your problem. Some companies offer gel seats that offer firm padding in a thin package.

Sheepskins

These fluffy seat covers, available as actual sheepskins or as synthetics that sell for much less, are designed to add comfort to your bike. A true sheepskin will be warmer on a cold day, and cooler on a hot one, than the standard seat cover. Look for a good, tight fit. Synthetic sheepskins generally don't work as well as the real thing, but the price is usually much lower. Be

certain to mount your seat cover securely, as a dangling end can become caught in a rear wheel with disastrous results.

Seat Covers

In the morning it's no fun to plop down into a seat, any seat, after a night of rain, or a morning of heavy dew. Especially with custom seats that offer large pores, a light evening rain or heavy dew can soak into the foam underneath, plopping you into a puddle of water. In order to prevent this, I recommend covering the seat with plastic, or with a special plastic cover specially shaped to fit the seat. The Honda Gold Wing SE offers such a seat cover as standard equipment. Until these covers become commonplace, the old garbage bag will have to do.

Backrests

Pity the poor co-rider. He or she must often spend hours and hundreds of miles sitting upright behind the rider with sometimes nothing to hang onto or lean against. If you like traveling with your co-rider, do him or her a favor by fitting a backrest if your bike does not already have one. It will give your co-rider something to lean against, which means he or she will no longer have to maintain that muscular tension of sitting upright against the forces of wind and bumps for hours at a time.

If your bike is fitted with a tail trunk, the trunk is probably already has a suitable pad. If not, aftermarket

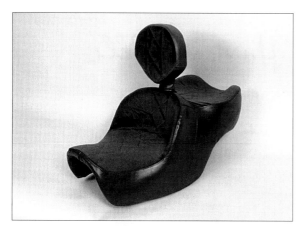

Several companies offer more luxurious touring seats that can be added to dresser motorcycles. (Photo courtesy of Hartco)

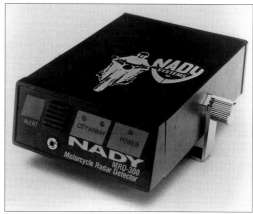

The radar detector can help remind you to check your speed. (Photo courtesy Nady Systems)

backrests usually consist of pad attached to a tube-steel rack that bolts to the back of the bike. Some luggage racks have them built in.

While I strongly recommend backrests for passenger comfort, you must also be aware of the downside. If the bike goes down, your best move is to get away from it so that it will not strike you as you slide. A backrest, however, tends to push the co-rider along, making it more difficult to get away. It's not a pretty thought, but nevertheless it's one about which you should be aware.

A few aftermarket seat companies offer backrests for the riders of major brands of dresser bikes. They usually pivot out of the way for mounting and dismounting of the co-rider and add some lower back support for the rider.

Radar Detectors

I believe in safe riding as much as the next guy, but I resent state governments and municipalities that use speed traps as a means of generating revenue. Second, our national highway system was designed for legal speeds in the neighborhood of 70–80 miles per hour, meaning that those speeds were deemed to be safe. The 55-MPH national speed limit was implemented to save fuel following the fuel crisis of 1973, and in my opinion was kept in force far beyond its useful life by several states more for the purpose of generating revenue than for any actual safety results. Some will tell you smugly and piously, "Speed kills!"

The fact is, speed alone does not kill. Bad driving kills. Bad riding kills. Drunken driving kills. If speed in fact killed, no one would survive a grand prix motorcycle race in which speeds of 150 to 180 MPH are common for every rider, every lap. The reason these riders can survive these speeds is that they're the best in the world, riding superior machines on closed courses free from outside traffic. My point is that speed can be managed safely under certain conditions, although I am certainly not advocating racing on public roads and streets.

You may not agree with my viewpoint, but I'm sure you'll agree that even the most law abiding of us will inadvertently speed at some place and some time. I believe that the driver inadvertently going 62 on a four-lane highway designed for 75 and posted for 55 is not endangering anything but his wallet and driving privileges. In such situations, a radar detector is a handy device to have as a reminder to check speed.

Law-enforcement officials in most localities use radar to enforce speed limits. In simplified terms, the radar gun sends out a burst of energy, a pulse. Part of this pulse strikes a moving object and is reflected, in a much fragmented pattern, back to the gun. The change in wave pattern caused by the vehicle's speed is read and translated to a number that is *usually* an accurate representation of the vehicle's speed. Sometimes, however, for complex reasons having to do with improper use or electrical interference, it's not even close.

The radar detector is a device that senses the radar gun's signal, and then howls or blinks a signal to the vehicle operator. The problem is that the detector cannot really help you if the officer is hidden behind a tree on a deserted road and zaps only you, using instant-on radar. Rather, the detector *can* help you if you're riding

The throttle lock exerts a constant drag to maintain a throttle setting.

On the six-cylinder Honda Gold Wing, the cruise control is incorporated within the handlebar controls.

a well-traveled highway and an officer is zapping vehicles up ahead regularly. The gun throws a wide beam that carries several thousand feet, often well beyond the target vehicle. It is this scatter that the detector can sniff out, and it can warn you of the presence of radar long before the gun is aimed at you.

Motorcycles are at an advantage when confronted with radar because of their relatively small size. Remember that radar depends upon reading a reflected signal; the larger the reflecting surface, the greater the distance the signal can be read. Huge tractor trailer rigs can be read from as far away as 7,000 feet, four-wheel-drive pickups from 2,100 feet, big sedans from 1,800 feet, and small cars from about 1,200 feet. Motorcycles, depending upon frontal area, should be invisible to radar until at around 1,000 feet.

It's important to mount your detector in a location that is easy for the rider to see and/or hear when the warning sounds, yet is protected from the elements. I recommend detectors designed specifically for motorcycles, as many of them offer an earplug to convey the signal to where it can be immediately noted. Also, they're properly protected from the elements and vibration.

It's also a good idea for the detector to be hidden from sight. If a police officer stops you and notices your detector, he or she may consider that a *de facto* indication that you have little respect for the law, and they'll be more likely to administer a strict interpretation of your case.

Throttle Locks

A throttle lock is a mechanical device that clamps onto the twist grip to maintain a throttle setting. Many long hours in the saddle holding the throttle in the same relative position can cause the right hand and wrist to become fatigued. In order to combat this, some riders mount a throttle lock (often mislabeled a "cruise control") on their throttles.

It's important that the lock be set with just enough tension to overcome the pull of the throttle return springs. The rider can simply rest his hand on the throttle grip without having to maintain tension, yet he can close the grip immediately when he has to.

Throttle locks are great when used on level, open roads, but less useful in hilly country. Every time the bike encounters a hill or headwind, it will begin to lose speed. The rider must then nudge in a bit of throttle to compensate, just as he must back off the throttle in downhill sections.

If used often and wisely, a throttle lock can help pay for itself in two ways. First, its steady hand will encourage economical operation of the bike. Second, dialing in a conservative speed will discourage inadvertent speeding, helping to preserve both your cash and your license.

Some motorcycles, such as Harley-Davidsons, come with a standard throttle grip screw in place that will function as a throttle lock. Older BMW twins also have a predrilled and tapped hole near the twist-grip into which a special spring-loaded screw could be inserted. Throttle locks are advantageous, but be

A tank cover protects your fuel tank, especially from the abrasions of a tank bag. Model availability is limited.

A smaller version of the tank cover is the tank bra. It prevents belt-buckle scratches on your precious paint. (Photo courtesy American Suzuki Motor Corp.)

absolutely certain in installing and maintaining them that there is no possibility of them impeding your closing the throttle.

Cruise Controls

Cruise controls are electro-mechanical devices that function like a throttle lock, but are much more sophisticated. With a cruise control you can dial in a cruising speed on your motorcycle, and the system will maintain that speed despite hills, curves, and headwinds. It constantly compares the bike's actual road speed with that you've preset and works the throttle mechanically to compensate. Your main duty with this device is to keep your eyes on the road and not be lulled into inattention.

In the 1980s, several companies offered aftermarket cruise controls, but they were expensive and difficult to install. Today, several makers of big dresser bikes offer them as standard equipment, which is much more convenient than trying to mount such a system after the fact. They're a real comfort for the long haul.

Tank Covers

The fuel tank is the central focal point for most motorcycles. Even if they don't notice the distinctive logo there, most in-the-know riders can identify motorcycles simply by the size and shape of their fuel tanks. One needs only to think of such classic shapes as the Harley-Davidson Fat Bob tank, the Triumph 500 and 650cc tank, and the BMW 6.3-gallon tank that was the standard on many of its twins for nearly two decades.

In order to protect their precious tanks from the elements and from being scratched by tank bags, some riders use tank covers. They're usually made of Cordura nylon, vinyl, or occasionally leather and are a great place for mounting club patches. Use a cover that's form fitting, and one that does not have loose corners. Remove it during your regular bike washings to clean and wax the tank, which will prevent it from being scuffed by dirt that is trapped under the tank cover.

Unfortunately, because these covers are so model specific, they're only available for bikes that have had a very specific following for many years, such as Harleys and BMWs, and occasionally Honda Gold Wings. The styling trend of recent years to integrate tanks into the bodywork has also worked against the continued use of tank covers. Let's just say that if such a cover is available for your bike, and you use a tank bag, get one.

Motorcycle Covers

Covers are an excellent means of protecting your bike if it must be parked outside, even while you're at work during the day. Usually made of cotton or coated nylon, covers can keep the sun and grit off your machine, but there are a few fine points to note about them.

Avoid covering your bike with a plastic tarp; it's too stiff and will scratch your paint when the wind blows. Also, it will hold in moisture and promote rust formation. A good tarp is soft and keeps moisture off, yet is porous enough to allow it to evaporate. Another drawback of plastic or untreated nylons is their tendency to melt when they come in contact with hot surfaces such as exhaust systems or engines. Many top-line covers are made of poplin with aluminized sections along the bottom that will not melt.

Look for grommets that will allow the cover to be secured with a bungee cord or cable lock. Without such a device, the cover can easily be blown off or stolen.

A fairing bra (or in this case, a lower bra) keeps the bugs and stone chips away. Frequently wash and wax the paint under it to prevent trapping dirt.

Fairing Bras

I know what you're thinking, but let's play this topic straight. Bras are usually vinyl, padded, form-fitting covers for fairings and/or lowers that protect them from stone chips and the elements. Like tank covers, bras can trap dirt underneath that, when combined with vibration and normal use, can damage paint. They should be removed during normal washings so that the paint underneath can be cleaned and waxed.

Custom Paint

To make your bike different from all the rest, you can't beat custom paint. "Good taste," according to my definition, "is knowing when to stop." Unfortunately, some people believe that if one stripe or chromed goody or light is good, a few dozen must be much better, often to the detriment of their machines.

I think tasteful custom paint jobs are wonderful and artistic, and I miss those of the late 1970s and early 1980s when touring was in its heyday. Back then, most bikes were sold bare and riders accessorized them with fairings, bags, and trunks. Because these items often came from several different manufacturers, it was necessary to have the whole bike painted to tie the lot together. The advent of the factory dresser spelled doom for this truly creative aspect of touring.

I strongly recommend, if you're considering custom paint, that you have it done by a professional. The application of the many different types of paint to the many types of surfaces on motorcycles today is an exact science that's now far beyond the scope of the backyard artist with a spray gun and a few sheets of sandpaper. I'm not saying it's impossible to get satisfactory results at home, but that with the technology in modern paints the prospects are becoming much less likely.

Custom paint can be a fine means of expression, but it can be a detriment when you decide to sell your bike. Not only do you have to find a buyer who likes the make, model, year, and condition, but he's also going to have to agree with your highly subjective sense of art. Don't expect to get your initial investment in paint back when you sell your bike, especially if your taste runs to highly emotional murals. Prepare to have your feelings hurt when prospective buyers discuss how best to remove your art and give the bike a "proper" paint job.

Bracing

With the advent of near race-ready street sports such as the Suzuki GSX-R, Yamaha YZF, and Kawasaki ZX series, racing technology has truly trickled down into street machines. These bikes use beam-style perimeter frames of steel or aluminum to promote ultimate rigidity. Still, even when these bikes are raced it's common for riders to add bracing of various types to stiffen their chassis even more. To understand the need for bracing, let's talk a little about handling.

The motorcycle rides on two tire patches that are held in relative constant relationship with each other by the frame. As long as those two patches remain in precise alignment relative to each other, the motorcycle will handle fine. However, if the bike is ridden hard enough, it's possible that the cornering loads will build up to the point that something will distort—and there are many likely candidates. The frame, the fork, the steering head, swingarm, and axles can, and will, flex.

When flexing occurs, the tire patches are momentarily thrown out of alignment with each other. The bike seems to not know quite where it's going, and the rider senses this uncertainty and loses confidence. He backs off the throttle. If you continue to push a flexing bike, you're asking for trouble. As parts flex they momentarily distort slightly, overcome the forces acting upon them, and flex back the other way.

Push the bike harder and the flexing increases in both rate and degree. Instead of a vague sense of unease, the rider feels an actual wobble. Push harder still and that wobble can actually overcome tire traction, causing a dreaded "tank slapper" in which the handlebar can be yanked from the rider's grip and begin a wild oscillation. The rear tire can also begin to hop and throw the bike seriously out of control. Wouldn't it be better to have a properly braced chassis and have avoided all of this?

A fork brace is a common accessory that fits above the front fender and links the fork tubes together. It was quite common for riders to add it to bikes back in the 1980s and earlier, but today's better chassis and thicker fork tubes make a brace less necessary. On most bikes the fork tubes are held together only at the upper and lower triple clamps, and way down at the axle. That leaves a lot of unsupported length of fork tubes below the lower triple clamp. Flexing fork tubes will cause the front end to wobble in turns, and a flexing fork can also be felt under heavy braking.

A fork brace properly installed will cut down on fork flex and help the bike keep itself pointed down the straight and narrow. The caution here is to install the brace properly so as to not cause fork binding. Make certain your fork sliders move in and out just as easily after you put the brace on as before. If they don't, loosen the bolts, check the alignment, and tighten the bolts again.

The triple clamps are the two metal clamps that attach the fork tubes to the steering stem. On the great

A street-bike fork brace links the fork legs together and passes over the fender.

This fork brace, on a BMW R100 G/S dual-sport, is located just above the tire to help peel mud away in rough going.

majority of bikes they are made of heavy cast metal and are plenty stout enough. Old pre-1987 BMW R100 and earlier twins, however, were notorious for having a very weak upper clamp made of a flat piece of 1/8-inch steel plate.

Beemer twin riders who like to ride hard often replace their standard upper triple clamp with a much stouter aluminum unit. These were readily available through the aftermarket, and most BMW dealers will know where to get you one for your old twin.

Frame bracing is needed on bikes that are ridden very hard, especially those not equipped with the new, high-tech perimeter frames. I'd rather not get into all the technicalities and aberrations, but let's just say that whenever a chassis part flexes, the result will be a wiggle or wallow, and a vague sense that the motorcycle does not quite know where it's going. This type of bracing becomes quite technical and usually requires welding, which means that only racers or very serious street riders pursue this avenue.

The swingarm is the unit that links the rear axle to the frame and is the other chassis component most likely to require bracing. In some instances, bracing is welded to the swingarm, and in others an entirely new, stouter aftermarket swingarm is substituted for the standard item.

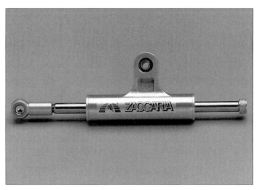

A steering damper helps high-performance machines handle better, but be certain your damper is not masking a problem that needs attention. (Photo courtesy Storz Performance)

A replacement windshield can be custom fit for length, tint, width, etc. (Photo courtesy National Cycle, Inc.)

If your chassis is causing handling ills, a fork brace is by far the least expensive and least radical approach, plus it will usually make a noticeable difference in stability. Changing the upper triple clamp is necessary on only a few machines, most noticeably old-style, air-cooled BMW twins.

It's easy to say that most riders do not ride hard enough to require frame or swingarm bracing, yet if you put them on a bike with a truly rigid chassis they will immediately feel more secure—even if they aren't sure why. These serious modifications are usually reserved for racers or the *very* serious fast riders.

Steering Dampers

A steering damper is device that helps to stabilize the motorcycle's front end by resisting forces that attempt to turn or twist the fork. It mounts between one fork tube and a frame member, or to some other solid part of the bike.

Steering dampers tend to be used today only on high-performance sport or racing bikes, and are rarely seen on tourers. BMW used to provide dampers on its larger twin-cylinder bikes up through the early 1980s, but no longer does.

Steering dampers have their place on sport bikes, but the majority of us will not have a use for them. My only caution is that you consult your dealer or other informed person if you believe your bike needs a steering damper. If you feel something is wrong with your motorcycle's front-end stability, have it checked out. A damper may simply be an attempt to mask a more serious problem.

Replacement Windshields

Many motorcycles now come with standard fairings and windshields, but the "one size fits all" mentality does not always necessarily work. The optimum situation is for the top of the windshield to be high enough that the main wind blast passes over the rider's head, yet low enough that the rider can look over it. As I stated earlier, it's best to see over it because at times dirt or rain can obscure your vision through a shield, and direct sun can cause it to "white out."

A few motorcycles offer adjustable windshields, but for the rest your best alternative is to replace the shield with one of the proper height. Your dealer can tell you if your motorcycle's manufacturer offers taller or shorter shields. If they don't, several aftermarket companies do.

A shield that's too tall can be cut down using the following method. First, determine exactly where the cut must occur, then cover that part of the shield with masking tape, and draw your cut line. Remove the shield and clamp it in a holding device, being very careful to pad it well so that the windshield is not scratched. Make your cut with a hacksaw blade, taking care to cut in a very smooth, even line. Finally, smooth up the cut with a file, carefully radiusing each edge slightly, front and back.

Trailers

Because of their size, motorcycles don't hold very much. When necessity appears, however, it tends to mother another invention. Rather than fight the continuing battle, some riders just accept the fact that they need to bring many items and get a trailer in which to haul them.

Riders outfit their motorcycles with either of two kinds of trailers—the camping or the utility trailer. The utility version is the lightest and least expensive, simply because it is a big empty shell into which the rider can load camping gear and other equipment.

A camping trailer is usually of the pop-up tent variety. The trailer top lifts up to form a roof, and the bottom a floor, with canvas or nylon sides. Some even provide a fold-out extension. The bottom area is usually available for storage.

Trailers are the answer to carrying things if you just can't travel light, but keep in mind how they will affect your riding. Because of the extra weight, slow down. Braking and accelerating will require more distance and time. Your freedom to maneuver is reduced, and you'll need more room to pass. In emergency maneuvers, the trailer will be a detriment, and under heavy braking some brands will try to lift the motorcycle's rear wheel. If you brake hard while in a turn, the mass of the trailer will attempt to continue traveling to the outside, forcing the rear of the motorcycle wide. In an extreme case the trailer could actually slide the rear of the motorcycle sideways, causing it to jackknife.

Tongue weight is the weight of the trailer's tongue upon the rear of the motorcycle. Observe the tongue weight recommendations with your trailer. Too much, and the rear of the motorcycle will be overly stressed as the front end rises, causing a severe case of understeer. Too little, or even negative weight, and the trailer will try to lift the rear of the motorcycle. This will result in a tendency for easy jackknifing, and very sensitive steering.

When loading, distribute weight in the trailer evenly from side to side, and with somewhat more weight on the tongue, according to recommendations. Secure the items in the trailer so that they don't roll around, changing weight distribution.

Be certain the high-pressure trailer tires are properly inflated and that your motorcycle's tires are inflated to their highest recommended pressures. Make certain the trailer's tail and brake lights are operational and that the lid is securely attached. Once you're riding along, it's very possible to even forget you have a trailer behind you. Note that trailers will cause your bike to use a little extra fuel, probably between 10

A cargo trailer allows riders to take along bulky camping gear, food and many of the comforts of home. (Photo courtesy of Kwik Kamp)

For real enjoyment in the wilderness a pop-up tent trailer allows the rider much more spacious living quarters, and the ability to take along much additional gear. (Photo courtesy of Kwik Kamp)

percent to 20 percent more, so be prepared to stop more often, and plan gas stops for reduced range.

Sidecars

Sidecars consist of a framework, bodywork, and seat attached to the motorcycle's right side in countries where vehicles drive on the right, and to the left side in countries such as Great Britain, Australia, and Japan where traffic drives on the left.

Sidecars (also often called "chairs" or "hacks") are popular in areas where the weather is wet or wintry, as that third wheel relieves some of the worry of skidding. A chair on the right side also means you can take left-hand turns at high speeds with the outrigger wheel adding stability. A skilled rider can also utilize the independent brake on some sidecars to help him around right turns. On right turns, however, the extra weight of the sidecar tends to push the motorcycle to the outside. In extreme cases the sidecar's wheel can come up off

Sidecars are great for riders who want more luggage or passenger capacity, and they're also favorites of handicapped riders. Here is a vintage 1920s Harley sidecar at the Griffith Park Sidecar Rally in California.

the pavement, causing the rider to lose control of the rig.

On the other hand, a favorite pastime of sidehack pilots is to put in an unsuspecting passenger, then intentionally lift that wheel off the ground and take them for a thrilling ride. With a skilled passenger (or "monkey" as they're called in racing) leaning his weight in the proper direction, a motorcyclist can hustle a sidecar around a racetrack quite quickly.

Use the sidecar to carry luggage or an extra passenger; I've even seen rigs with Mom & Dad on the bike, and two children in the sidecar—with most of their camping gear in the trailer!

In the past, sidecars have been attached using all manners of care and sometimes lack of same. If you intend to add a chair to your bike, be certain you're buying a unit with a proper attaching framework. Also, great advances have been made in front suspension systems, some of which do away with the telescopic fork in favor of a knee-joint affair that allows the bike and sidecar rig to be shoved into curves at pretty animated speeds.

The details of sidecars are much too complex to be handled adequately in a book of this scope. Rather, I suggest you check with your local motorcycle dealers for those who specialize in sidecars.

4
Motorcycle Components

WHAT TO DO WHEN THINGS NEED ATTENTION

When a motorcycle is put on the market, it is set up for Mr. Average Guy who will ride it his own way. The average tourer rides differently from the average sport rider, as well as from the average cruiser, and therefore places different stress and wear on his bike. Any motorcycle, therefore, may be built with a particular focus in mind, but with compromise as it attempts to fit the largest common denominator of riders. In this section we'll look at some of the components that can be replaced with aftermarket products to fine tune the bike to the way you ride. We'll also look at certain aspects of the motorcycle that are subject to normal wear and require replacement.

A great many component parts go into making one motorcycle. Let's address them in turn as they relate to touring and travel.

Brake Pads and Shoes

The pads (which attach to the calipers in a disc-brake system) and brake shoes (in a drum system) are what rub against the disc or hub and create the friction that stops the motorcycle. Not all brake pads are alike, and some are definitely better than others.

Several years ago, the standard pad on the market was impregnated with asbestos, which provided good braking action and wear. Research, however, showed that asbestos was a serious carcinogen (a cancer-causing agent), and brake pad companies were given a certain period of time to develop replacement materials for asbestos. As a result, organic brake pads were developed which perform very well and are friendly to the environment.

Some pads utilize sintered metal materials, but their drawback is that they cause a high degree of wear on standard disc rotors. Your best approach in this situation is to check with your dealer or another knowledgeable person regarding which types of pads work best on your bike without prematurely wearing the rotors.

Second, your riding style is another factor influencing brake pad choice that cannot be answered in a general book such as this. The rider who cruises around solo and never leaves town will not make the same demands upon his brakes as the sport rider who is out charging on mountain roads at high speeds. In addition, the tourer who rides in all weather may not make hard stops often, yet he's stopping a great amount of weight in all kinds of weather. His braking component needs will be different from other riders.

Racing brake pads are a common aftermarket choice of sport riders, and they can work well indeed. They tend to be softer and to grip the disc rotor better than standard pads, but the tradeoff is that they wear out faster. Still, I doubt anyone has ever been put in the poor house because he insisted on running premium brake pads. They cost a little more, but when you need to stop hard, you'll be glad you have them.

Finally, brake pads (and tires) may not provide optimum stopping performance until they have reached operating temperature. Every cognizant rider knows that his brakes work better and more predictably once they're warm. Some riders install serious racing brake pads, thinking they are really going to improve their braking. Yet these may not work well until they reach their operating temperature, which may be much higher than anything they could normally reach in even spirited street riding. For this reason, once again, it's best to rely upon the experience of knowledgeable experts when buying brake pads.

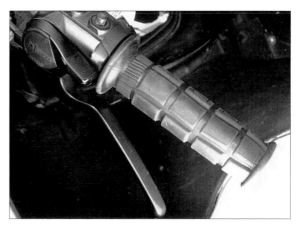

(Left) An accessory handlebar can fine-tune your riding position and leverage. (Photo courtesy Storz Performance)

(Right) The correct grip can ease fatigue and increase control.

Brake Care

Inspect your disc brake pads for wear at regular intervals. Their grooves act as thickness indicators; when the grooves are nearly gone, so are your pads and it's time to replace them. Failure to do so can result in decreased stopping power, and damage to the rotors.

Also, it's a good idea to replace your hydraulic brake fluid on an annual basis. Brake fluids eventually become contaminated with water; not only will water prevent the system from working optimally, but also it will encourage corrosion in the hydraulic lines and system.

Handlebars

The handlebar is the most important link between rider and motorcycle. Handlebar angle and length affect his comfort on the motorcycle and sometimes his ability to control the machine. For example, my back isn't the best, and while riding a used bike I'd just purchased, I found that the handlebar height put me in an upright riding position that sent road shocks right up my spine. This proved very painful, so I soon replaced the handlebar with a lower one from a different model. The forward lean put a curve into my back that allowed me to sit at a much more comfortable angle than the original handlebar had. Result: one back and one motorcycle saved.

A wider handlebar can sometimes help riders of sport bikes (which often have a very narrow bar) exercise better leverage against the bar and steer the bike with more authority. Likewise, if you find that you want to ride in a sporting manner, but you don't seem to fit on the bike right, often all that's needed is a handlebar change.

A lower bar bends the rider forward into a position in which the wind rush can help support part of his weight. Riders accustomed to a more upright position often believe that the crouching riding position common to sport bikes is uncomfortable, but the opposite has been my experience. As long as the position is not so extreme as to put a lot of weight on the palms and wrists, a crouch can be very comfortable for hours at a time as it curves the spine and spreads the rider's weight over the butt and the bottom of the thighs.

A crouching riding position also helps the sport rider in two other ways. First, by bending him forward he presents less of a profile into the wind. Second, leaning forward puts more of his weight on the front wheel where most of the braking takes place—and much of the steering. If the rear wheel slides a little in a turn, a rider can usually recover. Slide the front wheel, however, and you're in trouble. For this reason, a little extra weight out there will help keep the rubber planted.

Hand Grips

Hand grips are an oft-neglected area of motorcycling. The grips form an interface between the rider and the major controls of the bike and can be a prime comfort factor. The grips should be firm enough to provide a solid place to latch onto, yet soft enough for comfort.

In the last few years I've tried various foam grips that have been advertised as being able to provide some relief from vibration, but one brand was so thick that they were not comfortable for my hand. Another brand was so soft that I had to constantly squeeze them to grip them, and the relentless muscle tension tired my hands. After experimenting, I found that good old no-nonsense rubber grips, medium hard and of the proper

(Left) Countershaft sprockets are relatively small; the larger sprockets are drive sprockets. (Photo courtesy Sunstar Engineering USA, Inc.)

(Right) Here's where to direct the lubricant when you lube your drive chain.

thickness, suited my hands best. This is not to say that foam grips are not a good idea, but rather that grip choice is a very personal thing. Try different brands and types until you find what works best for you.

Remove old grips by slicing them. If you wish to preserve them, however, work the outside edges off, and then use compressed air to blow them away from the handlebar. To install new grips, lubricate the bar with a light layer of glue. Household glue should be adequate; epoxies can make removal difficult.

Chains and Sprockets

On chain-drive bikes, power is transferred from the gearbox to the rear wheel by a drive chain encircling two sprockets. The sprocket on the gearbox output is called the countershaft sprocket, and that on the hub is simply referred to as the rear or drive sprocket.

In order for your bike to stay on the road safely, the chain must be properly adjusted and lubricated. The instructions for doing so are contained in your owner's manual, but let's discuss some basics. As a chain wears, it elongates. Minute amounts of material are worn away from the insides of the rollers as they snick along the two sprockets thousands of times per mile. The sum total of these tiny wearings is a chain that has become elongated and then begins to hang loosely between the sprockets.

The term "chain adjustment" is a misnomer. You do not adjust the chain, but rather adjust the rear wheel and sprocket by sliding them slightly rearward to accommodate the lengthening chain, to take up the slack. If the slack becomes excessive, the chain will ride too high on the sprockets, which will cause the sprocket teeth to wear prematurely. In extreme cases, the chain

can actually skip a tooth or two, which can break off the ends of the sprocket teeth and damage the rollers.

You know it's time to adjust the chain, or should I say adjust the slack in the chain, when the amount of play or sag in the bottom row of chain exceeds what is called for in your owner's manual. The manual will explain this operation, which generally involves putting the bike on its centerstand, loosening the rear wheel's axle and locknuts, and sliding the wheel backward while making certain it is centered relative to the frame. Next, tighten the locknuts and axle nut.

Chains must also be properly lubricated. Note that the drive chain is composed of sets of inner and outer plates enclosing rollers that revolve around metal rivets. They hang out in the grit and water of a hostile environment and must be cared for.

The best time to lubricate your drive chain is when you have just finished riding your bike and the chain is at operating temperature. The heat will help the chain lubricant to flow into smaller nooks and crannies. Place the bike up on its centerstand with the gearbox in neutral and the engine off. You should now be able to spin the rear wheel freely with your hand. As you carefully rotate the rear wheel with one hand (which feeds the chain by at a controlled rate), direct the spray from a can of good quality motorcycle chain lubricant along the edges of the chain, between the plates. This will also allow lubricant to seep into the rollers. By spraying the top of the lower section of chain, centrifugal force as the bike (and chain) roll will help push lubricant into the rollers.

Good motorcycle chain lubes use a solvent carrier—a thin, volatile solution that cleans off dirt on contact and easily seeps into small places, carrying lubricant (often flakes of molybdenum) with it. Then the

Aftermarket exhausts can consist of complete systems, or of mufflers that slip onto stock exhaust headers. These slip-on mufflers are street legal and don't require carburetor rejetting; however, many systems are louder than stock and the decrease in back-pressure means the carburetor(s) must be rejetted. (Photo courtesy of Harley-Davidson)

solvent quickly evaporates, leaving the lubricant behind. Lubes not intended for chain use lack this solvent carrier and are not as effective.

In the 1970s, another type of chain called the *O-ring chain* came into popular use. The chain is manufactured with tiny rubber O-rings placed between its plates; thus the name. As previously described, these O-rings seal lubricant (that is placed there at the time of manufacture) inside the rollers, and make it difficult for dirt and water to get inside.

Note that contrary to popular belief, O-ring chains nevertheless do require lubrication to keep the rubber soft and springy. Also, the O-rings add a noticeable amount of rolling friction that does rob some power.

Why is it important not to get lazy and neglect chain care? A well-cared-for chain and sprocket system may last 20,000 miles or longer, but they all do eventually wear out. A system not given proper attention will likely be ruined within 10,000 miles, its rollers kinked and sprockets worn. Whenever one of these systems wears out, it's important to note that the chain and both sprockets *must* be replaced together as a unit; an old chain will wear out new sprockets, and vice versa. Replacing all of these items can easily total $100 or more.

Exhaust Systems

During the 1970s and 1980s it was very common for riders to replace their stock motorcycle exhaust systems with an aftermarket unit just as soon as they bought their bikes. These aftermarket systems were usually much lighter than stock, noticeably louder, and riders were convinced that they made their bikes faster and considerably more powerful. Well maybe, but maybe not.

When bikes were simpler, and before emissions standards became so tight, riders were usually right—an aftermarket exhaust system would indeed make their bike slightly more powerful, but there was a price to pay. This extra kick usually occurred high up in the RPM range, and at the expense of low- and midrange power. Also, the installer had to be pretty knowledgeable about such things as it was often necessary to rejet the carburetors to compensate for the change in back pressure caused by the less-restrictive pipe. Finally, these pipes invariably allowed much more sound through than standard exhaust systems, which annoyed many people and made a lot of enemies for motorcycling.

Today, with stringent pollution and noise standards in force, modern motorcycles are often complete systems in which the camshafts, carburetors, intake tract, and exhaust system have all been tuned together to create maximum horsepower while still staying within the legal noise and emissions requirements of the government. Changing simply one component, such as the exhaust system, may in fact have a detrimental effect upon performance. Also, such modifications are technically illegal, although these statutes are not likely to be enforced unless the noise is extreme.

Racers are willing to change cams, carburetors, and exhaust systems in search of greater power, but the casual street rider may not be. Besides, the motorcycles we ride today often make more than adequate power to keep all but the most jaded enthusiast interested. In short, I no longer recommend changing exhaust systems unless you *really* know what you're doing, and/or intend to race the motorcycle.

Carburetors

Carburetors are the devices that mix air with the fuel to deliver the proper ratio of each to the engine. Today, federal emissions statutes necessitate that most bikes have their carburetors set very lean by the factory, and changing these settings is virtually illegal. Because of the cost, complexity, and questionable results garnered by making such changes today, most riders simply live with the systems their bikes have and accept them as the price we pay for having breathable air in the future.

Some riders, however, who are heavily involved with performance, exchange their standard carburetors for *smoothbore* mixers. As the name suggests, the bore of these carbs is virtually smooth inside, keeping the

The addition of smoothbore carburetors (such as these shown with their throttle assembly) is certain to add horsepower once they're properly set up. Note that performance carbs may reduce torque at low rpm and increase power at high rpm.

With proper care, a motorcycle battery can last three or four seasons—or even longer. (Photo courtesy Yuasa-Exide Battery Corporation)

fuel flow from being interrupted by the convoluted bore shapes and protrusions of most carburetors. If ultimate performance is your goal, there is no question that smoothbore carbs are a plus. Again however, I don't recommend switching to these types of carburetors for tuning and legal reasons unless you're preparing your bike to race.

Batteries

The motorcycle's battery lives in a tough environment. It's subject to vibration and extremes of temperature, not to mention being bounced around while in use. It's a wonder they survive at all.

In my touring experience, my motorcycle batteries have lasted from two to four years before that dreaded "click, click" from the solenoid signaled their death. Batteries incorporate series of plates impregnated with lead; the spaces between the plates are filled with a liquid medium composed of sulphuric acid and water. When the motorcycle's electrical system sends electricity into the battery, a chemical reaction between the lead and the acid allows the battery to store the electricity, which is why they are often referred to as *lead-acid storage batteries.*

As a battery ages, some of the lead and various impurities flake off of the plates and fall to the bottom as a form of sediment. Sometimes a large piece of lead will become dislodged and jam between two of the plates, causing a short circuit. Or the level of sediment at the bottom of the battery will rise high enough to reach the bottom of the plates and cause a short.

This may not sound like a serious matter—after all, a 12-volt battery has six series of plates, each responsible for two volts. The problem is that if one series suffers a short, you now have a 10-volt battery, which is not sufficient power to crank over your engine. Your battery is dead, and your ride may be dead in the water, too.

Proper maintenance will prolong battery life. First, it's important that you maintain the fluid level by adding distilled water when the level drops. It's not necessary to add acid; more is formed during the regular operation of the battery.

Second, prevent your battery from becoming discharged completely. Once this occurs, the battery's overall useful life is drastically shortened. Be certain you have not left some electrical circuit in operation while parking your bike for long periods.

There is no truth to the old mechanic's tale that setting a battery on concrete will drain its energy. What drains them, rather, is long periods of idleness. They also do not like extremes of temperature. During winter storage, if your bike is left in an unheated environment in subfreezing weather, remove the battery and store it in a heated area. Mark your calendar every three to four weeks with a reminder to trickle charge the battery so that it does not run down. I know that some riders have gotten into the lazy, and wasteful, habit of leaving their batteries in their bikes all winter, and then just buying a new one each spring. It's nice if you can afford it, but with a little attention a battery can be made to last three to four times longer than one

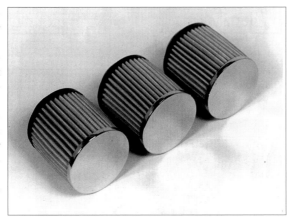

Be certain to service your air filter regularly. These are aftermarket performance individual units that replace the standard airbox and single air filter. (Photo courtesy K & N Corporation)

season. Or, use a "smart" charger that turns itself off when the battery reaches full charge, and turns on again when needed. It maintains the battery in a fully charged condition, and a fully charged battery will not freeze.

Keep battery posts clean by rinsing corrosion away with a weak baking soda solution to neutralize the acid. Brush away any corrosion with a stiff wire brush, and then coat the posts with petroleum jelly to prevent corrosion from returning.

Air filters

Engines are (in simplified terms) air pumps. The faster they can be made to take in large quantities of an air and fuel mixture and move it through the cylinder head, then out the exhaust, the more power they will produce. The usual limiting factors to greater performance are the engine's own valve and intake tract configuration, as well as the air filter and exhaust system. Freeing the heads to flow more is a major operation compared with opening the air filter or exhaust.

First, be aware the air filter is a major participant in the battle to keep your bike running well and staying healthy for many thousands of miles. The filter removes solid impurities that naturally hang in the air—dust particles and all manner of bits of grit. Yes, racing machines often run without air filters for the purpose of having absolutely no restriction to their engine's air flow, but keep in mind that racers are looking for even the slightest advantage if it makes the difference between winning and losing. They're willing to accept the expense and extra work involved in tearing down their engines frequently to repair the extreme wear and damage caused by racing and by running without an air filter.

As a motorcycle tourer and traveler, your primary consideration is reliability. If your bike doesn't run, your trip is over. Also, unneeded expenses are certainly not welcome when you're traveling. The point here is to keep your air filter on, and maintain it.

Two kinds of air filter are the paper and the foam varieties. The pleated paper type is not able to be cleaned, but is disposed of at regular intervals, or whenever it becomes so dirty that it impedes air flow. Ensure that it fits firmly in place so that no unfiltered air can slip past.

If a paper element becomes very dirty, it is possible to remove some of the dirt by knocking the frame of the filter gently against a solid object to dislodge the surface dirt. If you have access to an air compressor, blow compressed air through the filter from the *inside* toward the outside to push dirt away.

A modern foam filter uses oiled, pliable foam to trap dirt particles. When it becomes dirty, the filter element can be rinsed in solvent, oiled once again, and re-used.

The same cautions go for the airbox—the box in which the filter lives. Often, the manufacturer fits a rather restrictive opening on the box to help quiet intake noise—which can also literally cause the engine to run out of breath at higher RPM. Some riders drill holes in their air boxes to allow their engines to flow more air.

If you care to indulge in this practice, your bike will probably be a bit noisier than it was stock. Second, you must be careful that the air filter is still properly protected from the swirling water that is generated when the bike is ridden in the rain. Generally speaking, unless you're riding much more for sport than touring, ventilating your airbox can cause some potential problems.

Motorcycle Tires

The area of tire patch in contact with the road at any given time is perhaps five inches wide by three inches long, varying by size of bike, front or rear tire, and inflation pressure. This tire patch is the only part of your motorcycle that should be in contact with the ground, and it's the only means you have of controlling your bike.

The tire consists of a rubber carcass braced by cords that run around the tire circumferentially, and by plies that run across the tire (from bead to bead) at an angle of up to 90 degrees. The tread is the compounded rubber layer over the plies whose job it is to grip the road

A dual-sport tire offers a compromise that is usually balanced toward street performance. Tire makers understand that the dirt tends to be more forgiving of errors than is the street.

With its great tread depth and carcass design the Dunlop K491 Elite G/T is a mileage or "touring" tire, but it can still corner very competently. (Photo courtesy of Dunlop Tires, Ltd.)

and provide a fair amount of wearability. Let's consider some other basics about motorcycle tires.

One of the major complaints about motorcycle tires is that they tend to wear out so quickly. "I put a set of four tires on my car," a friend of mine says, "and they cost $300 and last 50,000 miles. I put two tires on my motorcycle and they also cost $300, then about 15,000 miles later they're junk. What's going on here?"

What's happening is that our friend is comparing apples with oranges. Yes, both types of tires are round and black, but that's about where the similarities end. Let's take an example. I've got a car out in my driveway that weighs 3,500 pounds and is powered by a 150-horse engine. In the garage, pampered and safe from the elements, is a 550-pound motorcycle that makes 65 horsepower from its twin cylinders. Why will that heavy car run 40,000 miles on a set of tires, but the bike may get 15,000 maximum? Let's look at the facts.

The car tires put down a contact patch that measures 6 inches wide by 9 inches long, which is 54 square inches per tire, or 216 square inches for the entire automobile. Each square inch has to handle 16.2 pounds of automobile. Even if you add a 160-pound driver, this figure increases to only 16.9 pounds per square inch. And for the rear tires, each of the 108 square inches of contact patch has to handle only 1.39 horsepower.

Now let's look at my motorcycle. Its front tire patch measures 2.5 by 6 inches, for a total of 15 square

inches; in the rear, figures of 3 by 7 inches provide a 21-square-inch patch. If the bike weighs 550 pounds, each of the 36 square inches must heft 15.2 pounds of motorcycle. Add a 160-pound rider and the average jumps to 19.7 pounds. Add a co-rider and touring gear, and it's like we're conspiring to mash that sucker flat! Finally, all of those 65 horses are herded through the rear wheel, and each of its 21 square inches must handle 3.1 horses.

Of course, such figures will vary depending upon the automobile and motorcycle you use for comparison, but these are pretty standard vehicles and, if anything, the bike is rather underpowered by today's standards. Therefore, while the weight figures are relatively comparable, the bike's rear tire must handle more than twice the horsepower per square inch. Now ask yourself, which vehicle gets used harder? You can bet I'm herding all of the bike's 65 horses much more frequently than I'm utilizing the car's 150. Everything's falling into place. Relatively short mileages on motorcycle tires is not a conspiracy by the tire companies, but rather a fact of harder usage compounded by greater weight and horsepower per square inch.

As for why motorcycle tires cost more, that's a simple economic fact of supply and demand. Motorcycle tires are manufactured in relatively small numbers compared with automotive tires, yet the development time devoted to them is relatively high. The company must recoup more of its costs per individual bike tire

than from its auto tires. Now let's consider a few facts about motorcycle tires.

As with anything in life, a tire is a compromise, especially if it's a touring tire. Every tire's prime purpose in life is to maintain its grip, therefore that quality must be given first priority during design. After all, what's the point of developing a motorcycle tire that will last 50,000 miles if, the moment the bike is leaned over, you go sliding about like a roller-skating bear? At the other end of the spectrum are tires made to grip like Velcro at insane speeds. Racing tires do this, but they may last only one 100-mile race—or less.

Tires wear out for many reasons, including road friction, destructive spinning and sliding, and squirm. As the tire spins, centrifugal forces elongate it slightly. This slight expansion promotes flexing, which causes heat, which in turn destroys the tire. To control this expansion, many tire manufacturers have developed belted tires, which include a circumferential belt of woven fabric, steel or Kevlar below the tread and all the way around the tire.

Another approach to improve a tire's mileage is to increase tread depth. Compare one of today's mileage units with an old Continental Twin from the 1970s; you'll find a real revolution in tread depth. Great depth is especially prevalent on H-rated tires, which are for continuous speeds of up to 130 MPH. Tread acts as an insulating blanket, and a thick tread such as these tires have would be a detriment on a V-rated tire—one designed to handle sustained speeds of up to 150 MPH.

High speeds generate tremendous heat—so much so that the tire may not be able to disperse enough of it—quickly enough—to prevent problems. As a result, H-rated versions of the same tire have greater tread depth than the exact same brand and size of V-rated tire. Generally speaking, if your machine is not capable of reaching 130 MPH, there is no real advantage to be gained by using V-rated tires, unless you're crossing over into DOT-approved racing tires that will give a traction advantage at track speeds. Unless you intend to ride on the track, or at sustained speeds of more than 130 MPH, H-rated tires are certainly adequate on a touring or sport-touring bike.

Tire Care

Because tires are essentially air bags that support the weight of your machine strictly with air pressure, it is absolutely essential that you check and maintain your air pressure on a daily basis while touring, and at least weekly if you ride less frequently. Tire researchers also note that the more pressure a tire carries, the more weight it can also carry. Therefore, if you intend to ride two-up and loaded, especially in hot weather, it's a good idea to inflate your tires to the maximum recommended pressure that's listed on the tire sidewall. Remember, tire pressure readings are to be made in the morning before the bike has been run and when the tires are still cold. Secondly, you may sacrifice some tire life and compliance (comfort) if you inflate them to maximum pressure.

So, why not go to an even higher tire pressure to provide yourself with even greater load capacity? Because tires are designed to flex a certain amount for grip and for other performance characteristics; overinflation will interfere with these abilities.

Radial Tires

In the 1970s and 1980s, the "radial revolution" swept the automotive world, resulting in tires that handled and rode better, ran cooler, lasted longer, and provided less rolling resistance for better fuel mileage. They were better in every way. So, why do most motorcycles still ride on bias-ply tires?

The reason is that motorcycles are not automobiles, and they do not turn like automobiles. Here's a simplified look at the situation. By definition, a radial tires is one whose plies run "substantially 90 degrees to their direction of rotation," according to the trade organizations that serve the tire industry. The plies run shoulder to shoulder, making for a very flexible sidewall. Bias-ply tires, on the other hand, have overlapping angles of plies that result in relatively stiff sidewalls.

Pliable sidewalls work very well on automobiles because, in a corner, the tire sidewall knuckles under to keep the tread flat on the road. Motorcycles, on the other hand, corner by rolling over onto their wraparound tread. In this situation, a pliable sidewall is a detriment.

In certain applications, however, a radial does work on a motorcycle. High-performance street and racing bikes now come standard with radials carried on very wide rims. These wide tires are very low in profile to provide a major amount of gripping surface, but a relatively short sidewall. The amount of flex, relative to sidewall height, helps to cushion the ride; however, there is not so much sidewall height that excessive flexing could result.

Radials are not incompatible with touring bikes, but the problem is that their pliable sidewall does not provide the load carrying capacity a touring bike needs. They do offer some advantages, although no dresser tourers have as yet been introduced with true, 90-degree radial tires. Radials are lighter than standard bias-ply tires, and run cooler. Their compliance can provide a more comfortable ride. In the handling department, the best way I can describe it is that a radial feels more "planted" as you set up for a turn—they inspire more confidence as they seem to grip better.

Radials do not necessarily offer better mileage, although the potential is there. In order to accommodate the low, flexible sidewall, the use of radial tires on touring bikes will have to be (as they were with sports) led by the motorcycle manufacturers. Existing radials, because of their low-profile sidewall, require a larger-diameter wheel. This change will have to be designed into the motorcycle; today's true radials will not retrofit older motorcycles that have wheels designed to fit standard bias-ply tires. That development has gained momentum through the 1990s.

Replacing Your Tires

When it's time to replace your worn-out motorcycle tires, don't just troop down to the dealership and order another set of what came on the bike. With a little thought and research, it's possible to tailor your tire

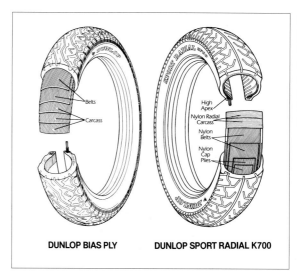

Here's how a bias-ply tire (left) differs from a radial in construction. (Photo courtesy Dunlop Tire Corporation)

DUNLOP BIAS PLY   DUNLOP SPORT RADIAL K700

choice to your kind of riding, and often to make a much better choice than your stock tires.

While all premium motorcycle tires are pretty good today, their performance characteristics vary. With such a variety of tires available, it's possible to fine-tune a set to the type of riding you do, allowing for differences in compounding, tire size, construction, and intent.

I interviewed a couple spokespersons for major motorcycle tire companies that sell both OEM and replacement rubber and asked them to tell me about the difference between the two kinds of tires. One spokesman told me his company supplies the exact same tires to two of the OEMs that it sells through dealers as its regular line of premium aftermarket tires in the United States. He went on to say that the parent tire company in Europe deals directly with a couple of bike manufacturers to design specialty rubber for several of their models sold in Europe. These same bike models are sold in the United States, but it's common for a bike company to contract for tires from several manufacturers to avoid becoming too dependent upon any one of them.

In some cases, the motorcycle manufacturer is designing a secret new model that it does not want anyone to know about. The bike company will ask the tire company to design certain sizes of tires to handle X amount of weight, horsepower, and torque; in addition, the bike company will specify its intent regarding touring, sport touring, or sporting use. The tire company makes up sample tires, the bike company tests them and then says, "Fine, but send another couple pair, one with two degrees more cord angle, and one with a slightly harder compound." The tire parade can go on for months. Finally, the bike manufacturer tells the tire company, "Sample 28 is fine—send us six thousand sets." The motorcycle company therefore decides which is the best tire for its bikes.

Another tire company told me that a particular motorcycle company just would not approve its standard tires for its line of heavyweight machines. "They take it up to 105 MPH on their test track," the spokesman said, "then take their hands off the bar and give it a whack. They want the bar to return to a neutral position within a set amount of oscillations, but our tire consistently went one oscillation too many. We had to redesign that tire with a different ply angle to meet their standards, and then rename it so they would approve that model for their bikes." This may seem like a lot of trouble to go through, but if you're like me, you're happy that the bike and tire companies do this for our safety.

Much of this testing is conducted on closed-course tracks because it's convenient and safer, and because in the case of a new model, it's much easier to keep it a secret. As a result, these particular tires that performed well on a test track with a professional rider may not act the way you want them to on the road. Stock tires are designed to meet very specific design parameters that may or may not meet the parameters you have for your riding.

Tire Basics

Tires come in many sizes, which read like the hieroglyphics on an Egyptian tomb. The old 3.50-19 size is gone, replaced by a sizing system that mixes metric measurements with inches. Now a front tire may read 100/90V-19. The 100 designates the tire's width measured in millimeters, while 90 is the height of the tire expressed as a percentage of its width. In other words, this tire is 90 percent as high as it is wide; this relationship is referred to as the "aspect ratio." The letter V is the speed rating; see the sidebar in this section for an explanation of that rating. Finally, the 19 indicates the rim diameter in inches.

Some riders may be tempted to mount racing tires on their motorcycles, believing that because they ride pretty hard, they need the extra traction that these tires offer. Many of the premium tire companies offer street-legal tires that are also used for production racing when offered in specific compounds. In order to be legally used on the road in the United States, any tire must have a DOT approval on the sidewall, and a grooved tread. These tires

are fine for riding hard on the road, but keep in mind that tread life will be relatively short.

If you're thinking of mounting slick tires such as those used in production and grand prix racing, forget it. They're not legal on the street, and for good reason. The slick tread grips superbly when warmed up to racing speeds (which is one reason competitors always take a warm-up lap before a race), but when confronted with water, oil, or dirt, slicks will not grip as well as conventional tires. All tires are designed to provide optimum grip while operating within a specific temperature range and, for racing tires, that heat range is relatively high. I have ridden on the track several times and can attest to the fact that you cannot ever ride as hard on the street as you can on a track. Leave slick tires on the track where they belong.

Compounding

Compounding is the complex chemical equation that determines the various properties the rubber in the tire tread will have. Generally speaking, a standard compound will tend to wear very well, and will exchange some tenacity in all-out grip for extended tread life. A sport compound will be biased toward good grip characteristics and, in general, may last half as many miles as a standard tire while being ridden twice as hard. A race compound is serious about grip at very serious speeds, and is willing to sacrifice all other considerations as long as mileage is sufficient to finish the race. Special compounds are designated "S" for sport, and "R" for race.

Tire Size

A general rule of thumb is that most bikes will accept a small range of varying tire sizes, although you should be familiar with the differences those sizes will make in your bike's steering and handling. Some bikes will accept tires that are one or two sizes larger (in aspect ratio, not in rim size), the limiting factor being the point at which the front tire will physically begin to rub on the fender or brackets, or the rear tire will rub on the swingarm or fender. Remember too that as tires are run they will "fling," or grow in size slightly, which can cause them to rub. A tire may fling about three percent at 55 MPH, and 10–13 percent at 125 MPH. Be aware, too, that as you mount wider and wider tires on the rear, the location of the tire's center point will begin to move out of line with the center of the front tire, and of the motorcycle. A spacer can be used to offset the rim and center the tire once again.

Larger rear tires are usually fitted to put more rubber on the road for better traction under braking and acceleration. Front tire sizes are usually changed to fine tune steering and increase confidence. If a bike tends to oversteer or feel twitchy and skittish in turns, a one-size-larger front tire may slow steering and increase confidence. Or, if the bike seems to change direction in slow motion or requires an inordinate amount of steering effort, a step down in tire size may speed things up. In general, it is best to stay with recommended sizes for both safety concerns and efficiency. Consult your owner's manual or dealer for alternative tire sizes.

WARNING. Never change tire sizes unless you have discussed it with your dealer or other knowledgeable person. A change in tire size *will* change steering geometry. A change to a lower aspect ratio will reduce ground clearance, which can cause the motorcycle to drag its parts on the ground and to lever its tires off the pavement at less severe lean angles than previously required. Put too wide a tire on a rim that is too narrow, and the rim could pinch the sidewalls so much that the contact patch size is actually reduced. Always confer with experts before making such changes.

Mixing Tires

Motorcycle tires are designed to be run in sets, so it's not a good idea generally to mix brands front and rear. Sets of tires from the same manufacturer will have compatible compounds, cord angles, tread patterns, and handling characteristics. However, Metzeler has designed a front tire, the ME33 Laser, specifically to act in concert with a variety of rears.

Because rear tires wear out two to three times faster than fronts, except for real hot-shoe sport riders, it's difficult to avoid mixing tire brands. I have done so, with the advice of experts, and while mixed pairs all feel slightly different, I have quickly adapted to the different feels of fronts and rears. In any case, radial tires are designed for very different characteristics, and I positively recommend you do *not* mix a radial tire with a bias-ply tire.

Also, keep tire wear factors in mind. When they're new, tires have a very rounded profile and will roll very easily into a turn. As tires wear they flatten out, especially the rear tire, which affects how the bike feels when you initiate a turn. If your bike tends to wear out

Tire Speed Ratings

What's in the alphabet soup

Motorcycle and automotive tires utilize four speed ratings in common usage. The ratings are S, H, V, and Z, and are a certification that examples of this tire have been tested and have met or exceeded the requirements for its speed rating.

The speed ratings mean that the tire has been able to survive a sustained speed of 112 MPH, 130 MPH, and 150 MPH for the S, H, and V ratings respectively, and in excess of 150 MPH for the Z rating. Don't laugh—some new superbikes have attained speeds approaching 180 MPH in closely supervised tests. ∎

two or three rears per front, be aware of how different the profiles will be between the new rear you've put on, and the front that has already survived one or two previous rears.

Choosing Your Replacement Tire

The vast choices available today allow you to select a tire design, speed rating, compound, and size that can tailor your tires specifically to your use. Here are some general guidelines.

First, never compromise on speed rating. If your bike is capable of sustained speeds in excess of 130 MPH, get V- or Z-rated tires. I don't care if you would *never* go that fast. Your bike's suspension and frame are designed to work with stiff-carcass tires, and an H-rated may not do the job.

In terms of tire design, your basic choices are among a sport-oriented tire, a mileage tire, or a standard. In general, a sport-oriented tire grips best, but wears out first. Mileage tires last the longest, but there's a question as to how far you can push them. Standard tires are designed for a broad variety of situations, and their wear factor is in the middle ground. Stick with sizes and aspect ratios that are very similar to stock. A very low aspect ratio may put more rubber on the road, but it could also put *you* on the road if this low-sidewall tire causes your bike to run out of ground clearance too quickly.

Use specialized motorcycle engine oil in your bike to help prevent viscosity breakdown, and to properly lubricate your integral gearbox.

Fork oil is available in a variety of viscosities. (Photo courtesy Klotz Special Formula Products, Inc.)

Generally, if you don't ride very aggressively and want more tire use for your money, get a mileage tire. If you really like to ride hard and aggressively on a sport bike, get V-rated tires in a sport compound. If you don't want to spend a lot, and don't expect to keep your bike long enough to wear out a set of mileage tires, standard skins should be fine. When it's time to buy new tires, make an informed choice. Consider your needs, check with the dealer, and talk with your riding buddies. After all, who knows better how you ride, the company that designed your bike, or you?

Motorcycle Lubricants

Without proper lubrication, a bike wouldn't last a mile. Parts would seize and overheat, and the whole thing would be reduced to a smoking, melted-together mess in a very short time. Let's cover some important points about motorcycle lubrication.

First, why is it that riders will hock themselves up to their forelocks to buy a $10,000 (or whatever price) motorcycle, then "protect their investment" by dropping in 99-cent-per-quart automotive oil they find in the discount store? Apparently, they don't know any better.

It's a fallacy that "oil is oil." Other than being dark and slippery, there are vast differences in lubricants. Even the best automotive motor oils probably won't protect your high-revving, multi-cylinder Japanese bike adequately because they're not designed to. The great majority of motorcycles sold by the Japanese companies share a common sump for the crankcase and gearbox. Automotive oils are designed only to protect the engine, not the gearbox, and their lubrication needs are quite different.

An engine oil requires good film strength (the ability to cling to parts and create a film) to provide a cushion between plain bearings and other engine parts. An automotive engine oil delivers that. A motorcycle gearbox, however, requires added zinc (more than is in automotive motor oils) to cushion the pushing and dragging motion of the gears. Companies that make specialty motorcycle oils add zinc to their products for this purpose. The most common situation caused by not using a motorcycle oil in this application is balky, clunky shifting.

A second situation caused by the common oil sump and gearbox is that of oil shear. Multi-weight oils contain polymers, long chains of molecules that provide varying viscosity (flow) characteristics (more about that later). With a 20W-50 motor oil, for example, the 20W ("W" means "winter") relates to the oil's characteristics at 210 degrees Fahrenheit. When an automotive oil is run in a motorcycle's common crankcase/gearbox, the gear teeth grind away at those polymer chains and wear them away, shortening them. In 800 to 1,000 miles, enough of the polymer chains have broken down to turn that 50-weight oil to a 40-weight. After 1,500 miles, it could be sheared down to a 30-weight.

As the oil thins, the engine can begin to suffer additional wear. A 50-weight oil can maintain its film strength at a higher temperature than when it has been thinned down to a 40 or a 30. As the oil breaks down it becomes thinner and does not lubricate as well. Specialty motorcycle oils include special shear-stable polymers that can bend in the gear environment, but resist shearing.

Once you accept the fact that motorcycles with common crankcase and gearbox require special lubricants, does that mean that Harleys and BMWs, which have separate gearboxes, can run on low-cost automotive oils? Not necessarily! BMW motorcycles run at

Motorcycle drive chains must be lubricated and adjusted on a regular basis, even if they are O-ring chains. The O-rings need lubrication to prevent them from drying out.

Motorcycle driveshaft and gearbox lubricants should be changed according to the recommendations in your owner's manual. Remember to recycle all lubricants.

much higher RPM than most car engines, and both brands put out much more power per cubic inch than auto engines. Oil must also remove heat, and air-cooled engines run hotter. Look at the size of the radiator in an 85-horsepower Toyota, and then check the one on a 100-horsepower BMW K100. Thus, use a true motorcycle oil in your Harley or Beemer. They're formulated to withstand higher heat and friction loads than cheap car oils.

Let's quantify these figures to illustrate the differences between auto and car engines. The Yamaha FZR600 is powered by a 599cc four-cylinder engine that is liquid cooled. It has been dyno tested at 77 horsepower at 10,000 RPM, on its way to its 11,500 RPM redline, where power drops to 73 horses. This 455-pound bike, with 150-pound rider aboard, has been tested at 11.74 seconds in the quarter mile, with a terminal velocity of 114.75 MPH.

By comparison, a family sedan I used to own was powered by an 1800cc four-cylinder engine producing 85 horsepower at 5,250 RPM. This will propel its 2,650 pounds (with 150-pound driver aboard) through the quarter mile at a relative snail's pace. Projecting those performance figures out, the FZR600 engine produces 128 horsepower per liter, and the sedan's only 47.2.

We've established that the motorcycle produces 2.7 times more horsepower from its given displacement; now let's consider how much oil is allotted to handle that load. The FZR holds only 3.2 quarts of oil to handle both crankcase and gearbox duties. The car's crankcase holds 4.0 quarts alone; a separate reservoir handles the gearbox.

Not only is there more oil to handle slightly more power in the automobile at lower RPM, but consider the use factor. Granted, the auto is heavier, but the motorcycle rider will be using more of his horses, more often, revving higher and riding faster than the auto driver will be. Aggressive riding creates much higher temperatures for the motorcycle despite its liquid cooling, and heat is the enemy of oil. Now, how do you expect oil designed for an automobile to properly protect this motorcycle?

As mentioned above, heat harms oil. Under extreme heat, oil additives begin to decompose, crystallize, and form abrasive materials. Inexpensive automotive oils will begin to break down at temperatures approaching 300 degrees Fahrenheit, but quality motorcycle oils are designed to withstand much higher temperatures.

Better quality oils are made from better base stocks that have been refined to a greater degree. In addition, they contain a higher quality of detergents, stronger EP (extreme pressure) additives, friction modifiers, and anti-foam agents. Foam is formed when air mixes with oil, and air does not lubricate.

Additive packages can create very different oils tailored to specific jobs. Diesel engines, for example, require lubricants that can handle contaminants. Automotive oils tend to go long periods between changes, and are used in liquid-cooled engines that are often run daily and at fairly constant RPM. Marine oils must handle engines that are exposed to a very harsh environment, sit idle for weeks or months at a time, then are run often at full throttle and high RPM.

A motorcycle may sit for months in the winter, then only be ridden on weekends, so it needs extra doses of anti-corrosives. Also, the temperature range of motorcycle engines varies a great deal. Bikes need higher grades of anti-wear additives that are designed for high RPM and high performance rather than for long drain periods. Motorcycle riders tend to be conscientious; they change their oil relatively often.

Synthetic Oils

Synthetics are tailor-made oils, built from the ground up, molecule by molecule, with a good quality additive package. They're designed to stay in grade longer than less-expensive petroleum-based oils. Synthetic-based oils may be based upon petroleum oil, plant matter, or gases.

When synthetics were introduced, there were some compatibility problems with existing automotive seals. The seals tended to leak, and the rumor was that synthetics were "thinner," which caused them to leak through. The rumor was false. Some companies that built early synthetic oils experimented with various chemicals, including alcohol and Poly Alpha Olefin (PAO). These were incompatible with seals and caused them to shrink, which caused seepage, and the belief that the oil was thinner. Today, any oil that passes the SF or SG rating of the Society of Automotive Engineers (SAE) standards is the same weight (or "thickness") as petroleum-based oils offering the same viscosity. Also, the seals were upgraded years ago to handle the new types of oil, and any car or motorcycle built in the last 20 years should not have a problem.

Another common fallacy is that an oil is a synthetic because it has synthetic additives. Many petroleum-based oils have various synthetic additives, but a true synthetic was built up from a synthetic base oil.

Oil Weights

I have already touched upon oil weights briefly, but it requires some clarification as there is a misunderstanding about oil viscosity. Some folks believe that if 10W-40 motor oil is recommended for their vehicle, they'll do it a favor and instead use 20W-50 because "it's better."

They're victims of incorrect assumptions. If your owner's manual calls for 10W-40, it's because testing has shown that in certain temperatures, this multi-weight performs best. A 20W-50 is a heavier oil, and it will not flow as well in a situation where a 10W-40 is called for. As a result it will not lubricate as well, and the engine will run hotter. Consult your owner's manual for the correct viscosity of oil at various temperature ranges.

Gear Oils

Special gear oils are used in the gearbox of machines that have separate gear cases, and in the rear hub and driveline of bikes that have driveshafts. BMWs, for example, use all three. These lubricants have been formulated with particular additives especially for the dragging and pulling action of hypoid gear teeth.

If you still don't believe that gear oils and engine oils are formulated for different duties, take the sniff test. Smell an open container of motorcycle hypoid gear oil, and one of engine oil. Not even close! The gear oil has heavy concentrations of sulpher and zinc, which the straight engine oil does not. These allow each of them to handle separate duties.

Fork Oil

The fork legs also require specialty lubricants for proper operation. In the past, bike manufacturers called for Automatic Transmission Fluid (ATF) to be used in their forks, but the lubricant manufacturers soon began offering much better specialty lubricants.

One benefit of specialty fork oils is that they're blended in increments of specific viscosities. By choosing the proper viscosity, an attentive rider can fine tune his fork for best results. Careful experimentation has proven to me that my bike works best with eight-weight fork oil. To obtain it I blend five- and ten-weight fork oils, slightly heavy on the ten.

Fork oil should have good lubricity and film strength, with anti-foaming agents and good shear stability so it won't break down while being repeatedly shoved through those orifices. Friction modifiers will help to prevent stiction—the static friction that causes a fork slider to momentarily stick before it releases and allows the slider to do its job. Some fork oils contain molybdenum, a soft, metallic chemical that provides greater lubrication.

5

Motorcycle Apparel

DRESS RIGHT, DRESS SMART

I've ridden in snow in the Alps, in 115-degree weather in the Mojave Desert, and have done 150 miles from Newcastle to Lincoln in the wettest 24 hours ever recorded in the history of England. In each situation I survived, relatively comfortably, and owe it all to the fine, high-technology motorcycle apparel now available.

The road is a harsh environment, especially on a motorcycle. It may be 40 degrees, windy, and raining just an inch from your skin, but inside your body it had better be approximately 98.6 degrees Fahrenheit, or you're in trouble. In my experience I've learned to dress properly for riding, but it was not always so. One June Sunday in 1976, I came face to face with The Enemy and only dumb luck saved me. I was going to ride solo from my parents' home in southern Michigan to where I lived at the time, about 200 miles to the north. The day was spitting rain, and my riding clothing consisted of a helmet, blue jeans and an insulated nylon jacket. My Honda CB550 Four was equipped with a fairing, so what was there to fear? "If it rains," I reasoned, "I'll just wait beneath an overpass until it stops."

When the first rain hit I did exactly that, then rode off again when it eased. When it hit the second time there was no place to hide and, though engulfed in rain, I just kept riding. Rain suit? Nope—felt I couldn't afford one. Besides, how bad could it get on a day in June?

After half an hour in the rain I could feel the wetness oozing across my back, dripping into my shoes and puddling in my crotch. I rode on, cold, shivering, and with my hands going numb. The fact I needed gas possibly saved my life. Hondas in those days had a gas cap release lever that had to be pushed down to spring the cap open. Not only could I barely feel my fingers enough to turn off the ignition, but also when I tried to operate the release lever my thumb collapsed—I could not control it. This caused me to realize the peril I was in, and I pulled into a restaurant to warm up.

At that time I had never heard the term *hypothermia,* but had just stared it in the face. Hypothermia is a dangerous lowering of the body's core temperature. It affects the extremities first, then the torso and brain, which leads to stupor, collapse, and death. Even if I hadn't been physically damaged by hypothermia, its effects such as my numbing hands could well have

The right riding gear not only looks good, but also functions well. (Photo courtesy of Harley-Davidson MotorClothes)

The action back is that additional pleat of leather behind the shoulders that prevents the sleeves from riding up when the rider reaches for the controls. (Photo courtesy of Harley-Davidson MotorClothes)

A variation on the ventilated jacket is the Perforated Summer Chief by Firstgear. Unlike a vented jacket, however, the perforations cannot be closed when the weather turns cool. (Photo courtesy of Intersport Fashions West)

To achieve good airflow, a jacket must offer vents both front and rear. These Daytonas are bomber-style jackets, and the rear vents are shown on the woman's jacket. (Photo courtesy of Intersport Fashions West)

caused me to lose control in a critical situation. There's more than one reason to fall.

Another consideration in riding is the wind-chill factor. It combines the effects of temperature and wind, and expresses them in terms of still-air temperature. For example, if you're out on a 50-degree day traveling at 55 MPH on your unfaired motorcycle, the combination of temperature and wind chill feel like 35 degrees Fahrenheit on your bare skin.

Apparel Basics

I'll cover all sorts of motorcycle apparel including leather, nonleather, boots, gloves, etc. For now, however, let's look at the basics about these items.

The job of any motorcycle apparel is to shut out the elements and keep you comfortable and dry. In order to do this it must seal well at all its openings. When you're shopping for motorcycle wear, note that it really is different, and is more functional in its specialized environment than are fashion-wear items. One desirable feature of a motorcycle jacket is an "action back," which is an extra pleat of fabric behind the shoulders to accommodate the arms-forward riding position.

Take a close look at the closures—without them, your motorcycle clothing will be drafty and cool. You need zippered or other closures on the sleeves and pants cuffs, a snug-fitting adjustable collar with a soft liner, and a waist that can be cinched down with a knit waistband, belt, or other closure. The front zipper should be backed by a storm flap of flat leather to block the wind coming through the zipper teeth.

A motorcycle jacket will also have slightly longer sleeves than a fashion jacket, and will be longer in back to cover the kidneys. The sleeves may be rotated forward about 15 degrees to accommodate the riding position. For protection, look for additional closed-cell foam padding over the shoulders and elbows; a stiff back pad is now being added to some racing jackets.

The more pockets in a motorcycle jacket the better. Experienced riders carry handy items in them such as ear plugs, a balaclava, silk glove liners for when it turns cold, a spare set of plastic screws in case they lose one from their helmet face shield, a business card for identification should their jacket be left behind accidentally, and a spare key for their bike lock. Each pocket should seal with a zipper or other closure, and there should be at least one inside pocket for valuables.

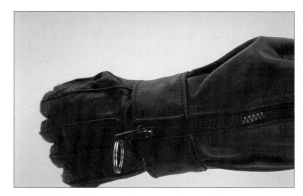

A good sleeve closure will prevent the wind from blowing up the arms and chilling the rider.

A riding jacket must have a comfortable neck closure that seals well to keep out the wind.

In hot weather, adjustable ventilation is a desirable feature. It consists of front-and-rear zippered jacket openings that are backed by perforated material such as leather or nylon to keep out the bugs. Usually the front vents are readily accessible by the rider, but he'll either have to remove the jacket or have a friend zip the back vents.

Motorcycle Suits

Motorcycle suits are available as two-piece or one-piece garments. The following factors apply no matter what they're made of. A two-piece suit consists of a jacket and pants that usually zip together to not only prevent the wind from getting up underneath, but also to keep the suit together for protection if the rider falls. A one-piece suit, of course, has no central split. There are two schools of thought about the relative merits of a one-piece versus a two-piece suit. Both arguments are valid. You decide which is best for you.

One-Piece Suits

Those who favor one-piece suits do so because they deliver maximum protection all the time. In general, a one-piece suit will be more wind- and weather-tight, as there is no waist opening, and it would be my choice if I often went on day-long rides in chancy weather. In a fall its middle can't ride up, but it's important to get a suit that's easy to get into and out of. It's a real plus if the legs open wide enough so that the rider does not have to remove boots to get the suit on or off. It's usually necessary to sit down to remove a full suit, and sliding your boots in and out can soil the insides of the legs, which in turn can soil your pants if you wear the suit over clothing.

Sporting and racing leathers are usually stylish and heavily protective, but may not offer many pockets or be as comfortable in the cold.

Two-Piece Suits

An advantage of two-piece suits is their flexibility—you can wear either the top or bottom without the other. Most riders wear a jacket most of the time, but find a full suit either too warm or confining, especially off the bike. When you stop to eat, it's much easier to get out of a jacket than an entire suit. If you ride to a rally or to visit a friend and want to walk around, sit by the fire or go to a restaurant, you may feel confined and conspicuous tramping about in a one-piece suit. In certain circumstances, such as when the road is still wet

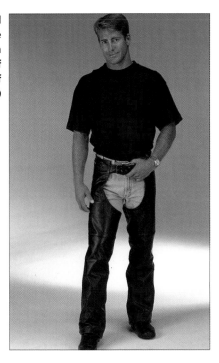

The traditional cruiser jacket takes on many forms, including the Commander (left) and Ventura (right). (Photos courtesy of Intersport Fashions West)

after a warm rain, you may prefer to wear just the lower part of the suit to protect your pants from road spray. And if the suit is bulky, well, the one-piece can't be split into two saddlebags. In general, select a one-piece suit for its greater ability to seal from the elements and to protect while on the bike, and a two-piece suit for its greater versatility and freedom off the bike.

A one-piece suit is often difficult to get up over your shoulders. To me, one of the things I like least is trying to pull on a one-piece rain suit alone. In the case of a nylon rain suit, it's particularly difficult to put on as it doesn't want to slide over wet leathers.

Finally, we've all heard the old joke about the man who buys a suit with two pairs of pants, then promptly burns a hole in the coat. If you buy a two-piece suit and damage one section, it's more convenient to replace one half of it than the entire suit. Also, if your bodily proportions fall outside the norm, you may be able to purchase separate tops and bottoms that fit your own proportions.

Leather Apparel

Think of people on motorcycles, and chances are the first thing that comes to mind is a leather jacket. The two items are as inextricably bound as John Wayne and westerns, as Thanksgiving and turkey, as hotdogs and baseball, and as sheep and wool. The look, feel, and smell of leather virtually evoke motorcycling.

The reason is that leather remains one of the very best abrasion-resistant materials available. When a rider falls, a good grade of leather that has been properly sewn will hold together and resist penetration as well as—or better than—any other type of material that is readily available and practical for motorcycle use.

Second, the smell, the feel, the suppleness of leather, and even the way it creaks, exude class and luxury. Ride in loose-fitting apparel that snaps and flaps in the breeze and you look geekish, but the leather-clad rider always looks cool, in control. Certainly leather is expensive, but when quality leather is properly cared for it lasts for years. I've heard of motorcycle-riding parents passing their leatherwear on to their children.

Back in my nylon jacket days I would replace my worn-out, dirty jacket about every two years. Today, a $400 leather jacket can easily last 10 years if it's not sent tumbling down the road. Now that nylon windbreakers can cost $70, leather is not all that expensive when its durability is factored in, and you can enjoy its benefit for many years.

Leather's long life is one reason that many riders prefer it in traditional styles. Leather jackets styled like those of the 1930s and 1940s remain popular today, especially for cruiser riders. Best of all, it looks good both on and off the bike.

Leather breathes, so it won't trap perspiration on a muggy day. If you do eventually suffer a get-off on your bike, it is repairable.

A high-tech jacket, this Firstgear Scout offers many features. They include a snap-out Thermoliner; front, rear and sleeve vents; and a sophisticated cargo system inside. (Photo courtesy of Intersport Fashions West)

Although it does not insulate well in and of itself, leather does block the wind efficiently. The addition of a lining can make leather apparel quite snug. For the sake of versatility, a removable lining enhances the value of leather apparel.

Motorcycle leather usually has a shiny finish to better shed the vagaries of a chancy weather environment, and it can be made more resistant to moisture and stains with special sprays. I don't recommend suede leather for motorcycling as it's made from split hides that pick up dirt and bugs, show the effects of rain, and require expensive professional cleaning.

Leather Jackets

Choose your leather jacket to fit loosely so you can wear a sweater under it if needed. Look for lots of pockets—at least a couple on the outside and one inner wallet pocket. The jacket should also have padding, such as at least another layer of leather on the elbows and shoulders. Thicker, rather than thinner, leather is a plus for safety and protection, but don't believe that thick leather can't be supple. Better quality leather jackets can be both marvelously supple and thick. Avoid large collars because they'll whip in the wind and jackhammer your shoulders.

Leather Pants

One-piece leather riding suits are best left to racers or sport-riding day trippers who don't expect to be out long enough for the weather to change drastically. For touring, two-piece leathers are much more practical.

Spray-Dyed Versus Vat-Dyed Leather

To find out, go scratch

Because of the strictness of laws that protect our environment, it has become increasingly difficult for tanneries in the United States to dispose of the chemical by-products of their trade. As a result, much motorcycle leather wear is now tanned, processed, and sewn in other countries such as Korea and Pakistan.

Some leather is still vat-dyed, which allows the dye to soak through it. Unfortunately, this process results in a major amount of by-products, although it's also a very good means of dyeing leather. Scratch or abrade leather that's been vat dyed and you'll notice that you cannot scratch off the color—it goes all the way through.

The other method of leather dyeing is to spray the dye on the surface. This process uses less dye, but only the surface picks up the color. If you'd like to find out what type of dye process you're dealing with, scratch the inside of the garment in an inconspicuous spot to see if you can scratch off the color. If you can, it's a spray-dyed garment. ■

Choose leather pants that fit snugly, but with a little extra room in the waist and upper thighs so they don't become too restrictive in the riding position. Also, look for a good seal at the waist and cuffs.

Padding is desirable in the knees and hips, with some type of expandable material such as Spandex in the lower hips and behind the knees for comfort. Pants that zip to matching jackets are a real plus for protection from the cold and a fall. As with jackets, pants pockets should zip or button shut for security.

Chaps

Chaps are versatile garments which are meant to be worn over pants to shield the fronts of your legs from the cold and wind; they're held on with a waist belt, plus straps across the backs of the legs. Once the weather warms, they can be easily removed and

Overpants are pants you wear over your jeans. They may be leather or textile, and offer additional protection from the elements. When the weather improves you slip out of them, so they must be easy to get into and out of. (Photo courtesy of Intersport Fashions West)

If your body type runs outside the mainstream, it may be necessary to have your leathers custom made. Many US manufacturers can accommodate custom sizes. The name listed on the order form for this suit was simply "Tiny." (Photo courtesy of Langlitz Leathers)

stashed in a saddlebag. Look for a good quality and thickness of supple leather. It's very important for chaps to be cinched down snugly so they can't rotate on your legs in a get-off, exposing you to injury. They also should be removable quickly and easily.

Overpants

An overpant is designed to be worn over other pants to provide additional protection and comfort. Overpants take chaps that final step forward by offering full, wrap-around protection.

To cover the rider's jeans, overpants are built a bit big and perhaps a little sloppy. If you work in an office environment, or anywhere in which you want to look your best, a jacket with overpants will protect your dress togs from bugs, dust and road grime.

The rationale behind overpants is that you put them on when the weather is cool or questionable, and take them off when things warm up. If you didn't intend to remove them in fair weather, you may as well just go for full leather or textile pants. Therefore, it's a real convenience when overpants can go on and come off easily on the road without having to remove your boots. They usually are supplied with long zippers up each side.

Look for zippers that are easy to operate, and pant legs that gape wide enough to allow adequate clearance for your boots. They should allow access to your jean pockets. The two main varieties are: textile overpants that are often waterproof and sometimes armored, and leather overpants that are designed more with style and overall abrasion protection in mind.

Textile overpants are often a deluxe version of rain suit bottoms that may offer such amenities as insulation, pockets, armor, and sometimes additional features. Armor refers to various types of usually closed-cell foam (sometimes backed with hard plastic) that is inserted into pockets in the garments to protect knees and sometimes hips from impact.

Leather overpants are cool, classy and comfortable, and look like "real" motorcycle wear. They provide great abrasion resistance, won't melt, won't flap as readily in the wind, and they smell great.

Nonleather Apparel

Much of what I've already covered about leather apparel also applies to nonleather in terms of design and what to look for. The features list also includes such things as closures and linings, ventilation and padding, pockets and one- or two-piece suits, and much more.

Hide Helper

Leather care and repair

Leather is very desirable apparel for the motorcycle rider from several standpoints, including protection, long life and style. In the course of its life, however, leatherwear will need care, and may need repair. Here is a brief summary of how to handle these needs.

Leather protects you—now you must protect your protector. Products such as these keep leather clean and supple, and help it resist water. (Photo courtesy Intersport Fashions West/ Hein Gericke)

Leather is a natural product that needs to be cleaned regularly. Most motorcycle leather apparel is treated to resist staining, and should be periodically wiped down with a damp rag. Commercial cleaning products are also available through your dealer. Do not *ever* allow leather to become soaked. This will wash the oils out of it, and cause the leather to become dry and cracked. If your leather gets wet, spread it out to dry (never use heat to dry it) and treat it immediately with a leather restorer that will replenish its natural moisture.

Once leather apparel has been cleaned, you can keep it supple and lubricated by rubbing in a light amount of petroleum jelly. Rub off the excess to prevent dirt from sticking.

Regarding leather repair, most individuals aren't prepared to take on the task, and it's sometimes difficult to find those able to perform the repairs. Your dealer may know of a repair shop, or the garment manufacturer may offer repairs. Simple abrasion marks that are the result of a low-speed getoff may be touched up with dye. Deeper holes, such as on a shoulder or elbow, must be patched with an additional piece of leather that will be dyed to match the garment. Dyes can usually be obtained through leather supply houses, such as the chain of Tandy Leather stores. They can also supply the heavy-duty needles and thread necessary for the task. Because leather is so hard to penetrate, most home sewing machines are unable to handle repairs.

The most common leather problem is a failed zipper, which must be replaced because it can rarely be repaired. This work can often be handled by a seamstress or tailor. For patch or dye work, a shoe repair store is more likely to be able to help. Unfortunately, both shoe repair and tailoring are dying occupations, and such shops may be hard to find. Check your Yellow Pages, and good luck. ∎

Let's consider the specifics of the other types of apparel, which are usually made of nylon, though occasionally other types of fabric are used.

Advantages

The major advantages of textile garments is that they can be less expensive than leather, and will not be ruined if they get wet. The most common type of material used for riding gear other than leather is nylon, in several forms. One common form is Dupont Cordura, a heavy, woven fabric available in different weights. In 1000-denier weights [denier (pronounced dén-yer) is a measure of the tightness and thickness of the weave] it is used for motorcycle luggage such as tank bags and soft saddlebags; apparel is made usually of 500-denier weights, though some is also made of 200 denier.

Inside the outer layer of Cordura nylon is bonded a layer of waterproof material. It's important to

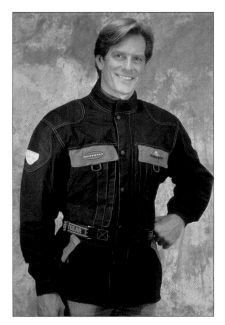

Dual-sport riders like a close-fitting, three-quarter-jacket with lots of pockets, armor and water resistance. Shown here is the Kilimanjaro jacket by Firstgear. (Photo courtesy of Intersport Fashions West)

A few companies, including Harley-Davidson MotorClothes, offer hybrid jackets that combine denim or other fabrics with leather for good looks and a reasonable price. (Photo courtesy of Harley-Davidson MotorClothes)

The Aerostich Darien jacket (pants are also available) is extremely versatile as it is armored and waterproof, and offers a Gore-Tex liner. Its fleece comfort liner is removable for warm weather, and can be worn solo as a casual jacket.

understand that while Cordura is a waterproof fabric, the apparel and other items made from it are not actually waterproof because water can seep through the stitch holes and past the zippers. Because of the waterproof layer, Cordura garments may not breathe well. Instead, some companies design their suits with a layer of Gore-Tex or other breathable membrane inside. These membranes resemble a sheet of clear plastic into which many microscopic holes have been punched. The holes are so small that they will not pass liquid water, but large enough to pass vapors. Therefore, water will not get in but the body's normal exhalations can escape.

Another method of making a fabric waterproof is to treat it with an impervious coating such as polyurethane. Many rain suits are made in just this manner, and the problem is that while they will not let rain in, they also will not let moisture out and can become quite clammy in use. For this reason I recommend the breathable fabrics, though they are usually quite a bit more expensive than the coated ones.

Man-made fabrics are also lighter than competition-weight leather and, if seams are sealed properly, garments made of Cordura and other fabrics can be made

quite rainproof. Leather, even when treated for rain resistance, is not to be considered a rain garment. Water can ruin leather, and treating it with water-proofing chemicals will affect its breathability. All rain garments are of man-made fabrics.

These textile fabrics are easy to clean—follow the instructions on the label so as to not reduce the fabric's rain resistance or other properties. Most are machine washable, but leather requires special care.

Though leather cuts the wind very effectively, it is not warm or insulating in and of itself. The same can be said of nonleather garments. Cold-weather suits tend to be of nonleather materials, with a layer of insulation sewn in between.

One disadvantage of non-leather garments is that they generally offer less abrasion resistance. Second, nylon will melt when exposed to high heat or friction. If a rider falls off his bike while wearing a nylon suit and slides along the pavement for some distance, the nylon may melt under the heat of prolonged friction. For this reason I strongly recommend that riders wear street clothing under their nylon suits. It's better to have the nylon melt against clothing than against your skin. Also, the nylon can melt if the suit is allowed to contact a hot engine or exhaust system, even for a short period of time.

In terms of ambience—the feel, suppleness, and smell—non-leather garments just can't match the attractiveness of leather. While leather is unruffled in appearance, looser garments that flap and flutter don't offer that same look of controlled competence. And as for color, both leather and textile garments can be made in many colors.

All-Weather Riding Suits

One of the more popular designs today is the all-weather, armored textile riding suit, designed with some closed-cell foam "armor" and a rainproof outer shell. These suits are very practical since they eliminate the need for an additional rain suit. They're often well insulated, but because of their insulation they can be bulky. Sure, they may look like "Dick and Jane at Hollyhill Farm," but when it's 40 degrees and raining, who cares what your suit looks like if it does the job and keeps you comfortable?

When trying out such suits, sit on a motorcycle in them and make sure that the arms and legs are long enough once you're in the riding position, and that there's enough room in the thighs and waist. Most are designed to be worn over street clothes, so wear your typical riding clothing when you try them.

Also look for a belt to keep the waist from billowing and costing you some warmth. A drawstring along the bottom of the jacket is also desirable. Large pockets should be sprinkled all over the suit, and seal well enough to keep the rain out. A distinct disadvantage of these suits is that they're quite bulky, and if you decide it's too warm to wear them, two of them could easily take up all the space in a trunk or saddlebag.

Rain Suits

Your first concern is to stay dry on a motorcycle. Remember my story at the beginning of this chapter about meeting up with hypothermia? When the weather turns wet, put on full rain gear or do not ride. Riders love to tell stories, and one of the most common is about the time they rode in a light drizzle, figuring it would stop. And of course it didn't stop, and eventually they became soaked because they just never seemed quite ready to pull over. Put on rain gear *before* it starts raining—after it's raining is too late.

Good rain suits offer a nylon outer shell and features such as tight sealing pockets, reflective striping and a tight seal on the cuffs and neck.

Rain suits differ from weatherproof riding suits in that the latter are usually lined and insulated. Rain suits are simply unlined oversuits usually made of a thin nylon coated with polyvinyl chloride (PVC) or polyurethane. Colors are usually a bright yellow, red, orange or a combination, and often they will offer one or more strips of retro-reflective materials such as Scotchlite. If it's raining, it's murky, and you're going to want both the bright colors and the retro-reflectivity.

Rain suits are available in one- or two-piece designs, with hook-and-loop or elastic strip closures at cuffs and sleeves. I've ridden in day-long rains, including one day in August, 1986, in England when Hurricane Charley delivered the wettest 24 hours in the recorded history of that wet island. Because my wife and I were wearing good rain suits, we stayed dry.

My advice, when it comes to comfort and safety items such as rain suits, tents, and sleeping bags, is to always buy the very best you can afford. Skimp on any of these items now and I can guarantee they'll cost you later in terms of discomfort, lost sleep, additional motel bills and possibly even injury.

Here's a tip: Because rain suits seal so well, they're virtually impervious to wind and water. When it's not raining, a rain suit can raise your comfort level a great deal on a very cold day by significantly reducing wind

Staying Warm

What to do when the cold gets serious

While this chapter covers motorcycle apparel, it requires some comment about what to do when it's *really* cold and you need to get serious about it. Your body manufactures its own heat, and the role of your apparel is to conserve it. This means not only insulating to preserve existing heat, but also filling in the cracks to prevent the wind from penetrating. Here is the short, condensed course (at the expense of some repetition) including concise tips for cold-weather riding.

The wind is a thief, stealing the heat your body makes, so it's imperative to form good seals where the wind can steal in. The neck area is of prime importance. Warm it with a dickie or turtleneck, then seal it with a windproof scarf or a product from the Aerostitch Rider WearHouse called the Wind Triangle. For sealing your neck better, and also to warm your head, pull out that silk balaclava that you've been saving in your jacket pocket. Sealing the edges of your helmet shield with duct tape will also prevent the wind from coming through, but don't seal it so well that your shield fogs.

Gauntlet gloves are the best means of sealing your sleeves, but if the wind still blows upward, try this. Put plastic bags (an old bread bag will do) over your gloves to stop the wind, and secure them with rubber bands. You'll find such bags quickly on the road at supermarkets. These plastic bags will not only cut the wind, but will also be effective in the rain. Be aware, however, that the plastic will make your hands slippery on the controls.

Most jackets offer good wind protection, especially if they're leather. If, however, you can feel the cold wind blowing through, a cheap and easily obtainable

Gerbing's Ultimate Jacket contains heating wires that make it one of the warmest jackets around. Heated pants, gloves and socks are also available from Gerbing's.

means of insulation is an edition of the local newspaper laid against your chest.

Here's a golden opportunity once again to make a pitch for electric clothing such as an electric vest, gloves and chaps. Your clothing traps the heat your body manufactures, and your body can only manufacture so much heat. Then consider that when you get cold, your pores slam shut in an effort to conserve heat. Electric clothing makes additional heat, and in so doing entices your pores to open, thus providing even more heat. Believe me, electric garments *really* work and I cannot recommend them too highly.

You've no doubt already decided that it's a good idea to put on as much clothing as you can, but have you considered your rain suit? Sure, it may be sunny bright, but when it's 45 degrees and you're shivering, that rain suit will help block the wind and trap the heat. Don't forget your rain boots and gloves, too. ∎

chill. I donned my rain suit one crisp, cold autumn morning in Nova Scotia and rode in comfort among the falling leaves. Rain suits are, after all, not just for rain.

Most rain suits weigh two to three pounds and have their own carrying bags. They fold up small enough to fit into a tank bag or small duffel carried on the rear.

Warm-Weather Suits

I have another story to help illustrate what can happen when a rider is not properly dressed. I moved to California from Michigan in 1978 and was completely inexperienced with the desert. I'd heard that it actually got too hot to ride, but couldn't believe such a thing. Wasn't riding always cooling in the breeze? Then I became immersed in my first desert crossing and learned what real heat was.

Riding a motorcycle is usually cooling because the air temperature is lower than the standard human body temperature of 98.6 degrees Fahrenheit. When the temperature nears and passes 100 degrees Fahrenheit, the hot breeze begins adding, rather than subtracting, heat. I didn't know this and made the stupid move of removing my shirt to get a nice tan. I even removed my helmet but quickly realized on both counts that I was even hotter now, as the sun was beating directly down on my skin. No clothing shaded me or blocked the wind. If you want to understand how to survive in the desert, consider how those who live there cope. The Arabs wear loose, flowing robes for shade and air circulation. Removing clothing is the worst thing you can do in the desert.

The boot covers furnished with some nylon rain suits protect well, but are slippery and not very durable.

If you ride in the rain, you need (clockwise, from left) Firstgear Overgloves, Rubber Overboots, Face Mask and Neckerchief. (Photo courtesy of Intersport Fashions West)

Staying Cool

What to do in serious heat

I've ridden in some serious heat, having crossed the Mojave Desert out West in June, July, September and October, which are among its hottest months. Here are some tips for staying cooler when the temperature gets up near, or passes, 100 degrees Fahrenheit.

The first rule in hot weather is to drink plenty of liquids, especially water and commercial thirst quenchers such as Gatorade, that are designed to replace the electrolytes the body loses in sweat. Stay away from alcohol; it's a diuretic that will cause you to lose more liquid than you retain, and the stuff's deadly when you're riding. Drink liquids before you get out in the heat if possible, and often while you're riding. If you're thirsty, you're already in danger. A bicycle water bottle is an excellent means of conveniently carrying water with you. It's light, inexpensive, and has an easy-open spout.

It's cooler in the shade, so to stay cooler you must stay dressed and shaded. Wear your helmet, jacket and pants. The worst thing you can do is to ride shirtless or without a helmet, which exposes you to the sun's direct rays and the wind's direct effects, both of which dehydrate you more readily. Don't forget sturdy footwear and ventilated gloves. Look elsewhere in this chapter for an at-length discussion of the benefits of warm-weather riding suits.

Besides drinking it, there are two ways you can use water to keep yourself relatively cool on a boiling day. First, soak a bandana or other suitable cloth in water and tie it around your neck. It will be in the breeze, and its evaporation (controlled by the tight knot) will cool you for hours.

The second method is one I've used, and recommend highly. When it's really hot, soak a sweatshirt or other heavy riding shirt in water. Oh, it'll make you shiver when you put it on, but don't be concerned how it drips on your pants—that will evaporate readily. And so would the moisture in the shirt if you rode with it exposed directly to the wind and sun. Put a windbreaker over it to keep the soaked shirt out of the direct breeze. Now, the water evaporating from the shirt will cool you directly, and you can control the rate of evaporation by how far you open the outer garment. ■

Boots with Gore-Tex liners, like these by BMW, allow the rider to continue on in wet weather without having to struggle into rain covers. They include retroreflective striping for visibility, and ankle padding.

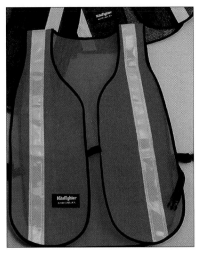

Retroreflective vests *really* reflect light and make riders visible at night.

To shorten my lengthening story, on this particular day I was weakening, getting groggy, and finally checked into a motel at the next town. There I slept the sleep of the stupid and exhausted, and eventually ate dinner at 11:00 p.m. before leaving at midnight. For specific information about staying cool or warm, see the sidebars in this chapter.

Today, special warm-weather garments are available that will make hot desert rides tolerable and more typical warm riding days enjoyable. In 1990, Hondaline (the accessory division of American Honda) introduced its Sena Madureira suit, named after a town in Brazil where the temperature and humidity both average in the nineties.

These suits are made of a polyester-cotton mix that breathes well while shading the rider from the sun, blocking some of the wind but allowing for full ventilation. They offer mesh-backed openings in the front that fold down to allow air in, and a similar opening in the back that allows it to escape, creating cooling air flow. If you can't find one of these, an alternative is a lightweight, light-colored mechanic's jumpsuit.

Because of its warm-weather nature, the warm-weather suit can be worn over just underwear. Find one that's cut a bit more generously, and it will fit over your work clothing for commuting. These suits will fold up to about the size of a rain suit.

Retro-Reflective Vests

One of the problems with being a motorcyclist is that auto drivers don't look for you, and this can put a rider in a very precarious predicament. The situation is even worse at night, especially for other motorists approaching from your rear or sides. For this reason, many riding suits and rain suits now offer retro-reflective striping that glows brilliantly when struck by a light source. The effect is so dramatic that it appears that the striping is illuminated from inside.

Some companies offer special retro-reflective vests that are worn over other riding gear and provide a huge amount of reflectivity. Usually they're made of an open nylon mesh that serves as a framework upon which to mount the reflective strips. The vests are sized large for ease of entry, and the strips are available in a variety of colors. One of the largest manufacturers of these products is Conspicuity, Inc., in Illinois. The name of the company (pronounced "con-spic-YOU-i-tee") is based upon the word "conspicuous." Some riders don't like the idea of the vests, perhaps feeling that tough guys don't wear Conspicuity vests. I have tested these products and can attest to the fact that, whether you like them or not, they really do reflect light!

Motorcycle Boots

Riding boots have a very specialized function, and I cringe when I see riders in cowboy boots, engineer boots, tennis shoes, or (God forbid) thongs. Motorcycle boots fill specialized needs that include keeping your feet warm, insulating and protecting your ankles from the engine cases, and protecting your toes from the shift lever. They're designed to grip the footpeg well and to grip the pavement whether you put your foot down in water, oil, mud, or gravel.

The upper section of the boot should be long enough to seal against the breeze, rigid enough to resist flapping in the wind, yet not so stiff as to chafe your

One approach to keeping hands dry in the rain is these Belstaff Glove Covers. (Photo courtesy of Belstaff)

Another approach to rain riding is these OSI Damdry (cute name!) gloves, which are also damwarm.

For seriously cold or wet weather, I recommend these heavyweight Tour Master Grand Touring Gloves.

Roadracing gloves, such as these by Tour Master, offer a combination of good tactile control with excellent protection across the backs of the hands, fingers and wrist bones.

calves. The boots also must be comfortable enough to hike in, and their soles must be suitable for walking on a trail.

My experience has been that the key to a comfortable boot is one that grips the ankle tightly to prevent heel lift. It's a plus if the boot opens at the side, as this allows them to be properly shaped at the heel. I strongly recommend that you buy boots in person from your local dealer, as fit is critical for comfort.

For the rain, some rain suits include nylon booties that are universally sized to fit over shoes or boots, but they shred easily if worn on stones or gravel. Pullover rubber boots, such as Totes, are rugged, watertight, and light. They fold for easy storage, and have a waffle-pattern sole for grip in wet weather. Another option is to select boots that incorporate a Gore-Tex or other breathable membrane that will keep the feet dry but allow inner vapors to pass through. Always protect your leatherwear in the rain.

Other Apparel

Motorcycle Gloves

When I go on tour, I carry four pairs of gloves—or at least a combination of gloves—to address four weather situations.

Cold-weather gloves are heavier, gauntlet-style affairs that are insulated and lined for the maximum in warmth. It's important that they be very well insulated at the knuckles for both warmth and safety. Be certain that the padding is well placed so that it does not bunch up in the palm, causing fatigue. They should not be so bulky that they hinder your feel of the controls.

Rain gloves usually consist of a coated nylon shell that either stows in the cuff pocket of a cold-weather glove, or is available by itself as a glove cover. The latter may be provided as part of a rain suit, but these are often coarsely made, being merely two halves of a pattern sewn together. Take care that when you use glove covers, you tuck the cover inside the sleeve of your

Racing boots, like these by AGV, tend to be light in weight, sporty looking and very protective. These offer replaceable plastic scrapers on the outside of the foot and top sections. That black area in the white consists of two ventilating scoops that are shown with their removable plugs in place.

Think of wrapping yourself in an electric blanket as you ride on a cold day. Better yet, get an electric vest. (Photo courtesy Widder Enterprises)

You say your hands get cold? Electric gloves are the answer. (Photo courtesy Widder Enterprises)

rain suit; otherwise rain can run down your sleeves and inside the covers. These covers can also be slippery on the controls.

Summer gloves go by several other names such as racing gloves or medium-weight gloves. They're usually unlined, lightweight gauntlet-styled affairs that are high on comfort and style. Of the various gloves you'll wear on a motorcycle, they're most likely to be in a color other than black and may be designed to match high-styled riding suits. These will also likely be your most comfortable gloves.

Racing gloves often will have several rows of metal studs on the palms as protection in case of a fall. They're effective in preventing abrasion on the palms, but won't be noticeable in normal wear. The studs are backed by a solid layer of leather—they will become very hot, very quickly, if you slide down the road on your hands—the leather's there for protection.

For hot weather, look for short, perforated gloves that allow for good airflow. Some companies offer fingerless gloves, and some combine leather with cloth. The fingerless variety offer a bit of palm protection, but none whatsoever for the fingers from wind, sun, or pavement. And non-leather gloves can literally fall apart under the stresses of a get-off. I recommend that you stick with full-fingered, perforated, all-leather gloves for hot weather. Just note that the sun shining through the perforations can cause a nasty sunburn—or certainly strange tan lines.

Electric Clothing

If your bed has an electric blanket, imagine that you could make a vest or jacket out of that blanket and wear it while you ride. The problem would be the miles-long cord, of course. If this sounds like heaven, though a bit far fetched, you'll really appreciate the reality of the situation. Practical versions of what I have just described have existed for more than two decades.

Electric clothing for motorcyclists was popularized by the Widder Corporation of Ojai, California, and the Gerbings company of Maple Valley, Washington, although other companies also manufacture it. The basic garment is the electric vest, which works on the principle that if you keep your torso warm, your hands and feet will stay warmer, too. Your normal clothing can only do so much; it merely traps the heat your body produces. Electric clothing manufactures additional heat.

Electric clothing is usually made of two layers of insulated nylon, with undulating electric wires coursing through it. In addition to vests, heated sleeved liners, chaps, and electric gloves are also available. I have considerable experience with these items, and have found the vest and gloves to be indispensable.

The electric garment manufacturer provides a wiring harness that makes his products easy to use. At one end, metal connectors slip over both battery posts, and at the other is a short plug that remains attached to the motorcycle. On the vest is a plug. In between is about a two-foot-long section of wire that includes an on/off switch or thermostat switch. When the rider wants to use the vest he plugs the switch cord into the battery harness and vest, and turns it on. I recommend thermostatic controls over on/off switches as they can sense the temperature of the outside air and adjust the heat accordingly, though some thermostats have not proven reliable over many seasons. In my experience Gerbing's products produce the most heat—so much that I strongly recommend the use of a thermostat with them. Other brands can usually do with an on/off switch.

A common concern with electric garments is the possibility that they may shock or burn the rider, drain the battery, or damage the electrical system. None of these concerns is really valid for a modern motorcycle's electrical system. I recently tested several electric vests, which drew from 40 to 50 watts. By comparison, a headlight draws 55 watts on low beam and 65 watts on high. An entire electrical garment setup that included a sleeved liner, gloves and electric socks together drew a total of 117 watts. Because they were thermostatically controlled, the garments operated only about 50 percent of the time. As a result, they were not likely to draw down the electrical system.

Any modern motorcycle manufactured since the late 1970s should generate enough electrical current to handle electric garments for one or two people, in addition to all the other duties it must handle. As for safety, the wiring harness of such electric garments will be provided with an in-line fuse. In the event of a problem the fuse will blow, protecting you from shock. Be certain that any electric garment you buy has a fuse, and never replace the standard fuse with one of higher amperage.

Electric clothing is usually made of unlined nylon, which feels clammy and cold against the skin. Also, this clothing can develop hot spots when held against the skin. For these reasons I recommend that you wear at least a tee shirt with a heavier shirt over it, to provide a means of spreading the heat and keeping the vest clean.

Electrical garments may cost about $130 including all hookups. While this is relatively expensive, I have used vests for 20 years and can attest that they really do work and are a wonderful luxury while on the road. The only negative is that these items occasionally require wiring repair, but it is usually simple and minor.

Note: I have worked for various motorcycle magazines testing bikes and other equipment for more than 20 years. At times, for just such observations as I've made above, I have been accused of being an elitist, of encouraging people to spend more money on products than is reasonable for the ordinary guy to spend. This, I have been told, means I don't have the best interests of the rider at heart.

To that suspicion I would reply that many of my dearest friends (including my wife) are also riding buddies. I absolutely have their best interests, and those of other fellow riders, at heart. The most important issue for me is that motorcycling is not a fashion show, but a very serious endeavor. Buy the wrong fashion from the Paris or New York designers and you may look ridiculous, but nothing serious is likely to happen to you. Buy the wrong rain suit, boots, gloves, or leather and in bad weather or a get-off (or as in my hypothermia example illustrated at the beginning of this chapter), you could be in very serious trouble. I do not advocate that you buy the most expensive riding gear, but rather the very best that you can afford. There is a difference, but often the most expensive is not necessarily the best. Your safety requires an investment in good equipment. Read the magazine tests to learn which is best.

Glove Liners

Usually made of silk, glove liners are designed to be worn inside your other gloves for additional warmth and comfort. I usually carry a pair in one jacket pocket as they weigh practically nothing, and are handy when you need them. They add a touch of luxury that helps keep blisters away when you're wearing unlined gloves, and add just that extra little bit of warmth to winter or rain gloves. They're priced at about $15–$20 per pair.

Silk glove liners add warmth and comfort.

A dickie provides real warmth, but it won't stop the wind by itself.

When combined with a dickey, Aerostitch's Wind Triangle warms and seals the neck.

Earplugs, such as these foam examples, will lessen your fatigue and can save your hearing. Check local laws regarding their use, however.

Balaclava

No, a balaclava is not a Greek pastry, but rather a one-piece face mask named for the town in the former Soviet Union in which it originated. Pronounced bal-a-CLAV-a, it fits over your entire neck, tucks into your collar and has an eyeport for unobstructed vision. It adds greatly to head and neck warmth, but to some degree it restricts turning your head.

Neck Sealers

The neck is the most vital area of your body that needs to be sealed in order to keep your torso warm. I've split this subject into two items, one for warming and the other for sealing.

A *dickie* is a knit turtleneck that pulls down over your head and chest. I wear mine not only when I ride in cold weather, but also much of the time in the house in winter. They cost $15–$20, and allow you to remain comfortable in much cooler weather. Dickies will keep you warm in still air, but wind will penetrate them.

Scarves and dickies are adequate for warming your neck, but I recommend a product called the Wind Triangle by Rider Wearhouse under the Aerostitch name in Duluth, Minnesota, for sealing your neck area. It's a nylon triangle with a layer of Gore-Tex underneath, lined with a heavy flocking material. At the back it joins with Velcro hook-and-loop fasteners. Wrap it around your neck, tuck it into your jacket, then strap your helmet over it and your neck is sealed—even in the rain. They're about $25, but worth it!

Hooded Sweatshirt

A hooded sweatshirt is a versatile camping garment and can also serve you while riding. At times, in very cold weather, I've donned my hooded sweatshirt with the hood up under my helmet. Yes, it really makes your helmet a close fit and makes it difficult to turn your head. A balaclava is better, although the sweatshirt is warmer. It will do in a pinch.

Back Protectors

A back protector is a fitted plastic or leather device with foam that is worn on your back to protect your spine in case of a fall. They were first used by racers, and now some sport riders wear them while riding on the street. Early versions were heavy and bulky, but later models have become lighter and more compact.

Earplugs

When you pull off the road after a long, fast ride, do you notice a ringing in your ears or temporary hearing loss? This problem is caused by the incessant wind noise inside your helmet, and it can lead to permanent hearing loss. Also, that constant droning can be very tiring.

To counteract these problems, I suggest using earplugs, either the foam or the custom-fitted variety. Although with earplugs you must respond to lower levels of sound, earplugs prevent temporary hearing loss, and keep it from becoming permanent. And, you'll arrive at your destination feeling less fatigued and more relaxed.

Foam earplugs can be found in sporting goods stores or gun shops, and at some factories they're readily available to employees. Hearing specialists can advise you where to go to be fitted with special

(Left) The hooded sweatshirt is great in camp, and can be worn under a helmet in an emergency.

(Right) The balaclava seals the neck and head for warmth and comfort.

custom-made earplugs. Please note, however, that in some locales, wearing earplugs while riding is restricted, so check local laws.

Helmets

Of all the types of motorcycle apparel, only one is indispensable—the helmet. Yes, in some states it is legal to ride without a helmet, and many riders do, but in the event of an accident a rider's head is likely to hit the pavement—it's hard to miss—and when it does, injury is virtually certain. Often the injury is severe. Sometimes it's death. With the vast array of lightweight, comfortable, attractive helmets available today, it's no longer necessary for you to feel claustrophobic or weighted down while wearing a helmet. A helmet is truly a necessary piece of motorcycle apparel.

Helmet Construction

The purpose of a motorcycle helmet is to disperse the energy of a crash impact before it reaches your head. The helmet's liner does this by crushing at a controlled rate. Of course, forces generated in accidents can be so severe that no helmet could possibly prevent injury. For this reason, keep in mind that while a helmet significantly increases your chances of surviving an accident, it does not make you immortal, and certainly is no substitute for careful riding. And, because helmets are designed to crush so your head won't, any helmet that

has been subject to impact should be either returned to the factory or distributor for inspection, or replaced.

The helmet's inner liner is made from expanded polystyrene, or EPS for short. It is actually closely related to the dense foam you find in those white beverage cups you can dent with your fingernail. EPS's specialty is absorbing energy by crushing, without feeding the energy back to the wearer. You wouldn't want a helmet that would momentarily absorb and store the energy in resilient foam, like a spring, then feed it back into your head. That would be simply delaying the inevitable.

While no one can predict how fast you'll be going, or what you might fetch up against in an accident, one likelihood is that you will be knocked from your bike. Because of this, helmet safety liners are designed to dissipate the energy generated by falling onto a hard, flat surface from the ride height of a motorcycle—rounded up to about six feet. This amount of impact energy corresponds to a linear speed of 13.4 mph, misconstrued by some helmet opponents to mean that a helmet will not protect you at speeds beyond this figure. Bullchips! Racers often fall from bikes traveling at speeds much in excess of 100 mph and walk away. What matters is not the rate of speed at the time of the crash, but the amount of energy with which the rider's head strikes a stationary object. As for falling, the amount of impact for a six-foot fall to the pavement is the same at 140 mph as it is at 40 mph.

A top-line, full-face helmet offers comfort, protection, controllable venting and a high-quality shield. (Photo courtesy of Shoei Safety Helmet Corporation)

A three-quarter (or open-face) helmet is lighter and can be more comfortable, but the tradeoff is a loss of frontal impact protection. (Photo courtesy of Shoei Safety Helmet Corporation)

The shorty (or half helmet) may be lighter and less expensive than other types, but it also offers the least protection.

The helmet has three major parts: the shell, safety liner, and comfort liner. The shell is usually composed of either fiberglass (often mixed with other components such as Kevlar to add strength without significant additional weight) or a polycarbonate mixture. Some people dismiss the latter as being merely "plastic" helmets, but in fact modern polycarbonate helmets are made of very sophisticated blends of resins designed for specific desirable characteristics.

A common fallacy is that the shells of some less-expensive polycarbonate helmets are composed of two halves bonded together—a bond, some people believe, that could potentially separate under impact. Their detractors will point to a slightly raised line running from the eyeport of the helmet, up over the top and back to the base, and will call it a "seam." Actually, this is not a seam, but a mold "part" line.

The helmet shell is cast as a single piece within a two-piece mold. When the mold closes, the polycarbonate resin is forced in under pressure, and some little bit of "flashing" material is forced into the area where the mold halves join. When the mold opens, this little part line is left. Most helmet manufacturers now buff off this part line as they don't want to give shoppers the false impression that this is a seam. Rather, a visible part line tells me that this helmet was made to sell at such a low price that the manufacturer did not even bother to invest the few seconds it takes to buff it off. The question to ask then is if they cut any other corners in its construction.

Fiberglass helmet shells are formed either by spraying chopped fiberglass into a mold, or by applying sheets of it in layers as a laminate. The latter costs more, but the advantage is that the fiberglass shell will delaminate under impact, which will absorb some additional crash energy.

The shell also keeps the wind and rain away, and often bears a graphics treatment to make you more visible. Attractive graphics may also make a helmet more appealing, and thus more likely that it will be worn. Under impact, the shell's job is much more important. It must spread the impact and resist penetration by sharp objects so that the EPS safety liner will remain intact to absorb the crash energy.

The comfort liner is the padding inside the helmet that rests against your head. It is usually made of an absorbent nylon or terrycloth material that breathes well. This material is very important for the fact that, if it does not do its comfort job well, you won't want to wear it, and the helmet can't perform its important task.

Helmet Standards

Two major helmet standards, and one minor one, have influenced the types of helmets Americans have worn since 1970. The basic standard is set by the United States Department of Transportation (DOT). It provides that any helmet sold in the United States must conform to its minimum standards, although helmet makers are encouraged to provide helmets that exceed the standard.

Helmets are tested by placing them in a sliding test rig, inserting a head form that approximates the weight of a human head and is fitted with sensors, then dropping it onto specified surfaces (such as a flat anvil or a pointed anvil) from specified heights. In simplified terms, the DOT standard states that a helmet dropped from 10 feet should pass no more than 400 Gs (400 times the force of gravity) to the headform inside, and that the major force of this impact must last no longer than a specific "dwell" time. This standard is going to be updated soon.

The other major helmet standard is that of the Snell Memorial Foundation, usually referred to as the Snell standard. It was named for racer Peter Snell, who died of head injuries in an auto race in the 1950s when his papier mache helmet disintegrated upon impact. Snell's friends united to form the foundation, which is dedicated to formulating higher helmet standards.

In simplified terms, the Snell Memorial Foundation standard states that, for a helmet to wear its coveted sticker, examples of that helmet must have passed tests in which no more than 285 Gs on average were passed to a head form in a 10-foot drop, followed by a second, lower drop onto the same spot on the helmet. On the surface it seems that the Snell standard is significantly more stringent than the DOT standard, but there is one major difference between them. The Snell standard has no maximum dwell time, but the DOT standard does.

Because of this, factions supporting either standard have attacked the other. Considerable heat and very little light has been shed upon the Snell versus DOT controversy in previous years. Proponents have lined up on both sides, saying things that only confuse the issue. Backers of the DOT standard accuse the Snell standard of inadequacy because it lacks a dwell-time standard, although in fact any helmet sold in this country, including every one that passes the Snell standard, must also pass the DOT standard.

Helmet manufacturers have told me privately that it is very difficult to meet both standards. To pass Snell testing, the helmet requires a relatively hard safety liner to handle two impacts; to pass DOT requires a relatively compliant liner to handle the dwell time. Snell backers retort that there is no proof that the DOT's dwell standard really means anything in terms of injury to the human brain. They say the Snell standard is

Pictured is a helmet testing rig for controlled drops onto specific surfaces. Sophisticated instruments measure the amount of force transferred to a headform.

This sticker, from the Snell Memorial Foundation, certifies that examples of this helmet have passed stringent safety tests.

better because it is more stringent, but DOT-helmet backers counter that a safety liner stiff enough to meet Snell's big-hit/little-hit standard is too stiff to absorb low-speed impacts. And on it goes, with the result that riders begin losing faith in their helmets, and the helmets' ability to do their job. Finally, both standards are essentially self certifying. Because of budget cuts, the DOT did very little helmet compliance testing in the 1980s. Snell does buy helmets at random and test them for compliance with its own standard, but not with the DOT standard. The DOT reportedly resumed testing in 1990.

I have what I feel is a reasonable reply to the controversy. Let's assume for a moment that both sides are correct. Let's even agree with its detractors that some Snell helmets can only marginally meet DOT dwell times, and accept that the Snell standard is more stringent. Let's also agree that a helmet that meets only the DOT standard can't handle a big hit as well as a Snell helmet can. Fine—so, as riders, which do we wear?

Imagine yourself riding at speed on your favorite road. Your speed may vary from 30 MPH in a particularly tight turn, to over 80 MPH on a short straight. As you ride you pass trees, rocks, soft sand, brush, curbs, and a hundred other obstacles, some hard and others more forgiving, that you could collide with should you fall off your bike at any given time. For these over here you might choose a Snell helmet, and for those over there you'd prefer a DOT helmet—assuming what we read about these helmets to be true. But you can't go changing helmets every couple of seconds as you whip by these objects now, can you? So what do you do?

What you do is choose a good, comfortable helmet, whether it bears just the DOT emblem or the Snell also, and you wear it religiously. You choose a price you can afford, an attractive style, and features such as ventilation, a good shield, a comfortable interior, etc. The point is that you like the helmet, and that you wear it every time you ride. THAT is the single most important action you can take to protect yourself. The rest—whether you eventually run your helmet up against a curb or a bush, a rock or sand, the pavement or nothing at all—is such a crapshoot that any attempt to deal with its specifics would be absurd. You pays your money, your wears your helmet, and you takes your chances. It's the best approach I can suggest.

Types of Helmets

Helmets come in three general types, the full-face, open-face, and shorty. The shorty was popular up until about the 1960s, and has regained popularity today with cruiser riders and to some extent with touring riders. It consists of essentially a bowl with straps, and is small and light, but offers no protection to your face and less protection overall than other types of helmets.

The open-face helmet was a natural evolution of the shorty. It grew to extend over the ears and encircle the back of the head, which increased its level of protection to a great degree. One researcher told me that it was very possible to lose an ear with a shorty helmet, but that an open-face protected this vulnerable area well. Open-face helmets accept face shields that snap or screw on, also offering protection from bugs and stones.

In the early 1960s Bell Helmets introduced a full-face helmet that was simply an elongated sphere with a tiny eyeport, and originally intended for use by drag racers. It did not offer much peripheral vision, and led to a belief that persists to this day that all full-face helmets restrict side vision. This is no longer true; in fact, all helmets must meet mandated eyeport standards to be certain they do not restrict side vision.

It's true that a full-face helmet offers more protection because the chinbar protects your face, but there's also another reason. Grab an open-face helmet by the ear flaps and attempt to flex it; it will have some degree of flex. Now try to flex a full-face helmet. Because the chinbar joins the helmet and completes the sphere, it braces the helmet overall. Also, as I said earlier, the job of the helmet is to distribute the impact over as great an area as possible. The bridge formed by the chinbar allows the impact to be spread over the entire helmet.

Full-face helmets are heir to a few disadvantages. They're heavier, they don't have a sunshade visor to keep the low sun out of your eyes, and they make it more difficult for riders and passengers to talk. Today's efficient intercom systems counter the latter problem, and a strip of duct tape will form a temporary sun shade. Finally, a rider's neck muscles will usually quickly adapt to a heavier helmet. And if you wear glasses you'll have to remove them to put on a full-face helmet, then work them back on once the helmet is in place. A few companies offer hybrid helmets, on which the entire frontpiece of a full-face helmet pivots upward so you can open it for convenience. Finally, full-coverage helmets tend to be significantly more expensive than open-face models, as expected.

Helmet Ventilation

The decade of the 1980s saw great progress made in moving air into, and through, helmets. Because full-face helmets have such great coverage, they tend to get stuffy in hot weather. Simpson started the trend in 1979 by cutting slots into the chinbars of some of its full-face models. The next step was to add a sliding plate behind the slots, so that the vents could be controlled.

The real breakthrough in helmet ventilation came when companies began adding controllable openings above the eyeport, air passages over the top of the head, and exhaust vents at the back of the helmet. Open the vents on a hot day, and a rush of cooling air caresses your forehead like a damp towel.

Mandatory Helmet Laws and Motorcycle Riders

The author's soapbox

The topic of mandatory helmet laws is the politics and religion of motorcycling. It's the one topic you don't bring up at polite gatherings, lest you spark a heated argument. I have strong opinions on the subject, also.

All available research points to one major fact: helmets save lives. Not only are they absolutely necessary in the event your head hits the ground, but they also help keep your hair from being tangled. When equipped with a face shield they'll keep bugs and stones from hitting you in the face, and they'll keep your head warm and dry in cold or wet weather. Finally, the rounded shell of a helmet moves through the wind stream more efficiently than does your relatively flat face, which means they're less fatiguing to wear. Don't make the mistake of thinking of the helmet only as a safety device that may come into play once or twice in a lifetime. Rather, it's a piece of riding apparel that serves its purpose each time you ride.

Some people object to helmets by saying the weight tires their neck muscles on longer rides. A typical helmet weighs about three to four pounds, and after a few days of riding with it the neck muscles strengthen themselves to accommodate the new demands.

Others state that helmets restrict their peripheral (side) vision. To be legally sold in this country, every helmet must meet the Department of Transportation (DOT) standards. One of these standards requires a minimum of 120 degrees peripheral vision; most people's side vision takes in an angle of 110 to 115 degrees. Sure, you can move your eyes and see each side of the helmet, but peripheral vision refers to what you see to the side while your eyes are looking straight ahead.

Another argument is that the weight of a helmet adds to the pendulum effect of the head in an accident, and can add to your injuries. A human head weighs about 20 pounds and a helmet no more than four pounds. If you get off your bike at speed, the least of your worries is going to be that extra 20 percent added weight on your head. And recent research shows that a full-coverage helmet will not cause collarbone injuries. It had been thought that the bottom edge of the helmet could break the collarbone, but very similar injuries in bicycle accidents indicated that researchers needed to look in a different direction. What they found was that the crash impact, not the helmet, was breaking collarbones.

Some riders don't wear helmets because they think they'll never have an accident. I've had three in the last 16 years. My friend Ken has had two. Chad has had one in five years, Joe three in five years, Paul one in eight years, Scott one in six years—I could go on through virtually every riding buddy I have. It's not that these riders are reckless or unusual, but we have more than a million miles among us. Think of your friends who rack up a considerable amount of miles and I'll bet they have stories to tell, too.

The fact is that if you ride, you eventually *will* go down. Dress for that inevitable crash as if your life depended upon it—it does.

Now for the second part of my sermon. For various and sundry reasons having to do with the fact I live in the United States, and because I feel that motorcyclists are being singled out for "special treatment" by our legislators, I am opposed to mandatory helmet laws. I once wrote a column for *Rider* magazine in which I noted that motorcycle deaths in the previous year had been about 3,900, while deaths from smoking-related causes in the same year were an estimated 395,000. In other words, the ratio of smoking deaths to motorcycle fatalities was 100:1. At that time, more than half the states had passed mandatory helmet laws, yet not one state had outlawed smoking. I interpret such actions as legislators wanting to control motorcyclists, whom the public doesn't like much anyway, as a means of illustrating to the public that they're doing their jobs. In my opinion, if these legislators were *really* sincere about saving lives on a grand scale, they would attempt to outlaw smoking. Since I wrote that column, anti-smoking legislation has become more common, and some states have actually repealed their helmet laws. Things have moved slightly in the right direction.

I strongly believe in voluntary helmet use, but am just as strongly opposed to mandatory helmet laws because I see the cynical hypocrisy and manipulation behind such laws. ■

6
The Tourer's Packing List

WHAT TO TAKE AND WHERE TO PACK IT

I've spent a considerable amount of time and verbiage talking about touring and travel thus far. Now it's time to get ready for a tour. What follows is a sample packing list for a single rider on a one- or two-week camping and/or motel trip. Consider it as a starting point only, then change it as you wish for your own needs.

The Basic Packing List

This list is based upon the one I have kept for years and which resides in a file folder in my desk. I've used it and it works. There are no other secret ingredients or magic whizbangs—this is 99 percent of what I carry on any given trip, with some slight modification for particulars that apply to a specific season or destination. Now let's look at some of these items in detail.

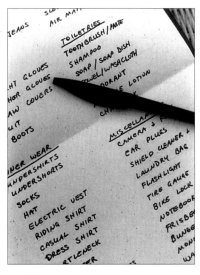

Each well-equipped tour begins with a list. Make it, use it, update and keep it.

Outer Wear	Inner Wear	Camping Gear	Toiletries	Mechanical	Miscellaneous
Jacket	Undershirts	Tent	Toothbrush and	Motorcycle tool kit	Camera and film
Riding pants	Undershorts	Sleeping bag	toothpaste	Master link, chain	Maps
Helmet and face	Socks	Sleeping bag liner	Shampoo	lube (if chain drive)	Ear plugs
shield	Hat	Warm sleepwear	Soap and soap dish	Fuses	Shield cleaner
Spare face shield	Electric vest	Mattress	Shaving kit	Bulbs	Rags
Boots	Riding shirt	Matches	Towel	Spark plugs	Laundry bag
Light gloves	Casual shirt	Hooded sweatshirt	Washcloth and bag	Tire repair kit	Flashlight
Midweight gloves	Dress shirt		Deodorant	Duct tape	Bike lock
Cold weather gloves	Turtleneck		Moisture lotion	Tire gauge	Notebook and/or
Glove rain covers	Sweater		Lip balm		notepad
Rain suit	Dickie		Medications		Frisbee
Rain boots	Wind Triangle				Bungee cords
	Bandana				First-aid kit
	Casual shoes				Swiss army knife
	Casual pants				Money
	Dress pants				Water bottle
	Balaclava				More money
					Credit cards
					Lots more money

Travel Snacks and Emergency Rations

Road food

It happened to me in Port Clinton, Ohio, in 1976. I was heading home to Michigan from a ride to Pennsylvania, when I was caught in a violent thunderstorm in the early evening. I had not yet eaten dinner, the campground was in the boondocks, and I'd just made it there in time to set up my tent before the storm hit. It was a violent, tornadic thing and, once it had left, everything was so soaked and muddy (including me) that I just didn't want to go into town to eat. So I ate in camp, even though I wasn't packing cooking gear. Here's what I ate.

> One can of chili
> One apple
> One banana
> One can of peaches
> One granola bar

No, I didn't eat the chili cold, but built a small fire with some dry wood I'd found. I opened the can with a backpacking can opener before setting it in the coals, and stirred it with my spoon. Once the can was bubbling, I retrieved it with the pliers from my tool kit, and greedily consumed the hot chili.

While solo touring, when you can set your own schedule, it's possible you'll want to do something like this rather than spending the time and money for a restaurant meal. Your basic supplies include a can or two of soup or other such concoction, can opener, fork or spoon, and matches. A much more civilized alternative is to pack one or two freeze-dried backpacking meals, with a pot in which to boil them.

For snacks on the road, fruit will help keep you regular, provide quick energy, and it tastes good. Apples last a long time and are refreshing. Oranges travel well, but are so messy I'd not eat one unless I had a water supply handy for cleanup. Peaches are tasty, but delicate, as are pears. Raisins and trail mix are other popular favorites. Bananas are fine if you don't let them get too old. Little-known fact: bananas are an incredibly tasty dessert with chocolate. Stuff a banana with some pieces of chocolate in your chops and enjoy. Yum! ∎

Outer Wear

Most of these items were covered in detail in Chapter 5. That leave us with the following items.

Face Shields

If you ride behind a fairing or windshield, you may not need a face shield on your helmet for pleasant weather, but you will certainly need one for rain. Without a fairing, you'll need a shield all the time. Sure, I know some guys ride with just sunglasses for eye protection, but whenever I flip up my shield and ride in only my glasses, it seems I pick up a piece of dirt in my eye within three blocks—without fail. With my shield down on a full-face helmet, I hardly ever pick up junk in my eyes.

Shields are available in clear and tints, the latter for use specifically in bright sun, but never at night. In the desert, a tinted shield lends a bit of shade for the face and reduces glare.

Open-face helmets utilize a variety of flip-up or snap-on shields, the former being the most versatile. The better the optical quality of the shield, the better.

Clean your shield frequently, as your unobstructed vision is your only hope for survival on the road. Clean your shield whenever it becomes dirty enough to notice, to be a distraction. If you can stop, rinse the shield in plain water and wipe it with your bare hand; if you use a rag you can rub grit into the shield and scratch it unknowingly. If you wear a ring, be careful not to grind it into the shield. Every evening on tour I remove the shield from my helmet and give it a thorough cleaning, inside and out. Because it is possible occasionally to lose a screw that attaches your shield to your helmet, carry a spare in your jacket pocket or tank bag.

A mini flashlight is small enough to carry in your jacket, or certainly a tank bag, and is indispensible for camping.

This electronic air-pressure gauge will list tire pressure with an accuracy of within one psi.

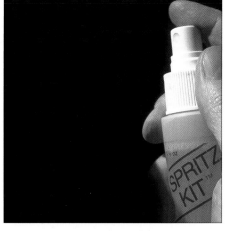

I always carry a small spray bottle of plastic cleaner and a rag for cleaning my windshield or helmet shield. An option is to mix automotive paste wax 50/50 with water and apply it with the fingers (it's too thick to spray). It's abrasive enough to clear off bugs without scratching the shield, and leaves a wax finish.

Bugs and grit are a constant on the road and can befoul your shield at any time, which is why it's a good idea to carry shield cleaner and a rag with you. Mine goes in the tank bag so that if I need it, I can pull off the road and grab it immediately.

For cleaning your shield buy a small container of liquid paste wax. Pour out and store about half the contents of the bottle for future use. Now add water to the half-full bottle of paste wax until it is full. Shake well. The diluted wax makes a good cleaner as it still has some of the grittiness of the wax, yet it's soft enough not to scratch, and it leaves a wax coating to which dirt and dismembered bugs will not cling easily. It's also easy to obtain and inexpensive.

Inner Wear

Most of the items here are self explanatory, but let's say an additional bit about a few.

Hat

What can you say about a hat? It keeps your head warm, and the sun and rain off you. Hats are indispensable if you camp. A knit one is great to wear when sleeping in cold weather. One with a floppy brim is best in rain. At rallies, you'll want a leather one full of rally pins. The baseball style with mesh is preferred in hot weather. The older I get, the more I wear hats.

Riding shirt

My favorite type of riding shirt for anything but hot weather is a good, heavy combination of wool and flannel with a couple of good sized, button-down pockets. It looks casual, yet the nicely made ones are very presentable, especially when worn over a turtleneck sweater. The pockets will hold your notebook and pencil, film canisters, lip balm, passport and sunglasses. They're also a secure place to carry your wallet in the shady part of town.

The chamois shirt is one of my favorites for riding. It has large pockets, is heavy and offers rugged good looks.

The Cowboy's Friend

You can call it "neck helper"

Cowboys are often pictured wearing bandanas around their necks, and for good reason. A bandana was a true friend out on the trail, and it can likewise be a real neck helper for the motorcycle traveler. You can find these at many five-and-dimes and gas stations, and they usually are priced under $2.

When it's cold, use a bandana around your neck as an extra means of keeping the wind away.

When it's very hot, soak a bandana in water and knot it around your neck. That slight evaporation will make a noticeable difference in keeping you cool. Also use it for dripping water down your shirt or wiping your face. After a few days on the road your neck may become sunburned; tie the bandana in such a way that it drapes over the back of your neck as a shade.

When you awake in the morning and are packed and ready to leave, the bandana can be used to wipe the dew from your seat before you plop yourself down. It can wipe up many other things, and even be used to clean a windshield or face shield, although it's usually not sufficiently absorbent to do a good job with them. In all this cleaning, be mindful that your bandana needs to be cleaned, too.

In camp use it to grab the handle of a hot skillet (you didn't bring a potholder), and drape it around your neck to keep the mosquitoes off. The only uses I don't recommend for the bandana are as a (ahem) repository for nasal debris, and for use in wiping your dip stick. You've got to draw the line somewhere. ∎

A chamois shirt is a similar shirt made of heavy cotton that is very handsome and usually available only in solid colors. Most have long tails, and are so heavy they can be worn as a light jacket in camp. Also, darker colors hide the dirt.

Dress shirt

By listing dress shirts I don't mean a real dress shirt, like what you'd wear with a suit and tie, but rather something more presentable than your functional riding shirt. It's the shirt you would wear for going to dinner in a decent restaurant. It's the shirt you would wear when staying with friends and going out on the town with them. Or it's the shirt you would wear just because you don't want people to think that motorcyclists are dirtbags.

Turtleneck

Two types of turtleneck garments are useful to riders. One is the full knit turtleneck sweater that looks classy when worn under a sport coat or other jacket. The other is more of a polyester and cotton light garment that can be worn under a riding or dress shirt.

In a cold climate, the turtleneck sweater looks good, is warm, and seals your neck well. It can be bulky and take up a significant amount of space in the luggage. The light turtleneck garment can be worn most anytime, looks good, and is a real plus in cool weather. I have taken either, and both, on trips and find that the sweater is the ticket when it's cold and expected to stay cold.

Casual shoes

Casual shoes can be any comfortable shoes that you wear when you're not riding. You will need at least one pair, as your boots will become unbearable after a time. With the limited packing space available on a motorcycle, most riders can afford to bring only one pair per person.

They must be comfortable and versatile. You'll want to hike in them, and wear them to dinner, so I suggest a lugged sole. They should be adequate for keeping your feet dry if you're caught outside in them,

A turtleneck is warm and stylish.

although you'll probably switch back into your boots if it rains in camp. If you run for fitness, it's obvious what kind of shoes you'll bring. Their being washable is also a plus, as are many athletic shoes.

Socks

Although cotton is more comfortable, wool socks insulate very well and will keep you warm even when they're wet. In cold weather, wear a pair of each if your boots aren't too tight with cotton on the inside for comfort, and wool on the outside for warmth.

Camping Gear

I'm pretty uncomfortable attempting to cover the topic of camping in one small section of this book when there are many excellent volumes already available on the subject. Instead, I would rather direct you to your local bookstore or library to seek out those books.

Basically, motorcycle campers have much in common with backpackers in terms of having limited space available, and being able to carry limited weight. If there is any advice I can offer, it is to follow the lead of these relentless pursuers of high-tech perfection. If it works for them, chances are it will work for you.

Sleeping Bag Liner

Most sleeping bags are made of nylon, which is cold and clammy against the skin. For this reason many campers use cotton or flannel sleepwear that's much more pleasant. Another alternative is to use a liner of the same material inside the bag. Not only is it more comfortable, but also it's washable and provides an extra layer of warmth on those chilly nights.

Some riders use a single bed sheet as a liner. My advice is to consider products designed as liners, as they're sewn into the proper shape and often include tie-downs so they can maintain their position inside the bag. One of the most frustrating situations is to be tossing and turning inside your sleeping bag, then to realize that your liner has become twisted around your legs like a giant snake.

Hooded Sweatshirt

If you camp in very cold weather, a hooded sweatshirt can be a lifesaver. Not only is it comfy around a campfire with the hood up and your hands in the hand-warmer pockets, but also you can sleep in it and keep your head warm (see page 104).

Dressing on the Installment Plan

Layering your clothing

When planning for any type of activity in changeable weather, layering is the most useful concept. The idea is that, rather than wearing one big, heavy jacket, you wear layers of clothing that can be peeled off or added to as the weather changes. For example, in cold weather my ultimate layering consists of a cotton tee shirt, polyester-and-cotton turtleneck with dickie, electric vest, riding shirt, sweater, Aerostitch Wind Triangle, and jacket. If I'm still cold I'll put my rain suit on over my clothing, even if it's not raining.

As the weather warms, I have the option of peeling off the appropriate number of layers, beginning with turning off the electric vest. Layering offers tremendous versatility. ■

The pocket notebook has many uses.

A bicycle water bottle fits in a tank bag or fairing pocket and offers quick refreshment with its unique nozzle.

Toiletries

Pack your toiletries into a small, easily carried pouch that can be taken to the outdoor biffy when camping. As for items needed while riding, keep your lip balm and moisture lotion in your jacket pocket or tank bag. Check that you have an ample supply of any medications, and take along the prescription and emergency phone numbers should you have any medical problem on your trip.

Towel

Here's the problem—how do you dry your towel and washcloth during the day while you're riding? One method I use is to keep them accessible in my luggage, then drape them over the bike in the sun while I'm having breakfast or making other lengthy stops. Don't forget to wash and dry your towel frequently.

Miscellaneous

Notebook or Notepad

Notebooks and notepads have so many uses: to record names and addresses of people you meet on the road, note your fuel mileage, make a "things to do" list, check off your postcard list, note mechanical items that need attention, and take notes on the places you've been and things you've seen.

Frisbee

Once I get in for the night I become restless, wanting to stretch and run around a little bit. One of these ubiquitous flying discs, by this or several other brand names, is an excellent opportunity for two or more people to stretch and move around a bit. I favor the Night Lighter model that glows in the dark once exposed to a light source.

Water Bottle

When traveling in hot climates, or just because you like to take a refreshing drink when you stop, pack a water container in your tank bag or fairing pocket. The best kind I've found are sold in bicycle shops, and are designed to fit to that wire bracket that rides on a bicycle frame. These bottles are plastic, cost well under $10, and have a unique stopper arrangement that can be sealed tightly, or easily opened for drinking.

Besides drinking, water can be used to soak the bandana around your neck, clean your shield, wash out a cut, or flush grit from your eyes.

Swiss Army Knife

Swiss Army knives are among the most versatile do-anything items ever invented. The basic units will have a couple blades, a punch, bottle opener, screwdriver blades, toothpick and tweezers, all for under $25. I've also seen extremely elaborate ones in Switzerland that also included saw blades, scissors, magnifying glasses, feeler gauges, jackhammers, and welding torches. Well, perhaps I do exaggerate a touch, but be informed that these are very useful items that can clean a spark plug electrode, cut a gasket from a sheet of cork, tweezer out a sliver, cut the insulation from a wire for splicing, and perform many other tasks.

Another handy item is the Leatherman Tool, a survival-type tool similar to the Swiss Army Knife that will carry pretty sturdy pliers, knife blades, cutters and other implements of destruction, depending upon model. Ask for them at better hardware and gift stores.

Taking Care

A basic first-aid kit

Motorcycling is risky business, and accidents do happen. For that reason, carrying a first-aid kit makes sense for when things go wrong.

The most common injuries for motorcyclists involve burns and scrapes, the former from brushes with hot engine parts, and the latter from falling off and hitting the pavement. For this reason, my first-aid kit is heavily biased toward taking care of these two emergencies. For minor burns I recommend antiseptic creams. The burn should then be covered loosely with a gauze bandage taped in place.

Pavement scrapes (affectionately referred to as "road rash") are also a type of burn. They're constitute major skin trauma and can be very painful. Such injuries should be washed out immediately with soap and water, then covered with a proper antiseptic cream. Again, attach a loose gauze bandage that promotes airflow. Have any type of injury checked by a physician as soon as possible.

In addition to antiseptic cream and various types of bandages, your first-aid kit should also include tape and scissors, cleaning agents, and a booklet of first-aid tips. This subject is so complex that I recommend readers take a first-aid course, especially one of those sponsored by the American Red Cross. ■

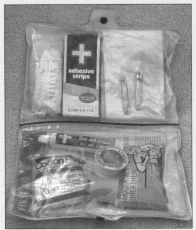

Pack your first-aid kit with items that pertain to burns and scrapes, which are the most common injuries for motorcyclists. And take a Red Cross First Aid Course.

For a truly unique tool that can perform many duties, bring along a Swiss Army Knife.

Mechanical

Motorcycle Tool Kit

Most motorcycles are furnished with a tool kit from the factory, and those tools tend to not be very good. I'm convinced there is a taffy plant somewhere in the Orient that produces a rather tough mix of the stuff that is poured into molds to form the wrenches that are provided with these OEM tool kits.

Once you buy a machine, inspect its tool kit and ask yourself if you would rely on these items to get you going again in an emergency. If you've given them a vote of no confidence, troop on down to your hardware store and replace that kit with real tools that not only work well, but will not round off the edges of nuts as their own edges gradually spread apart. Use these tools for maintenance work so you can become familiar with them.

Tire Gauge

Here's another opportunity to remind you that your motorcycle runs on a set of matched air bags known as tires. The air pressure inside, rather than the tires themselves, support the machine. For this reason it is imperative that you check the air pressure in each tire daily.

Pencil-type gauges have been around for years, and sell for a few dollars. Dial-type gauges are much heavier and more expensive, but they're also much more accurate. The most accurate these days are the digital gauges, some of which are gauranteed accurate to within one-half psi or less. Once any air-pressure gauge is dropped, it should be checked for accuracy against a digital gauge. Keep the gauge in a pocket of your tank bag, and use it often.

Fuses and Bulbs

Ever try to find an auto store open on a Suturday night, just after you've blown your halogen headlight bulb? How about finding a taillight or turn-signal bulb when you need one? Impossible? Not quite, but close. I make it a point to carry one of each of these three bulbs with me when I travel, as they're inexpensive and take up little room. Also, take an inventory of the various types of fuses your bike requires, and carry several spares of each type in a 35mm film cannister packed with cotton.

A word about halogen bulbs—they burn at very high temperatures and must be clean when installed. Even the oil from your fingers can cause the heat to concentrate, resulting in premature failure. Wipe the glass surface of the halogen bulb sparkling clean before you install it, and don't forget to clean the inside of your headlight glass, too.

Note that the reflector portion of the headlight is very soft and should not be touched. Clean it with a soft brush, compressed air, or by immersing it in soapy water and rinsing, but do not wipe it dry.

Duct Tape

This wide, silver tape has so many uses I've lost count. It's wide, strong, and sticks to nearly anything. It can patch a hole in a duffel bag, hold a cracked taillight together, seal a saddlebag lid against the rain or retain a side cover that has lost its grip. This is the ideal product for all-around baling-wire fixes when you're on the road.

The pencil-type tire gauge (left) is the simplest and least expensive, but also the least accurate. The round gauge is relatively accurate, but an electronic gauge should be the most consistently accurate long-term.

The Basics of How to Pack

Where the Weight Goes

When you pack your motorcycle, where you put the weight matters a great deal. As I mentioned in Chapter 3, a tank bag is an excellent place to carry items, as it is located securely and between the axles. However, it's also not a good place to carry solid objects because of the possibility of being thrown into them in an accident. Here are some other packing considerations.

Pack and Roll

Make little ones out of big ones

It's nothing to do with music, nor is it a basketball play. To pack and roll refers to one of the best ways I know of to pack clothing.

In order to keep your clothing wrinkle free, roll items into tight cylinders. Lay your pants and shirts out flat, fold them, then roll them cylindrically, being careful to smooth out any wrinkles as you roll. Keep them tight with a rubber band at each end. Your clothing will fit into a much smaller space so you can pack more, and it will arrive wrinkle free. ∎

Garbage Packing

The inside story

No, it's not what you think. Rather, I'm talking about a way to keep your belongings dry in your saddlebags during a rain storm, whether you pack in hard or soft bags. The trick is to place your belongings in plastic garbage bags (other types of plastic bags work equally well, though garbage bags tend to be larger and thicker).

Don't make the mistake of wrapping the garbage bag around the outside of soft saddlebags. The plastic rattles and frays in the wind in a few hundred miles. Rather, pack your belongings into the plastic bags, then insert them into the soft bags.

And if your soft bags have rain covers, be very sure you fasten them securely. I have seen a number of rain covers blow off soft saddlebags. ■

The inside of this BMW saddlebag shows the amount of room available, and that some space is stolen by the convoluted interior shape.

dress shirt, a bike lock, light gloves and a camera. They're very useful, but just short of essential.

When your luggage is stuffed to the breaking point and you really *must* leave something home, that's when you consult your C list that includes such items as the frisbee, hair dryer, firewood and television. From this point it's a matter of considering bulk and weight as opposed to usefulness.

Where Specific Items Go

A dresser motorcycle offers six specific areas in which to pack items, or five if you're traveling two-up. These six are the saddlebags, trunk, tank bag, fairing pockets, your jacket pockets, and the passenger seat for solo riders. The latter is a very useful area that can hold a great deal. It's wonderful to have a guest along, but bringing a passenger not only nearly doubles the amount of luggage you need to carry, but also deprives you of a major luggage carrying area. Let's consider the kinds of items that should be packed in each area.

Saddlebags. As I've mentioned, saddlebags are a good place to carry weight as they're located close in to the bike and between the axles. If they're hard-shell bags they're likely lockable. Pack heavy, basic items such as clothing, extra tools, and cook stoves. Much of your gear will be carried here.

Trunk. Because it's high and behind the rear axle, use the trunk only for relatively light, bulky items such as rain suits, sleeping bags, and tents. It's also good for items you may need in a hurry. Non-dresser bikes may have a luggage rack here instead of a trunk.

Put your heavier items in the saddlebags because their bracketry places the weight between the axles where it belongs. Also, centralize mass by placing heavier, denser items closest in toward the motorcycle—toward the inner portion of the bags. Of course, both bags should be loaded with approximately the same amount of weight to equalize forces when turning.

Packing by Priorities

Packing by priorities means that when you're dealing with limited space availability, it's best to arrange your items in a priority system so that if something needs to be left behind, you'll already have selected the items most likely to be left. Make A, B, and C lists of items with the A list being the essentials, the B list including what's really handy to have, and the C list things you would like to bring, but could do without.

For example, the A list would include such things as your helmet, jacket, rain suit, boots and underwear; you would not go touring without those items. The B list would include major items such as dress pants,

A tank bag (like this one by Roadgear) is the very best location in which to carry soft items that you want handy on tour.

A lockable fairing pocket, such as this on a Honda GL1500 Gold Wing, is useful for storing small objects that you want to access easily, but keep secure.

Tank bag. Not only will your tank bag display your map, but it's the best place to carry items you'll need often and quickly on your ride such as gloves, shield cleaner, rags, tire gauge, notebook, water bottle, moisture lotion, dickie, and a camera. Because of the possibility of smacking into your tank bag in an accident, pack that camera near the front of the bag so it's padded by the items behind it.

Fairing pockets. If you ride a dresser bike, chances are its fairing offers a pair of small pockets. Use them for items you will need quickly and frequently. Any of the items listed above for a tank bag could just as easily fit into a fairing pocket. Note that the items carried here will be subject to a lot of vibration, so only pack items that will not be effected by it.

Jacket pockets. Jacket pockets are good for small items you will need frequently. I use mine to carry my ear plugs, balaclava, spare keys, film, moisture lotion, lip balm, and other small odds and ends. Do not carry hard or sharp objects that could injure you in a fall.

Passenger seat. If you're not packing double, use that rear portion of your seat for carrying. It's a wide area that can handle an object as large as a duffel bag, or as small as a tailpack. It's a good place to carry weight because it's situated between the axles. Depending upon my needs and loads, I have used this area to carry my camping gear (tents and sleeping bags make for a comfortable backrest), my camera case, and overflow items from the tank bag when I'm weekending alone and traveling light without saddlebags or a trunk.

In Praise of Calculator Watches

Your wrist computer

I recall when the first calculators appeared. They were about the size of small radios and cost hundreds of dollars. Today, I wear a significant amount of technology on my wrist that tells the time, functions as a basic calculator, and serves as an alarm, too. All this for as little as $10!

A calculator watch has been my indispensable traveling companion since I first saw these tiny wonders at an affordable price. I use the calculator to figure gas mileage, check restaurant bills and keep track of the leak in my wallet. When traveling overseas it's invaluable for converting currency exchange rates to "real" money. As a person who prefers to awake early and get a few hours in before breakfast, I find the alarm is also a useful feature. Now if they'll bring one out that can find the nearest gas station and motel, they'll really have something! ■

Carrying Your Camera

When you need more than just the Brownie

Touring is travel, and travel means going to exotic and exciting places. Places you'll want to remember in photos. For most people, carrying a camera is as simple as grabbing the little disc or 35mm camera and slipping it into a pocket. But most people aren't motorcyclists.

Consider that your pocket is a great place to keep a camera handy, but the problem comes if you happen to suffer a getoff and land on the camera. Second, modern cameras are hardy but precision instruments that must be sheltered from the killing vibration generated by a motorcycle. If you have a sophisticated camera system that consists of several lenses and bodies, these parts can be damaged if allowed to vibrate against each other. Third, the delicate mechanisms inside can have their little brains scrambled by bad vibes.

Because I test and travel on motorcycles for a living, and have to provide photos with my articles, I bring along a considerable amount of camera equipment. My equipment includes two camera bodies (one as a backup), two wide-angle lenses, a 50mm, a telephoto zoom, and a large 300mm telephoto.

All but the 300mm fit into a standard-looking camera case—with one important difference. Before putting my equipment in the case, I filled it with two blocks of solid foam rubber, then figured where the various bodies and lenses could be placed to float in

foam, separate from each other. I cut out areas within the foam to house those pieces. An electric knife is the ideal means of cutting foam; with other knives the foam does not offer enough resistance, and compresses against the force of the cut.

My camera case goes behind me on the seat, or in a tail trunk. It's not as easy to access, but is more protected from the elements, and I'm protected from it. The ideal location to carry less bulky camera equipment (such as a single camera with lens) is in a tank bag, providing the equipment is not so large or heavy as to pose a hazard to you in the event of a frontal collision. In the tank bag, the camera is available on short notice should you want to photograph a deer grazing beside the road or a friend who has just fallen face-down in fresh cow flop.

One problem I had was that, because of its bulk, I was leaving my wonderful professional camera equipment at home on non-business rides, and getting no photos. Instead, I have had very good luck recently with disposable cameras. They cost in the $10-15 range, fit easily in a pocket or tank bag and some come with a flash. Sure, they don't produce transparencies or professional-quality photos, but they do offer presentable prints

Keep in mind that film will be damaged if subjected to excessive heat. For this reason, store your film in the part of your bike that remains the coolest in hot weather. ∎

7

Planning a Tour

ESTIMATE YOUR TOUR EXPENSES:
IT'S ALL JUST TIME, DISTANCE, AND MONEY

Planning a tour is like planning any endeavor. You set your goals, and then you determine the means it will take to reach them. On a tour your goal is to travel a certain distance within a certain time, having an enjoyable experience if all goes well. The three basic units you have to work with are time, distance, and money.

Time

Time is immutable for all except space travelers moving near the speed of light. For them it is possible, through concepts perhaps only scientists can understand, to leave on an intergalactic voyage and return years later before their fathers were born—or something like that. We, however, are caught within the constraints of standard time. Still, there are tricks to getting more from your time.

First, a one-week vacation actually equals nine days if you leave on Saturday, then return on the Sunday of the following week. Best of all, these nine days probably cost you only five days of vacation. Likewise, by using both the beginning and ending weekends, a two-week vacation totals 16 days, while costing only 10 work days. If you get three weeks of vacation per year, taking three separate one-week vacations will buy you 27 days on the road at the cost of 15 vacation days. Three weeks taken as one block, however, would get you only 23 days of travel for your 15. Still, having three consecutive weeks at your disposal certainly opens up more possibilities.

When you're traveling, and assuming you're eating in restaurants, here's another time saver. Americans are trained to eat three meals per day with breakfast at about 8:00, lunch at noon, and dinner at 6:00 or later. Enter a restaurant at these prime times and chances are you'll wait awhile as the waitresses try to seat everyone, distribute menus, and the cooks attempt to keep up with demand.

My alternative is what I call *slow-time grub*. By this I mean that I eat only twice per day, avoiding the main rush-hour meal times that seem to be religion for the masses. To get me going in the morning I pack some fruit, such as a banana, apple and peach, with a 12-ounce can of juice. Throw in a couple of bagels if the fruit isn't enough. Then, around 10:00, I stop for a big breakfast once the restaurants have cleared out. Additional fruit keeps me satisfied during the day if necessary, then I stop for a leisurely dinner around 5:00–5:30. Alcoholic beverage consumption is reserved for the evening once I have secured my stop for the night and am within walking distance of my bed.

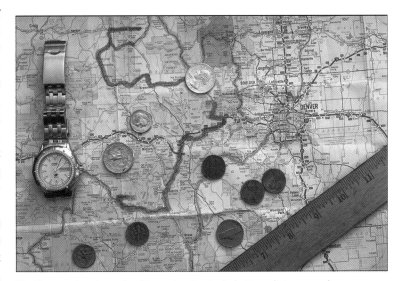

The three major elements of tour planning include time, distance, and money. Blending them well is the key to a good ride.

Taking Note

The rider's pocket friend

I'm a stickler for organization, and one of my indispensable tools is a pocket notebook. I keep one on both of my bikes at all times. In them I record gas stops, tire changes, tuneups, oil changes, parts replacements, and the usual business of riding and running a motor vehicle.

But there's more to a notebook than this when you're on tour. During these times the notebook goes into my tank bag, where I can get to it quickly. There, it's easy to reach for gas stops, and for recording that little delightful road I just took, the name of that little shop my wife liked so much in Lake Tahoe, the campground that was tucked away in the woods.

Also, the notebook is fine for recording the name and address of that couple who offered to put you up for a few days if ever you passed through Anchorage, the name of that restaurant they said you *must* go to in Seattle, and the specifics of that new touring item on their bike that you simply *must* have. ■

We're all aware of the immense tragedy and heartache caused by drinking drivers each year. Motorcyclists, unfortunately, are over-represented in such statistics, probably because of the greater skill level required to operate a bike, and the huge amount of performance available in bikes at relatively little cost. As responsible, well-meaning adults we *must* accept the fact that once we have partaken of alcohol, we absolutely cannot operate a vehicle as safely and effectively as we could have before consuming it. The best policy is to never drink and ride. It's the responsibility of each of us, my friend. Live by it!

Distance

Once you have established the time available for your trip, you'll need to choose a destination that fits your time constraints. How many miles do you wish to cover in a day? Do you plan any layover days? Mileage is a very personal consideration; here are some of the parameters.

The major consideration in daily mileage is whether you will be traveling to reach a destination, or whether the travel is, in and of itself, the purpose of your trip. For example, when my wife and I travel in the Alps it seems each moment, each kilometer, is crammed with images and feeling, gorgeous sights and intriguing places. We want to stop in every little town to walk, take photographs, have a cup of cappuccino. The roads kink up and over such romantic sounding places as the Susten, Grimsel, Grossglockner and OberAlp passes. Ride through a series of 40 switchbacks within two miles, and I can guarantee your tongue will be hanging down on your tank bag in a short time. In the Alps, a series of 125-mile days can be exhausting.

On the other hand, the roads in the American West allow you to gobble up the miles like a bear going through a trash can. Los Angeles to Phoenix, which is approximately 500 miles through the desert, is a day's ride. The Grand Canyon to Los Angeles, approximately 800 miles, is two days when all you want to do is get from one place to the other on the four-lane. If you prefer to eat well, sleep late, ride the back roads and stop at places along the way, you'll need more time.

Your pace will depend upon the type of trip you're taking, the bike you're on, how tight your schedule is, and how much stamina you've got. As an experienced tourer, I find that when I plan to get somewhere, anything short of 200 miles per day is positively dawdling, and that can be very pleasurable. Most of my "gotta git there" travel days range between 200 to 400 miles, with the latter being tops if my wife accompanies me.

On long, cross-country rides alone I've found that I can still enjoy a 500-mile day, but that anything beyond that becomes work. I have done several 600-mile days when I've had to be somewhere on schedule, and even one 700-miler, but they were not really a lot of fun. I just rode and rode and rode, stopping only for gas and quick, unsatisfying meals. Sure, I've heard of stalwarts who join the "Thousand in One" club by traveling 1,000 miles in 24 hours, but I have no desire to join them. I travel by motorcycle because I find it enjoyable; to me the enjoyment drops off precipitously beyond 500 miles, and the trip becomes an ordeal. Your mileage may vary; ride your own ride.

Plan your travel days depending upon your own personal likes and dislikes. I recommend a maximum of 400 miles per day, especially if you're traveling with

Squeezing the Tank

Tips on improving your fuel mileage

At one time, the motorcycle was regarded as a prime economical means of transportation because two-wheelers got such great fuel mileage. Over the years, fuels have become more expensive as motorcycles have seemingly lost their ability to squeeze distance out of liquid dinosaur. One reason is that bikes have become bigger and heavier, with larger-displacement engines, and the other is that they have become more powerful. In everyday riding, my 20 years of motorcycle testing experience tell me that the great majority of bikes of 600cc and larger will turn about 40 to 50 miles per gallon in general use, and sometimes less.

Here are some basic techniques to consciously squeeze your tank:

1) Have the bike tuned up, and replenish all lubricants. A bike that runs well runs most efficiently.

2) As the tires roll they flex, and this flex creates rolling resistance. To lessen the effect of this resistance, pump your tires up to the maximum allowable inflation pressure as listed on their sidewalls. Keep in mind that the higher pressure will make the ride a bit more harsh and may adversely affect tire wear.

3) Slow down. Any vehicle will burn noticeably more fuel at 65 MPH than at 55. As speed increases, so do wind resistance, rolling resistance, and friction losses.

4) Most chain-driven bikes today offer O-ring chains that seal in the lubricant more effectively. However, all those little rubber seals add a slight amount of friction; racers tend to use the non-O-ring type because there's less friction loss. I'm not suggesting that you go back to a non-O-ring chain, as they usually won't last nearly as long and require a lot more care. Rather, be sure to properly maintain and adjust your chain. Lubing your O-ring chain will keep the rubber "live" longer, extend chain life and lessen friction loss.

5) Moderate your riding by avoiding quick starts and hard stops. Learn to anticipate changing traffic patterns and smooth out your riding whenever possible. Back, two-lane roads are much more interesting and I prefer them for touring, but if you really need to save gas, limited-access, four-lane highways with no stoplights or cross traffic are the solution. ∎

others. You'll find that the more persons you add to your group, the more frequent your stops become, and the longer they last. Travel in company and you're always at the mercy of the most careful eater, the latest sleeper, the most prolific photo taker, the slowest rider, and the smallest bladder. Travel alone and you ride by your own schedule.

Need I say more? Certainly traveling with others adds to your enjoyment of the ride, but groups and high-mileage days do not usually mix.

A nine-day tour of 3,600 miles requires a 400-mile daily average, and will be absolutely grueling! If you wish to return from your vacation feeling rested, consider instead a ride in which you spend about three days on the road, arrive somewhere and spend a few days, then ride two to three days back home. A 2,000–2,500 mile round trip will be much more comfortable, yet it will demand that you stray barely more than 1,000 miles away. In a pinch, you're only two days' ride from home. You could also do it in a day if you hook up with one of those guys who likes that sort of thing—only don't invite me.

Table 7.1 Maximum Daily Mileage for "Enjoyable" Trip				
Trip Duration	Iron Butts	Cycle Jocks	Casual Riders	Touring Novices
One day	1,000	500	300	200
Two days	800	400	250	150
One week	600	300	200	125
Two weeks	500	250	150	100
Three weeks	400	200	125	100
Four weeks	350	170	100	100

Money

Of our three factors, only money can be manipulated. Most of what you need to spend on tour will go for food, fuel, and lodging. Let's play with some figures here to predict our cash flow. Let's say you and a friend are planning a nine-day ride from your home in the Chicago area to visit friends in Georgia, about 1,000 miles away. Here's how to estimate your expenses.

Dining in this splendor is likely to cost a bundle, but sometimes it's worth it.

Fuel

Let's say the world oil situation, tax legislators, and the oil companies have established the price of gasoline on your trip at an average of $1.45 per gallon. Your bike uses a gallon every 45 miles, and the trip will cover approximately 2,000 miles. Simple division shows that your bike will consume approximately 45.5 gallons of fuel, so round it up and call it 50. At $1.45 per gallon, you'll spend $72.50 for gas. Round it off (always round off high on your money estimates) to $80.

Food

All right, despite my best efforts to persuade you otherwise, you *insist* upon eating three meals per day on your tour. Well, let's see what it should cost you. Depending upon your eating habits, breakfast will probably cost the two of you about $15 per day if you have a nice, big one. For lunch you plan to spend about $12, but for dinner you like to splurge. A nice meal with wine, but no more riding, may cost $45. Better yet, call it $50. You expect your meals to total $77 per day, but hey, figure it as $85—just in case some lobster tails crawl across your path.

You plan to allow three days to reach your destination, and three days to return; six days at $85 per day is $510. When you arrive you'll eat dinner with your friends, so delete $50. Your last night there, you'll treat your friends to dinner, so add $100. Or take them to McDonald's for $15.

On your trip back, your friends will give you breakfast, and you plan to return home early enough to have a home-cooked meal. Delete one breakfast and one dinner ($65), and find that your meal total comes to $495.

Lodging

Lodging is another major source of expense. Camping, of course, will save you a lot of money, as it might average $15 per night. You'll have four nights on the road, so plan $65 for lodging if you camp.

If you plan to stay in motels, the amount can vary dramatically from below $30 to $100 or more. For many of the national chains you can expect to spend $65 per night, for a total of $260. Let's stay there.

Your basic tour expenses for fuel, food, and motel lodging come to $80, $495 and $260, a total of $835. For incidentals, entertainment, and whatnot, I'd be prepared to have another $200 available. Round it off at $1,050.

If this is more than you care to spend, well, you have the facts available that will help you decide upon how to economize. You know that camping can save you a bundle. Also, with your meals looming as the single biggest expense, perhaps you'd be ahead of the game by cutting down on those big dinners—and buying the kind of wine that has a screw cap instead of a cork. Or maybe you'll take my advice and cut back to two meals per day. Finally, your most economical way to eat is to prepare your meals in camp, provided you have enough luggage space to carry cooking and camping gear.

Remember that whenever figuring expenses, always estimate high. When in doubt, check the final item in the packing list in Chapter 6.

Your decision to camp or to stay in motels will have an effect on your touring budget.

8

Co-Riders and Group Rides

GIVE YOUR PASSENGER OR GROUP A GOOD RIDE

I know of many male riders, too many, whose wives used to ride with them but don't anymore. The men still like to ride, but for many reasons their wives either don't do so any longer, or in other cases never did. In terms of enjoyment for couples doing things together, and for normal resentments when they don't, this is a really sad situation. I don't pretend to be "Dear Abby" on two wheels, but perhaps some of the points in this chapter will help riders understand their co-riders' needs better.

Second, motorcyclists often ride in groups, and certain basic principles will help make group rides more enjoyable. I'll cover that subject here, too.

Sampling the great outdoors on a motorcycle is all the more enjoyable when you can share it with a friend.

Co-Riders

First, I used the term "co-rider" because the term "passenger" really isn't adequate. The person on the back really isn't in the passive role of the person who rides along in an automobile. The co-rider really can be an active partner with the motorcycle operator, and in fact I've seen couples in Europe riding along very aggressively, the woman on the back shifting her weight and actively participating in the ride with the man in front. Sure, most of our co-riders in the United States tend not to become actively involved in the ride, but perhaps they'd enjoy it more if they did.

The easy part of co-existing on a motorcycle is in leaning together and for the passenger to know that, when the bike comes to a stop, she (I'll use the female pronoun, as the great majority of riding couples involve a male rider and female co-rider) should not take her feet off the pegs. Instruct an inexperienced co-rider that, when a curve is coming, to look over your shoulder in the direction of the turn. It's much less frightening to look into the turn, plus this action causes a subtle weight shift by the co-rider into the turn, which is desirable.

The difficulty is in sharing a vehicle on which fatigue, discomfort, worry, and aggravation are more likely to occur. Throw in the difficulty in communicating, and its resultant frustration, and you can appreciate the potential for trouble.

Ask a number of co-riders for their major riding complaints and you'll usually hear one or more of the following statements:

"I hate it when we leave so early and I spend half the morning shivering."

"He rides so fast I get scared."

These friends, who rode to the Americade rally in upstate New York, are waiting to go on a guided tour. The rally also offers lunch and dinner tours on the tour boats in the background.

Color, camaraderie and excitement are all part of a rally parade, such as this one at Americade. Parades also offer the closest form of formation riding.

"I get so tired by the afternoon, and he gets mad when I want to stop."

"He gets to handle the controls, and that's fun for him, but I get so bored on the back."

For those of you riders who would like for your co-rider to come along more often, keep in mind that although it may be your motorcycle, it's her trip, too. With so many dual-income couples it has become common that the wife earns a major portion of the income, and has a major say in how it is spent. If you want her to keep riding with you, you'll have to consider her special needs, too. Be sensitive to them, act on them, and there's no need for your co-rider to be afraid, uncomfortable, or overly tired. Or maybe it's time for her to have her own motorcycle.

Unity of Purpose

The purpose of any tour is enjoyment. The plan to achieve that purpose may involve several weeks on the road, several days, or just a few hours to complete a circuit. In any case you, your co-rider and the group will all enjoy yourselves more if you feel united in your purpose. This can be achieved by agreeing upon the trip's major plan *before* you leave.

How far afield can two people be on their unity of purpose? If they don't agree on any of the variables they can be very far afield indeed, like this couple.

He: "Wow, two whole weeks to tour! We're going to hit Yellowstone, then ride over to Minnesota and stay

with old Uncle Gustav a week. We can make it home in three days, even though that means three straight 500-mile days. It'll be rough, but we can handle it. And we can save money by camping."

She: "Two weeks on a motorcycle? I'm definitely not thrilled, but I supposed it won't be so bad since Minnesota isn't *that* far. At least he didn't say anything about seeing that Uncle Gustav creature—when you look up the definition of the word 'slob' in the dictionary, you find *his* picture. With no real schedule we can take it easy and stop to rest every 100 miles. It'll be tiring, but with a good night's sleep in a motel I can handle it."

Group Rides

Here's a good place to bring in the subject of group rides, because they and the concerns of co-riders merge at about this point. The difference is that usually co-riders accompany a rider on a longer trip, but group rides are most usually day trips. Of course, many of the points that follow will apply to both co-riders and groups.

Obviously, the lack of communication here could well turn the trip into a disaster—if it ever occurs at all. Here are the items that must be discussed and agreed upon by any couple or group traveling together a reasonable time before the trip occurs.

The bed-and-breakfast feels like a home because it *is* a home!

Destination and Route

State exactly where you're going, how you wish to get there, and how long the trip will take. Include any side trips and visits to friends, relatives, or local attractions. Think of the various routes and plans possible between, say, Denver and San Francisco.

The route you plan will be the deciding factor in your mileage, scenery, riding style, and who and what you'll see. Have a map session to plan the route, including probable rest stops and overnights.

Hours

Personal habits have a lot to do with how compatible people will be on a trip. Two couples want to tour together for the first time. Kathy and Mark never hit the hay before midnight, and believe there's no such thing as bright and early—only bright and surly. They need an hour to get ready, then prefer to eat breakfast. They never get on the road before 10:00.

Dave and Joy turn in early and are up with the sun. They repack before bedtime, lay out their clothes for the morning, and are out the door in a half hour. After a couple hours on the road, they'll have breakfast about 10:00. What do you think are the chances these two couples will have a happy ride together: slim or none?

Daily Mileage

Riders vary in their physical and emotional makeups. Once you've chosen your destination, estimate your total mileage for the trip and break it into a daily amount.

Daily mileages are discussed elsewhere in this book, but I would strongly recommend no more than 500 miles in a day with a passenger; 400 miles is about the outside limit of comfort. Three hundred should definitely be comfortable, 200 is downright leisurely, but much less feels like you're not getting anywhere. Actually, the number of miles doesn't matter so much as the fact that the pace is agreeable to everyone. Definitely be flexible and willing to compromise.

Frequency and Kinds of Stops

The Iron Butt Rally is a grueling, competitive motorcycle ride that begins and ends at pre-set points, and rolls through about 10,000 miles in 10 days. Riders have to reach several checkpoints, and can earn points by taking side trips. Obviously, the Iron Butt is not for everybody, but it serves as another example of the extremes some people are willing to endure in search of their riding pleasure.

Some folks like to stop at every postcard shop, while others don't like to stop for anything but gas. Some like fast food, and others prefer gourmet. Balance your stops to coincide with prevalent likes and dislikes. If it's not possible to balance these, perhaps you'd better not ride together.

Inclement Weather

Show me a rider who likes riding in the rain, and I'll show you a duck on two wheels. Riding in rain is gloomy and chilling, and worries about skidding make it a tense experience. Without proper clothing a rainy ride is damp and shivery at best, and dangerous at worst.

To avoid problems, riders must see to it that everyone in the group is adequately equipped for bad weather. And discuss ahead of time what to do when the weather is suitable only for ducks.

Accommodations

People's tastes and wallets differ, and for this reason overnight accommodations must be discussed in advance. Some folks are motelers and love to stay at little cabins in rural areas or outside small towns. Others are hotelers, and prefer to stay near the center of a city where the action is. Others prefer to camp whether it be for the savings, the ambiance, or both.

When we welcome a new rider into our group, we have only one rule: Don't crash.

Riding in the rain is never fun, but it can be tolerable if you're equipped for it.

If the group agrees to camp, one member should be designated to research the campgrounds available along the route where stops will likely be made. If people agree to stay within four walls, they should agree upon hotels, motels, cabins, or whatnot, and what price range they prefer. To keep people happy, you might designate a motel steward who is in charge of finding a place each night, or put this responsibility on a rotating basis so everyone can suffer exposure to the possible ribbing, joshing, and complaints they're going to have to take for their choices. Avoid any place called The Bates Motel.

Another option that should be considered is the bed & breakfast. For a price that is often lower than, or competitive with, a motel, you get a private room and light breakfast, but the bathroom is usually down the hall and shared by several guests. European B&Bs often have a sink in each room.

I've stayed in such places all over Europe, and a few in the United States and Canada, and find them delightful. The guests stay right in the home with the owners, who can tell you where's a good place for dinner, what there is to see, or where to have your bike serviced. Usually there is a common room where the guests and owners will gather in the evening, which may be the site of an impromptu piano or guitar recital, or someone will regale the assemblage with tales of travel.

In Europe and Canada, B&Bs are intended as a low-cost alternative to hotels, and are simply furnished. Breakfast is usually something simple that may (or may not) require any cooking. In the United States, however, B&Bs are much too few and far between.

They tend to proliferate in tourist areas, and are often in large, older charming homes with many rooms that have been totally redecorated and furnished with antiques. As a result, prices tend to be higher than at motels.

Speed

Depending upon how formal your group is, you may or may not wish to establish a few formal rules for the ride. On larger group rides you may wish to establish a lead rider, with the caveat that no one should pass this rider. And one or two riders in the rear can perform the "sweep," which is to help anyone who experiences difficulty and has to stop.

Depending upon how well you know the others in your group, a good policy is to ride a mellow pace at first in the twisties until the ride leader gets a feel for the group's ability. If all seems well, he can pick up the pace to brisk. How do you tell if a person is riding over his head? It's not so much in his speed, as in his smoothness and his lines. A person riding smoothly, no matter what the pace, is in control. A person who nails

Near the end of a great day of riding in Colorado on a pair of very competent sport tourers, Rick and Todd enjoy the view near Crested Butte, Colorado.

The Victor McLaglen Motor Corps. offers a new perspective on the group ride. How about 12 riders on four motorcycles! They often perform at motorcycle events.

the brakes coming into a turn, tiptoes through, nails the throttle coming out and is all over the road is not in control, and is a danger to himself and others. Slow the pace.

I ride with a fairly constant group of close friends, all of whom know each other's habits. We are all veterans of a high-performance riding school that is conducted at various race tracks throughout the year, and have taken it a half-dozen times. As a sporting bunch, we like to ride pretty fast. We know who's faster and who's slower, and no one's ego gets bent out of shape trying to prove otherwise. Whenever a new person rides with us, we let them in on the only rule: "Don't crash." And we tell them very sincerely, "Ride your own speed. We're glad to have you along. If you want to pass someone, and it's safe to do so, go ahead. But if you find us going faster than you want to go, ride your own speed and you'll find us waiting on up ahead where there's a fork in the road. We really don't mind one bit waiting for you to catch up; we mind a lot having to wait for an ambulance if you screw up."

Size

Larger groups should break up into smaller, individual groups so as to not create traffic congestion for other motorists who may want to pass. Larger groups of eight or 10 two abreast are fine for four-lane highways, but on two-laners you might want to keep the groups to about six so that faster traffic can pass.

The Plan

If you're organizing a breakfast ride, for example, it's important that you have a plan. Be sure that people know where to meet, where you'll be going, when you'll be leaving and what you'll do after breakfast.

Through trial and error, our group has arrived at an inviolable rule: We leave at the appointed time. We're all busy people, and sometimes our schedules don't allow for slack. For that reason, if we're leaving from the 76 station at 8:00 for a breakfast ride to Camp Scheideck Lodge, it means we *leave* at 8:00. If you want to chat or get gas, you'd better arrive at 7:45.

At 7:59 the group leader starts his engine, which signals everyone else to do the same. Our feeling is, "If you want to chat, let's do it over breakfast, not in some gas station." If anyone arrives late, well, they know where the group is going, and they're welcome to come join us.

9

Motorcycle Camping

THE ENJOYABLE ALTERNATIVE

There are many reasons for camping. It brings you in touch with nature. You can hike and fish. You can meet people. Campfires are such a wonderful experience. It's less expensive than moteling and saves money. It's the enjoyable alternative.

I don't know about you, but I love camping, especially by motorcycle. I camp for all of the above reasons, and probably several I haven't even thought of yet. In this chapter I will cover how camping relates to motorcycling, rather than attempt to provide the be-all, end-all thesis on camping. You see, there are numerous books on the subject of backpacking and camping, certainly by people who are more experienced in those specialized areas than I. My recommendation is to consult those sources for information about types of tents, the pros and cons of down versus fiber-filled sleeping bags, how to cook a meal in camp, etc. Those experts have already fought those battles and won. Let them tell you how to camp. Let me tell you how to integrate camping with motorcycling.

Campers and riders have a lot in common. Both have limited space available, and both like to travel light. We have the same problems with carrying food and with facing inclement weather.

But motorcyclists have some different considerations. For us, the weight of our equipment is less of a consideration than the space in which to carry it, especially when we're traveling two-up. By carrying a co-rider we lose the valuable storage space on the back of the seat, and increase the amount of equipment we need to carry. It's essential that you purchase your camping equipment with an eye toward its fold-down carrying size, with weight considerations secondary.

For solo riders, the rear of the seat is the obvious place to carry large items such as the tent, sleeping bag,

Now *here's* a man who has his priorities straight.

and pad. For two-up tourers these items are usually too much for a luggage rack to handle, so I recommend you mount the tent and pads on the rack, with the sleeping bags carried atop the saddlebags. Several companies offer aftermarket racks or eyelets that bolt to the tops of saddlebags, and to which sleeping bags can be attached. Of course, you must protect all of this equipment with a waterproof carrying device, usually a nylon bag inside a very sturdy plastic bag. Because you're carrying several items, some of them perhaps loose, here's an excellent situation in which to use a net cargo carrier rather than bungee cords.

Camping Equipment

Rather than attempt to get into all the nuances that the camping books can tell you so much better, I would like to cover the three basics that you need in order to spend the night in camp—from the motorcyclist's perspective. These are the tent, sleeping bag, and pad.

Camping is inexpensive, and you can't beat the ambience.

To handle the extra equipment needed for two to camp and cook, a trailer is a welcome addition.

Among luggage consisting of saddlebags, a tank bag and tail bag, the careful packer can find room for enough camping gear to enjoy moments like this.

A typical down bag (right) will stuff down to a smaller package than a fiber bag. The fiber bag can be stuffed down smaller than is pictured.

The Tent

The tent should obviously be small, and tailored to your use. Buy a tent that is one person size larger than you actually need so that you can stow some of your gear inside and have room to maneuver. The solo rider should consider a two-person tent, and the couple a three-person. Tents much larger than these may not pack small enough to conveniently carry on a motorcycle.

I suggest you get as good a tent as you can afford. Back in my cheap days I used to get along with the base model of everything, and I can't tell you how many nights I tossed restlessly, uncomfortable because I'd bought inexpensive, inadequate camping equipment. The good stuff will last for years, but a cheapo tent will tear more easily, it may not go up as well or resist the wind as well, and it may allow the rain to seep through. A cheap sleeping bag will likely leave you cold because of a lower level of insulation that mats down, breaks down or shifts.

Sleeping Bag

When deciding upon your sleeping-bag needs, figure the coolest temperatures you will be camping in, then subtract about 20 degrees. At higher elevations, temperatures drop drastically at night, especially in spring and fall. On the other hand, if you use a cold-weather bag it may be uncomfortably hot in milder weather. What to do?

My wife and I solved that problem by buying two sleeping bags that zip together, one a down-filled bag insulated for cold weather, the other a fiber bag for milder weather. When we camp together, we use the bag that most suits that night's temperature on top as a blanket, and the other on the bottom. When I camp alone, I choose the one bag that most suits my expected temperature. This combination gives us great flexibility.

Because nylon is clammy against the skin, and sleeping bags tend to be made of the stuff, I strongly recommend using a sleeping-bag liner or sleeping in cotton clothing. In most cases a liner is only a cotton sheet sewn into mummy shape for each person. You can bring a flat sheet from home to use as a liner, but if you toss and turn in your sleep, your legs will soon become entangled in it. If that's a concern, bring safety pins and pin the sheet to the inside of your sleeping bag. Or, buy a purpose-made liner that ties in place.

Pads

Some people can sleep on the bare ground in their sleeping bags, but I'm not one of them. I need a sleeping pad, and several types are available. I prefer an inflatable pad because its pressure can be adjusted for comfort. The kind I use is foam filled so that it provides some loft and insulation in and of itself, and it has three separate air chambers that can be adjusted individually through separate valves.

Inflatable pads are relatively comfortable and can be folded to a fairly small size but have a couple of drawbacks. First, obviously, is the possibility that a puncture can ruin your night's sleep. Most come with a patch kit, but choose a rugged one regardless. The other disadvantage is that this air bag under you does not insulate well and can become very chilly on a cold night, which is why foam inside will help.

The closed-cell foam pad is an alternative to the inflatable variety. It is light, folds out flat, insulates well, and is surprisingly comfortable. It doesn't always fold to a small size for packing, which is a disadvantage for motorcycling. It's also great as a pad to sit on around the campfire or at the picnic table. And you can be sure that, at least, it will never spring a leak.

The most exasperating problem I've found with camping is finding a suitable pillow. For years I tossed and turned, awakening with a stiff neck, before discovering a solution that works for me. As mentioned above, I sleep on an inflatable pad that inflates in three sections. One of them has a pillow, but it's not adequate by itself. What works is that I fold my leather jacket (or you can use your dirty clothes bag) and place it under the head of the mattress, then pull the sleeping bag over it. The jacket and pillow combined add enough elevation, and the sleeping bag enough comfort, for a good night's sleep. An alternative is an inflatable pillow.

Cooking

Don't expect to eat like a gourmet around me. The problem with cooking in camp while motorcycling is in carrying all that gear and keeping food fresh. If you really insist upon eating in camp, I suggest you learn from the backpackers who now can select from among some pretty tasty prepackaged freeze-dried and other types of meals. You heat up some water and pour it into the bag of freeze-dried food for a piping hot meal, which means you'll need to carry a stove and fuel. Some of these meals will cost you about what a

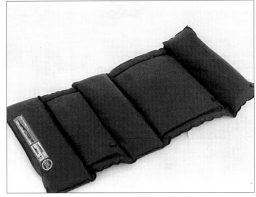

The multi-chambered air mattress allows the camper to adjust it to his particular comfort needs.

mediocre meal would cost in a restaurant, but nothing can beat the ambiance of a campground meal—at least as long as it's a good one.

If you find backpacking food a little too rich for your wallet or fat for your tastes, here's a menu tip I learned while my wife was in the hospital giving birth to one of our children. One of the most versatile items in grocery stores today are "Ramen" style noodles that come dry, packaged with flavorings—usually chicken or beef. When plunged into boiling water they make a great base for a soup to which you can add sliced vegetables or even a selection of mixed frozen vegetables. They're nutritious, inexpensive and very tasty.

10
Touring Security

KEEP YOURSELF AND YOUR BELONGINGS SAFE

One of the worries associated with touring is that every time we park our bikes and leave them, we're leaving a great deal of valuable equipment exposed to damage, theft, and vandalism. It's not at all comforting, but with a little forethought we can minimize the risk.

Common Sense Security

Problems will most likely occur while leaving your bike unattended in populated areas. Use common sense to minimize your exposure to loss in these situations.

A high-quality lock, such as this U-lock by Kryptonite, is your first line of defense against the theft of your motorcycle.

Whenever you intend to leave your bike, assess the situation. How safe does this part of town look? Certainly there are parts of most major cities in which we would be loathe to leave our machinery, or to even walk around except in a group—unless the group was the Third Airborne. Seek out areas that are well lighted, and where traffic is relatively heavy. Ne'er-do-wells are less likely to strike where they feel they can be observed. Park near where people are working, such as gas stations, restaurants, or construction sites. Give the impression that the owner is probably close by.

The only reasons we tend to leave our motorcycles are to eat, to sleep, or to take in some attraction. For gastronomic situations, keep in mind that most restaurants have parking lots, and many have windows. I prefer places that feature both. For attractions, the safest are those that charge for parking. They are staffed by attendants, and casual thieves are less likely to hang around where they have to evade these people.

In cities, hotels often have secured parking areas. If they don't, find a pay parking lot with attendants; leave your bike close to the attendant's station and take a cab back to the hotel. At motels, leave your bike as close to your room as possible. If you have a bike cover, use it. They make a bike difficult to identify, and out of sight can be out of mind for some thieves.

I discourage riders from taking their bikes into their rooms because they can leave a mess, which discourages the motel operator from accepting riders in the future.

Motorcycle Security

Your major concerns in leaving your motorcycle are preventing vandalism, preventing theft of items from the motorcycle, and preventing the theft of the bike it-self. Visibility discourages all three problems, and taking loose items such as a tank bag with you will remove the most obvious temptation. Still, there is no way you can absolutely guarantee security unless you chain Arnold Schwarzenegger to one side of your bike and Sylvester Stallone to the other, and arm them with machine guns.

Thieves

Consider the likely troublemakers. There is the casual walk-by jerk who has virtually no equipment and little imagination. He may try to run off with your CB radio, tank bag, or duffel bag on impulse, and will usually give up easily if things don't go according to plan. The best way to thwart these weasels is to cover the bike, and don't leave your helmets just sitting around. Use your helmet locks or, better yet, lock them in the saddlebags if there's room.

Professional thieves are at the other end of the scale. They often steal to fill an order because a customer needs a specific part off a particular bike. The big iron is in demand, specifically Harley-Davidsons and Japanese muscle bikes. Thieves may steal a sport bike because a friend of theirs dropped his and now needs the complete plastic bodywork that would otherwise cost about $1,000. If yours has what they want, they'll try to take it.

The common ritual is to snip the security chain with bolt cutters, break the fork lock by twisting the front end hard, and hot-wiring the ignition with a length of wire and connectors. Some can even do it with a safety pin! Another method is to freeze locks with liquid nitrogen so they become brittle, then break them with a good whack. Modern power tools can eventually defeat even the best locks—if there's time to use them.

If the professional thief really wants your bike, he can have it free and into a van in a minute or two. Your job is to make his job harder, to slow him down and increase the odds against him, to cause him to shrug his shoulders at your bike, and go off to find easier pickin's. None of these methods will make your bike impossible to steal (check if Arnold and Sylvester are still available), but they can possibly tip the scales in your favor and make a potential thief decide it's not worth the risk.

Another form of motorcycle lock is the cable type, but be certain it's a sturdy one. (Photo courtesy Kryptonite)

Locks

Whenever leaving your bike use the fork lock; it's your first line of defense against the casual thief. Next, especially when leaving your bike overnight or for long periods in the city, use a quality aftermarket bike lock. Be certain any lock and chain you use is *case hardened,* which is a heat-treating process that makes the surfaces very hard and resistant to bolt cutters. When possible, position the lock and chain high enough off the ground so the thief can't use the extra advantage of standing on the handles of bolt cutters. If you carry only a shorter chain and lock, slip it tightly around the rear wheel and frame to immobilize the bike.

The thief will appraise the situation and attack the weakest link. Chain your bike to a small tree and he may cut the tree down. Loop it through a chain-link fence and he'll cut the fence. Lock the front wheel to a stout fence and he'll remove the front wheel and truck the rest of the bike away, leaving you with an expensive and oversized key chain. Immobilize the front wheel by looping a chain through it, and the thieves may place a skateboard under the wheel and push the bike away.

A hidden switch wired to the hot lead and coil will discourage hot-wiring. To improve your chances, mount the switch under the locking seat.

Alarms

Alarms may scare off the casual thief, and will draw attention to the bike. But unless the alarm is loud enough for you to hear personally, how much good will it do?

An alarm system, such as this one by Gorilla, is easy to install and emits a piercing shriek when disturbed. The question: will anyone come to your bike's defense when you're not around?

Suppose you heard a bike alarm go off and responded, only to see a large, hairy man tampering with a motorcycle? What would you do? He'd probably tell you it was his bike, that he'd lost his keys, so bug off. Some alarms have pagers that will alert the owner several blocks away if the bike is tampered with. The owner can inform the large, hairy man that it is in fact *his* bike, and we can hope the man leaves quietly—in a squad car.

Suppose I told you that I could steal your bike easily if you locked the ignition and fork lock, and that I could do it in seconds without breaking anything. Would you believe me? You should if you ride an older bike on which the key number is stamped on the ignition, gas cap, or seat locks. Many brands did this, and all a thief needs to do is note the key number and drop into his local dealership to have a key made. Check your bike for key numbers immediately; if they're listed, write them down and then use a file to remove the numbers.

One reason the national recovery rate for stolen motorcycles is low is that stolen parts are so hard to identify. When a theft ring is broken, the police often find garages and back lots filled with motorcycle parts—seats, forks, carburetors, engine parts, and so forth. All are no doubt stolen, but there's nary a traceable serial number to be found. Could you identify your own bike's seat, tank, wheels, or carburetors from among a pile of like equipment? Could you prove they were yours, beyond a reasonable doubt, in a court of law? To improve your chances, enscribe your driver's license number in an inconspicuous spot on these items with a metal stamp or vibrating tool. Use a state prefix, such as CA, MI, PA, or NJ, so the police will know where the part originated if it turns up in another state.

Note: Do not enscribe your social security number on the parts. With privacy laws today being so strict, it is very difficult and takes months for a police department to obtain such numbers from the federal government. Drivers license numbers, however, are readily available to any police department.

In case the tips in this chapter don't work and your bike is stolen, notify police immediately. A joy rider could still be in the vicinity, and professional thieves could have it stripped down to its component parts in a matter of hours. Time is important.

11
Motorcycle Safety

KEEP THAT SHINY SIDE UP BY MANAGING RISK

Some people regard motorcycle safety as an oxymoron, a contradictory play on words like "jumbo shrimp." In actuality, motorcycling can be relatively safe, and much of that is under the control of the individual rider by managing risk. The first part of managing risk is to understand the problem.

A major study has concluded that slightly more than half of all motorcycle accidents are caused by other motorists. Does this mean that safe riding is out of your hands? Not at all! The rider can lessen his chances of becoming a statistic by becoming cognizant of the signs that other motorists are about to do something dangerous, and then by taking appropriate action before the danger becomes real.

In the latter part of the 1980s, motorcycle deaths declined drastically from more than 5,000 per year to under 4,000. One reason for the decline was that fewer people were riding motorcycles during these years. However, of those who remained, many were now long-time riders, which meant that the experience level among all riders was gradually moving upward. Experience is a powerful teacher for riding a motorcycle well.

Sure, we understand that motorcycling is not as safe a means of travel as the automobile. Riders are more often hurt and killed on a per-mile basis because they aren't surrounded by walls of steel that can absorb an impact. Auto travelers are often belted in, which gives them a further advantage, and many cars now have air bags. Finally, an automobile usually stays on all four wheels in an accident, but a motorcycle is usually knocked over, which means its rider(s) will be thrown off. That means they'll probably be hurt. Add the slip-sliding factor of oil, water or sand on the pavement that is of little concern to the car driver, but extremely important to the motorcycle rider. Now factor in the relative comfort factor brought about by heating and air conditioning, and the car guys have all the advantages.

Or do they? Almost any motorcycle above 400cc can out-accelerate and out-brake almost any car on the road, and can out-maneuver the car. Bikes take up less space in the lane. These benefits arise because of a motorcycle's small size, but that size also means that other motorists don't notice them. The most common type of

If you're an inattentive rider, evil can befall you before you even notice. (Photo by Mike Florian)

The inattentive left-turning driver causes the majority of motorcycle accidents involving another vehicle.

accident involving motorcycles is one in which a motorist doesn't see the bike and pulls out into its path.

Causes of Motorcycle Accidents

If we knew what caused motorcycle accidents, we could readily avoid those situations and be much safer riders. The fact is, we *do* know what causes them—a very accurate picture of motorcycle accidents is available from two studies.

The Hurt Report

Hugh M. (Harry) Hurt, in conjunction with the University of Southern California, issued a famous report in 1979 that, as of this writing, still remains the definitive work on motorcycle accidents. Though its official title was "Motorcycle Accident Cause Factors and Identification of Countermeasures," the treatise has popularly come to be known as "The Hurt Report." Hurt, or his team of investigators, studied 3,622 motorcycle accident reports and visited the site of 899 accidents, where they garnered information. They concluded that in 51 percent of the cases, the motorcyclist was *not* at fault. The accident was caused by an auto driver who usually claimed he did not see the rider in time to avoid a collision. These incidents usually occurred at intersections in broad daylight, most of them between 4:00 and 6:00 p.m. Many of these people were on their way home

from work, on a familiar route, in a hurry, driving on "automatic."

In the most common scenario the car is poised, ready to pull out into an intersection as the motorcycle is coming through with a green light. The auto driver doesn't check adequately and pulls into the rider's path. The rider perceives the danger, panics, and underutilizes the front brake while locking the rear—which throws him into a skid. The motorcycle's marvelous ability to avoid an accident is neutralized by an operator who is too frightened or inexperienced to react effectively.

Because the rider is relatively unprotected, he's injured 98 percent of the time according to the Hurt study. In 45 percent of these cases, the injuries are serious; 13 percent are groin injuries caused by the rider flying forward and striking the instruments, handlebar, and controls. Remember what I said about loading only soft articles in a tank bag?

Sixty percent of the accident victims in the Hurt study were not wearing helmets, but unhelmeted riders accounted for 77 percent of the deaths. The other 23 percent were wearing helmets, and in the entire study only one rider who was wearing a helmet died of head injuries. **Wearing a helmet is the single most important factor in saving your life in an accident.**

Seeing the Light

Anti-Fogging Treatments

In rainy and cold weather, fogging is a universal problem affecting helmet face shields and windshields alike. Fogging is caused when the moisture in warmer air (such as your breath in the case of helmet shields) strikes a cold surface and condenses on it. This happens to all cold surfaces, but we notice it more on shiny ones or those we have to see through.

A number of companies offer products that, when applied to face shields, effectively keep them from fogging. They're usually available in spray-on or wipe-on applicators, and usually need to be re-applied after the shield has been cleaned, if not every day. They work by dispersing the big drops into sheets of fine, tiny droplets you can see through, and most do their job effectively. However, when I tested a number of these products for a motorcycle magazine, I found that their ability to disperse water varied widely. Before you purchase any of these products at your motorcycle shop, I suggest you apply the product to a small area of your helmet shield, then try to fog the shield with your breath. Keep a small container of anti-fog handy in your jacket pocket or tank bag. ∎

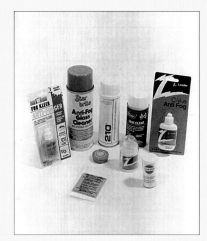

Also consider that, in the more than 20 years since these accidents occured, major advances have been made in helmet construction and design.

With only 12 percent of the accident-involved riders were alcohol or drugs a factor, yet those impaired riders figured in 45 percent of the fatal accidents. Riding drunk or stoned increases your chance of an accident, especially a fatal one, dramatically!

Motorcycle Safety Foundation

A Canadian study by the Motorcycle Safety Foundation (MSF) selected riders randomly for a telephone interview. Of the 2,277 interviewed, 28 percent said they had been involved in a motorcycle accident at some time. These accident-involved riders were then placed in one subgroup, and nonaccident-involved riders in another. The differences between them were then evaluated, and the MSF made some interesting findings.

Accident-involved riders averaged 22 years of age; the noninvolved averaged 26 years. Single riders crashed more often than their married counterparts. The accident-involved rode more miles annually—they had more exposure to accidents. The conclusions drawn from these and other factors in the study were that the most important factors relating to the chances of having an accident are age, riding while impaired, length of time licensed, and marital status. Maybe it's because you can no longer afford to go out on the town when you're married—or don't care to.

The MSF study then drew composite profiles of a very safe rider, and of one who was essentially an accident looking for a place to happen. The safe rider is a 30-year-old married man who has been riding more than 10 years and does not mix drinking and riding. At the other end of the spectrum is a young man of 18. He is single, newly licensed, and has had a few drinks. His statistical chances of having an accident are 18 times greater than those of the first rider.

Insurance company studies tell us that single male drivers under the age of 25 are a much higher risk than females or older married men. The reason for this conclusion can be summed up as, "boys will be boys." Guys under 25 are risk takers, while women and older men are less so inclined. Put these guys behind the wheels of cars and they'll also crunch *them* up at a much higher rate than average.

The important point here is that in the great majority of situations, *you* the rider control your chances of being involved in a motorcycle accident. Knowing that, there are a number of things you can do to improve your chances, and to reduce the possibility of injury should you be involved.

1) Wear a helmet and proper riding gear every time you ride, and insist that your passenger do likewise. Proper riding gear consists of a jacket (preferably of leather or other heavy material), heavy pants, sturdy footwear (preferably boots), gloves, and eye protection.

2) When approaching an intersection, be mindful that this is where the majority of all motorcycle accidents occur, according to the Hurt Report. Slow down. Watch for motorists who are poised to pull out in front of you. Try to establish eye contact with them. Change your position in your lane so the driver *has* to perceive your movement. Ride with your headlight on high beam, or turn it to high beam if you don't like the situation. Do not flash your high beam, as this may be interpreted as a signal to the other motorist to go ahead. Be ready to hit your brakes. Be conspicuous by wearing a light-colored jacket and helmet.

3) Take a riding course to help improve your skills. The MSF offers basic and advanced RiderCourses in which even the most skilled riders will pick up some hints they've never heard of previously. Also, attend a performance riding or safety school that offers racetrack instruction. See the accompanying sidebar for details on these courses.

4) If offered an alcoholic drink soon before you'll be riding, refuse it. You might think that just one won't hurt, but even one drink will adversely affect your reaction time and judgment.

5) Always ride within your limits. Talk to yourself while you ride, and critique your riding. If you begin riding too fast for your ability or conditions, tell yourself you're doing it, and then back off. "Showing" somebody what a fast rider you are, getting the ol' ego involved, is exactly why so many young, immature riders crash. Still, it bites a lot of older, immature riders, too.

6) If you're single, get married! (Only kidding.)

Target Fixation

Have you ever had one of those days?

Has this ever happened to you? You're riding along a winding road, having a good time, when suddenly you round a turn to see a small rock in the road ahead. You know it's there, you have plenty of time to avoid it, yet you run right over it! You can't believe you could do such a stupid thing.

Greetings! You have just been a victim of a phenomenon known as "target fixation." It was noted and defined during research concerning aircraft pilot training. When operating simulators, certain pilots were observed to see obstacles in their paths, but fly right into them despite the fact there was plenty of time and room to avoid them.

What's happening here is that we tend to steer in the direction that we look. We see a rock in our way, we look at the rock and bingo—we run over the rock. The solution is to work some mental discipline. When you see rocks in the road, force yourself to see a *path* through rocks rather than a scattering of rocks. Tear your eyes away from the obstacle and force them to see the solution.

Finally, use target fixation to your advantage. Have you ever gotten into a curve too hot, braked hard, looked at the ditch, and then followed your eyes right into it? When you get into trouble, tear your eyes away from what you can hit and force yourself to look where you want to go. This little bit of mental discipline has saved me a number of times. ■

Learning to Ride the MSF Way

Start with the basics and learn them well

The Motorcycle Safety Foundation (MSF) of Irvine, California, is a nonprofit organization dedicated to the proposition that a trained motorcyclist is a better, longer-living motorcyclist. And they're most definitely correct. The MSF offers two types of motorcycle RiderCourses, one for the beginning rider and the other for the advanced.

The beginning RiderCourse is designed for people who have little or no recent experience on motorcycles, but who want to learn to ride. For a very reasonable fee (usually around $150 or less) the novice rider will be provided with the use of a helmet and motorcycle, and a weekend of instruction that includes hands-on operation. They need to bring only the desire to learn.

Classes are often conducted at schools that can provide both classrooms and spacious parking lots for riding exercises. Classes are non intimidating, the student-to-instructor ratio is no higher than six to one, and there's plenty of time for one-on-one questions.

The advanced school is conducted much like the beginner's, except that riders may bring their own bikes and the curriculum is much more advanced. Several of my riding buddies, all good riders, have taken the advanced course and each has reported that he enjoyed it and learned a great deal.

If you would like to know more about the MSF, or take a class, make a toll-free call to 800-447-4700. In California the number is 800-CC-RIDER. ■

The Motorcycle Safety Foundation offers classes for both beginning and advanced riders. Take the Experienced RiderCourse even if you've been there, done that.

Another major factor in accidents is the rider who, as written in the accident report, "failed to negotiate a turn." A motorcycle journalist I know serves as an expert witness in court cases involving motorcycles. "The rider's story usually goes," he says with a tired smile, "that the motorcycle enters a turn and, at the apex, the brakes just strangely lock up—all by themselves."

His smile is not for the riders' misfortunes, but for human nature's inclination to blame misfortune on bits of machinery that can't talk back, rather than to accept responsibility for doing something dumb. Motorcycle brakes do not lock up by themselves—these riders have gotten into a corner too fast, panicked, locked the brake(s), and gone on their ears. It's human nature, but bad form, to blame it on the motorcycle. Once again, immaturity in action.

The Performance Riding Schools . . .

An exciting way to improve your skills

Each of us harbors a little dream in our souls, a little belief in our softball games that we're actually playing in the World Series, in our football tossing that we're in the Super Bowl, and in our sport riding that we're actually wailing up the main-straight hill at Laguna Seca Raceway at 160 MPH at some international race. Well, most of us will never actually do any of these things, but even a wizened old touring guy like me actually *has* gone over the hill at Laguna Seca (oops, never say "over the hill" to a wizened old touring guy) at a pretty tame 110 MPH. And so can you.

Several people offer the opportunity for riders who want to learn to ride better, safer, and more smoothly, to do so on an actual racetrack and with professional instruction. I have taken such schools on several occasions and will report unequivocally that they absolutely made me a much better rider, and they did so after the *first* day!

The schools I've taken include California's Leading Advanced Safety School, or CLASS for short, and Freddie Spencer's High Performance Riding School. CLASS is run by Reggie Pridmore, a three-time U.S. Superbike champion in the 1970s who can still turn a pretty mean lap. Reg conducts his schools at various tracks around the country, including Laguna Seca, near Monterey, California, where the U.S. International Grand Prix was held for several years through the late 1980s and early '90s. There likely is a CLASS school at a track near you. Spencer, a three-time international Grand Prix champion, conducts his classes at the Las Vegas Motor Speedway in Nevada.

As the title of his schools suggests, Pridmore is not trying to turn anyone into a racer, although his son Jason has won several championships and is now competing at a fairly high level, in addition to serving as an instructor at the CLASS schools. Because it is *not* a racing school, there is no reason for a participant to feel intimidated. Yes, it's conducted on a racetrack, and good riders can generate some pretty serious speeds, but no one needs to feel they're expected to go any faster than they want. Participants ride their own machines, and are able to use them to their fullest potential on the track.

With Spencer, you ride his specially prepared Honda CBR600F3s and the emphasis is a bit more technical, but still street oriented. Both instructors offer advanced schools aimed more toward racers.

(continued)

Can you ride like this? Me either. This is Nick Ienatsch, moto-journalist, multi-time race champion and instructor at Freddie Spencer's High Performance Riding School. The goal at most schools is not to make you into a racer, but into a much more competent street rider. And it works!

Freddie Spencer, a three-time world Grand Prix motorcycle champion, teaches performance riding and racing schools at the Las Vegas Motor Speedway.

... The Performance Riding Schools

One real eye opener is to get a ride on the back of a bike with Pridmore or one of his instructors. You may have thought you were going pretty quick all day, but a few laps with an expert will cause you to realize how much faster smoothness allows you to go. The gem I have taken with me from each of Pridmore's schools is his one golden rule: "Don't concentrate on trying to go fast—concentrate on trying to be smooth. Once you become smooth, you will become fast." To learn more about this school, contact: CLASS Motorcycle Riding Schools, Suite C24, 15500 W. Telegraph Road, Santa Paula, CA 93060-3051, 805-933-9936, www.classrides.com

Freddie Spencer's High Performance Riding School offers a very analytical approach to riding fast and well, and will benefit both the street rider and racer alike. Contact the school at Box 36208 in Las Vegas, NV 89133, 702-643-1099. You can e-mail to ffreddie@anv.net or check the web site: fastfreddie.com.

Another fine school, although one I have not taken personally, is Keith Code's California Superbike School. Again, although California is in the name, schools are conducted at various tracks around the country. Code was a successful Superbike racer in the 1970s, and now wants to help other riders become successful racers. Some of his students are now competing in the big time, and are doing well.

Because Code's is a racing school, the emphasis is on racing techniques and there is considerable instruction involved. The school provides Kawasaki Ninja motorcycle for all riders, plus leathers if needed. Because of the heavy emphasis on instruction, riders may not get as many track miles as they would in a typical CLASS school. However, Keith Code now offers several programs of one or two days duration that are designed to meet a wide variety of needs. For more information, contact the California Superbike School at Box 9294, Glendale, CA 91226, 818-246-0717. ■

Inclement Weather

According to the Hurt Report, only 2.2 percent of motorcycle accidents occurred in inclement weather. This certainly doesn't mean it's safer to ride then, but that most riders stay off the road or take the car in bad weather. If you're touring, and have a schedule to keep, you may have to ride in bad weather. Your first line of defense is to dress properly and thus stave off hypothermia. There is no reason you can't ride safely in rain, but you must adjust your riding accordingly in terms of speed and lean angles.

Virtually all riders are aware of the grease strip in the center of the lane, caused by the oil dripping from thousands of car crankcases passing overhead. Keep in mind that this is not the only place that lubricants fall. Gobs of grease drop off of steering linkages. Fluid spits from leaky shock absorbers, brake fluid from leaky hoses, and antifreeze from rusted radiators.

Consider the pavement to be an enormous greased griddle. Oil floats on water, so when the first sprinkle of rain brings that characteristic oil and rubber aroma, watch out. After a steady rain has fallen for a time, the road surface slime eventually flushes away, but the grease strip is a permanent fixture.

Water is a lubricant that lessens the tire's grip on the pavement. Under cornering loads, the tires will slide much sooner than if they and the road were dry. Slow down in the wet, especially in curves, and allow more stopping distance.

Brakes can lose effectiveness in the rain as the exposed rotor and pads of a disc brake become coated with a layer of water. When you first apply the brakes in the wet, the pads may skate along the disc before the water layer is scraped away, and the brakes begin to grab. A rider who finds his brakes not working well will apply them harder and harder, sometimes in a panic, and then suddenly when the water is pushed aside they may grab suddenly and lock the wheel.

The Neglected Routine

Your main means of support

Think about it—what supports the weight of your motorcycle on the road? Your tires, you say? Well, what happens if your tires lose their air? Obviously, it's the air pressure within your tires that supports you as you ride. Therefore, tire pressure must be maintained religiously.

To work effectively, tires are designed to accommodate a range of loads, temperatures and pressures. The sidewall of every street-legal motorcycle tire carries the information as to the maximum amount of load it can carry, and the maximum inflation pressure allowed. They're related: the more pressure a tire carries, the greater the amount of weight it can support. However, don't over-inflate a tire as that takes it beyond its design parameters and can induce handling and other problems.

Check and adjust your inflation pressure on a daily basis on tour, and at least on a weekly basis otherwise. A nail in a tubeless tire can induce a slow leak that will become apparent if the tire is checked each day. If left too long, the tire will become dangerously low on air, which would lead to instabilities. ∎

A little time spent checking your tire pressure on a regular basis can return big dividends in better handling and longer tire life.

Motorcycle manufacturers have attempted to alleviate the problem by ventilating the disc with slots or holes to let the water escape so it won't build up a layer, and to cool them. They have also developed pad materials that are more prone to grab the disc in the wet.

Drum brakes also suffer from exposure to water, but the method is a little different. Because the brake shoes are enclosed in the hub, that first little drizzle usually does not decrease their effectiveness. However, a prolonged rain or a ride through a puddle may cause water to enter the hub. Next, the shoes begin to skate on the water, and braking power diminishes a great deal. Unlike a disc brake, a drum does not dry out quickly. Any brake that has lost its effectiveness because it has become wet can be at least partially restored if it is applied several times to generate enough heat to clear the shoes or pads.

Finally, riders in the north and east are eager to get their bikes out on the road at the first opportunity as winter begins to wane. But be wary of early spring roads and streets that are puddled over. Those puddles can hide frost heaves or missing chunks of pavement that have broken off during the winter.

Know Before You Go

The pre-ride inspection

Sure we love to ride, and we're often in a hurry, but it takes only a moment to perform a pre-ride check. Here are some quick checks to perform daily, and others on a weekly basis. If you don't understand some of these, consult your owner's manual or your dealer.

DAILY

Fuel supply: That it is adequate, and that petcock(s) are turned on.

Engine oil supply: That it is adequate for proper lubrication according to your dip stick or oil sight glass.

Inflation of both tires: Use an accurate gauge to check that inflation is within the range stated in your owner's manual, but does not exceed the maximum pressure listed on the tires' sidewalls. Always check inflation when tires are cold.

Brake master cylinder: Check the fluid level via the see-through sight.

Clutch master cylinder (if so equipped): Check fluid level.

Headlight, taillight, brake light, turn signals, horn: Check operation.

WEEKLY

Battery level: Check electrolyte level in each cell; add distilled water if necessary. Check terminals for corrosion; clean if necessary. While on tour, carry an old plastic shampoo bottle with a tight-sealing lift-up top that forms a narrow spout; it is perfect for shooting water into the battery. Buy distilled water at the grocery store; it's very inexpensive.

Clutch adjustment: Check per owner's manual, and adjust if necessary.

Wheels, including spokes if so equipped: Notice if wheels are out of round or damaged. If your bike is equipped with spoked rather than cast wheels, check that spokes are sufficiently tight. Do this by placing the motorcycle on its centerstand or other suitable stand suffient to raise each tire off the ground. Spin each wheel and lightly run a screwdriver or wrench along the spokes as they whirl past. Tight spokes will make a pinging sound, but loose ones will clunk. Adjust according to the owners manual with a suitable spoke wrench.

Drive chain: Adjust and/or lube according to your owner's manual.

Cables: Check for fraying and broken housings. Lubricate when needed, and replace when necessary— *before* they break.

■

Push Right, Go Right

Understanding Countersteering

This particular phenomenon is not understood by most motorcyclists, and many even deny its very existence, yet I assure you it is real. The official term is "countersteering," and it relates to the mechanics of how a motorcycle is steered.

Most riders are under the impression that in order for the motorcycle to turn left, they turn the handlebar to the left as they do at very low speeds. However, when speeds rise much above a walking pace and the gyroscopic action of the wheels begins to take effect, the motorcycle will turn by countersteering. By this, I mean that you turn left by turning the handlebar slightly to the right, and vice versa.

There isn't room here to go into all the complexities of this phenomenon; let's just cover it enough to make the point and illustrate its usefulness. As you're riding along at, say, 40 MPH and want to turn left, you will lean your bike in that direction and the handlebar will cock slightly to the right. To what degree this happens will be dictated by the vagaries of the motorcycle's rake and trail and general steering geometry.

As the motorcycle leans, the front tire's contact patch moves slightly rearward, which causes the fork to swing slightly to compensate. Bicyclists who ride with no hands are very familiar with this phenomenon. Next time you're out riding, hold the hand grips very lightly as you bank into a turn, and notice how the bar subtly reacts—in the supposed opposite direction to which it should. If you want to see countersteering in dramatic action, attend a dirt-track race. There you'll see riders cocking their front wheels completely away from the direction of the turn, yet all the time turning nonetheless.

What's useful to realize here is that the phenomenon exists, and how to use it. Some riders have been known, in a panic situation, to fight their machine's ability to turn by attempting to wrench the handlebar in the direction they need to move to avoid an obstacle. Instead, because of countersteering, they find themselves turning into the obstacle they're trying to avoid.

To prevent this sort of thing happening to you in an emergency, change your thinking about turning. Think of leading with your shoulder into the turn, or even of initiating the turn with your hips. Imagine that you're planting your rear tire to the outside of the turn with your lower body, which in turn allows the fork to seek the appropriate orientation in relation to it. Better yet, take an MSF class and really learn to do it right. ■

12
Motorcycle Rallies and Clubs

FOR THE GOOD TIMES OF YOUR LIFE

What is a motorcycle rally? It's a gathering of riders, a party that may last a weekend or a week, and involve anything from a few dozen to many thousands of riders. Rallies are usually one of several kinds.

Brand Rallies

At brand rallies, such as those for BMW riders, and the Harley Owners Group (HOG), anyone who rides the particular brand is welcome. Riders of other machines may have to be accompanied by a rider on that certain brand to be allowed in. Some marque clubs split hairs even finer, specifying a particular model such as the Venture Touring Society for Yamaha Venture owners, the (Kawasaki) Concours Owners Group (COG), and several organizations for owners of Honda's Gold Wing. Some vintage clubs cater to owners of the Vincent, BSA, or Indian; many other brand clubs exist.

Touring Rallies

Some popular touring rallies are Americade, held in Lake George, New York, and those put on by *Rider* magazine at various locations around the country. They're designed for touring riders, but all are welcome.

Club Rallies

These are sponsored by motorcycle clubs, and often are distinct from marque clubs in that they welcome all riders who belong to the club, which is not based upon riding a particular brand. The American Motorcyclist Association now sponsors a rally for all motorcyclists, and has a motorcycle museum at its headquarters in Pickerington, Ohio. The Retreads is a club for riders age 40 or older. Women on Wheels (WOW) is for, well, you know.

Finally, there's another category of motorcycle festivals that take place over a larger area and lack the closed-off area in which rallies usually occur. Examples would be those associated with major events such as Daytona Motorcycle Week, and the huge annual gathering called The Black Hills Motor Classic in Sturgis, South Dakota, every August. The latter is put on by the town of Sturgis and is open to all, but probably 80 to 90 percent of the participants arrive on Harley-Davidsons. It is one of the largest motorcycle gatherings anywhere, and the 55th anniversary celebration in 1995 drew an estimated 250,000 participants.

At a rally, the parade is often the grand finale. (Photo courtesy *Rider* magazine)

Your Representative in Washington

The American Motorcyclist Association

Almost every association has its own lobbying group in Washington, D.C., and at state capitols. They keep track of the various proposals and bills making their way through Congress, and you'd better believe that when a bill comes along that can potentially affect them, the National Avocado Growers Association representative will be there, or someone from the National Beef Council, or from the Grape Growers Association.

As motorcyclists, we have our own watchdogs and lobbyists, too, in the American Motorcyclist Association (AMA). Located in Pickerington, Ohio, the AMA membership in 1998 was well over 200,000, which is good and bad. It's good that that many people have invested the money to join this worthwhile organization, but it's awful to think that with several million riders in this country, only a small percentage have bothered to support the group that supports them.

The American Motorcyclist Association does much for riders by fighting to keep riding areas open, to educate them, and to fight bills that would unfairly or unreasonably restrict motorcycling activities. Some examples of such legislation include those that would restrict motorcycles on certain public roads, parks or beaches, or those that would force mandatory helmet use. Excuse me, but motorcycle riders are adults who can make their own decisions about what head wear is appropriate.

Also, the AMA sanctions most of the motorcycle racing activity that occurs in the United States, including both road and offroad racing. If you'd like to learn more about the history of your sport, the AMA Heritage Museum features many exhibits of machines and motorcycling lore. Finally, the AMA has begun sponsoring a national rally in Ohio for both members and non-members alike that involve tours, dual-sport rides, field events, demo rides and all the other rally activities.

If you would like to join or learn more about the AMA, you can write them at 13515 Yarmouth Drive, Pickerington, OH 43147. Or you can join toll-free by calling 800-AMA-JOIN. Tell them Bill sent you. ■

What Goes on at Rallies

The most frequent question I get from riders who haven't attended them yet is, "What goes on at rallies?" All rallies are different, but often they are bound together by common threads. A true rally usually is held on a closed site such as a fairground, resort, campus, or private facility. Riders pay to get in, and are given a wristband that allows them to join rally activities. The color of the wristband may indicate the package of activities in which they will participate.

Rally participants may be given a rally packet that usually includes a rally pin and patch to wear on caps or vests, some meal tickets, a schedule, door-prize tickets, a local map, plus information about the rally and the area.

Door prizes will be motorcycle-related items such as gloves, boots, radar detectors, radios, helmets, leather jackets, rain suits, T-shirts, and virtually everything you can name. At major rallies, the grand prize may be a European tour or a new motorcycle.

During the day you'll be busy with mini-tours, seminars, poker runs, and more. Seminars are conducted by industry experts about such subjects as tires, batteries, apparel, and general touring topics. A poker run is a scenic ride with frequent stops. Participants draw a card at each stop, and by the end of the ride assemble a poker hand. Those with the best hands win prizes, but there are often lesser prizes for worst hand, most cards of one suit, and other variations.

Mini-tours are day trips that may be guided by a rally representative, or self guided. They take you to local spots of interest such as waterfalls, historic sites, restaurants, crafts areas, scenic roads, etc. Guided tours will be group rides, and will tend to follow a

In just a few seasons of riding and touring a rider can assemble a nice little collection of pins and patches.

Rallies are a good place at which to buy items for yourself and your bike. Here is a small portion of Tour Expo at Americade 1998.

The light show is very popular at rallies, and gives riders a chance to show off their rigs. Be sure to enter your machine in the bike judging, too.

schedule, but self-guided tours provide enough information for you to travel at your leisure.

A banquet or dinner may be served as part of the rally package. Larger rallies may offer theme meals such as a chuckwagon dinner, barbecue, or shrimp roast, depending upon geographic location. Americade offers dinners on large cruise boats that provide a scenic view of the area.

In the evening a dresser rally might provide a light show. Many riders like to deck their bikes out with decorative lighting, and an evening light show gives them the chance to ride slowly past the crowd in the parking lot, showing off their stuff.

Field events are tests of skill that will be held in a parking lot, and they are really enjoyable. They're all low-speed, nonthreatening events.

The *slow race* is just what it sounds like. Riders line up behind a line, and the object is to be the *last* rider to cross another line a few dozen feet away. You must stay in motion, and anyone who touches a foot down is disqualified. Here's a tip: you'll do better in the slow race if you simultaneously slip the clutch and drag the rear brake. Not recommended for those with marginal clutches.

The *wiener bite* is an entertaining event. A hot dog is suspended by a string, and the end dipped in mustard. Contestants, be they rider or co-rider, must ride up beneath it and take a bite out of it without stopping. Any miscalculation results in a big swatch of yellow mustard on their face, which is great fun for the crowd.

Riders may ride up to a clothesline strung overhead to which numerous clothes pins have been clipped. Their co-riders will have to pluck as many of them off as possible, without the rider setting a foot down. They then proceed to a second clothesline where the co-rider tries to put the clothes pins *back* on the line.

At a rally you're likely to meet people with interests similar to your own. It is heartening that these two hard-core riders can together indulge themselves in their special passion for riding colorful, spring-loaded plastic animals.

Bring your children to the rallies! Obviously, young Kyle here is being brought up right.

In addition to these types of rallies, there are also specialty events for sidecar owners, campers, or others with special interests. In the *blind sidecar race,* the rider is blindfolded while his passenger talks him through a course laid out with a series of cones. The couple that finishes in the shortest time, having knocked over the fewest cones, wins. My advice is definitely to attend a rally when the opportunity presents itself. They're really a great deal of fun and a good way to meet new friends!

A poker run is an excuse to take a nice ride. At each stop, riders draw a card.

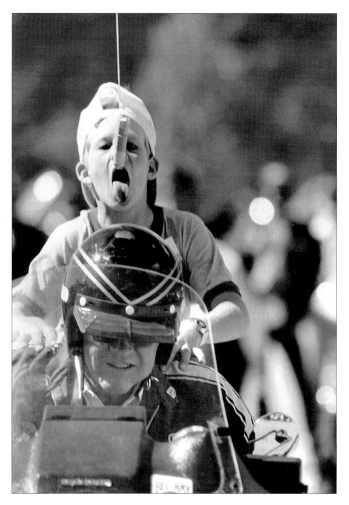

The wiener bite is an entertaining field event.

Clubs

Motorcycling is essentially a social activity, which is why rallies have become so popular. Many riders have joined clubs to add to their riding enjoyment, to learn more about their sport, and to meet others to ride with. Clubs are usually associated with a specialty, just as some rallies are. There are clubs for the riders of various marques and models, women, Christian riders, political groups, touring riders, sport riders, and any way, shape, or form in which riders can be specialized.

Just as with rallies, riders join clubs for many different reasons. Clubs often sponsor rallies, and may adopt a charitable organization such as a home for disadvantaged youngsters or a campaign to eradicate disease. Often the club is conscious of motorcycling's image and attempts to improve it by conducting toy runs and other charitable activities.

13
Organized Tours

LEAVE THE PLANNING TO THEM

Motorcyclists are independent sorts, but under certain circumstances we like to join forces to save time or take advantage of the knowledge of others. Some companies offer organized motorcycle tours that feature a prearranged route, accommodations, some meals, and air transport. The tour company can also help you arrange for a bike to buy or rent in certain far-away locations, and facilitate arrangements for insurance and registration. If you wish to take your own bike out of the country, the company may be able to make similar arrangements ahead of time and take care of the paperwork so that you can ride off with a minimum of hassle.

Today, organized tours are available to many locations including Europe, Australia, Russia, China, South America, and of course various areas of the United States and Canada. Whitehorse Press, which publishes this book, also offers one called *Motorcycle*

Touring: An International Directory that is a compendium of tours offered in various locales around the world. It includes schedules, prices, trip itineraries and other information characterizing the many organized motorcycle tours available. It also lists places where you can rent a motorcycle for traveling on your own. If you simply *must* have your own motorcycle along on your trip, the book also offers helpful information on shipping your motorcycle. For more information, contact Whitehorse Press at the address listed in the front of this book.

Why an Organized Tour?

You could take an organized motorcycle tour for any of the reasons detailed above, but friends are really what such tours are about. Many American riders fantasize, for example, of touring the Alps but have no idea of how to arrange such a trip. But even if they knew how to ship their bike (or arrange for one there), there are still endless details about arranging accommodations, dealing with border crossings, currencies, insurance, languages, visas and the *carne du passage,* that can become mind boggling. Most of us get two, three, or perhaps four weeks of vacation per year, and that's just not enough time to make the necessary arrangements for such an adventure. Dream tours such as these are best when shared with others with similar interests, plus there's safety in numbers. It's much more fun seeing Salzburg, Venice, or Guanajuato with others, especially if you have a flat tire or run out of gas somewhere on the road.

Sometimes, a turn-key organized tour just makes everything so simple that it's the only way to go. (Photo by Linda Broadstreet of Freedom Tours, Longmont, Colorado)

How Tours Work

Organized tours offer many advantages. Once all the arrangements have been made, you could board an airliner with a group of 10 to perhaps 40 other riders in your group and have a chance to get acquainted in the air. You'll step off the plane with just your helmet and enough gear to fit into two saddlebags and little more.

Your group will be picked up by a bus and taken to your hotel to freshen up, or to rest if it's been a transoceanic flight. There will likely be a reception to allow everyone to get better acquainted, and so that the tour director can convey some information about the specific details of the tour.

Here is where the tour director can become invaluable. Assuming you're in a foreign country, the director can help you understand the traffic regulations, local hazards, currency, some handy phrases in the local language, what to see, where to get gas, how to use gas coupons (if required), where to cash traveler's checks, how to know when the exchange rate you're being quoted is too unfavorable, how much to tip, and where the restrooms are likely to be cleanest—need I go on? With enough homework and preparation, you could have learned many of these general facts for yourself, but even so, you would not have discovered some of the specifics unless you knew someone who had been over these roads recently.

Many tours also utilize a luggage van, which is a real plus. Sure, your motorcycle will likely have saddlebags but, as anyone who tours knows, your luggage is always stuffed to the gills when you leave. Where do you put the gifts and souvenirs you pick up along the way? Also, in European hotels, a sport coat or suit and tie is considered appropriate dinner wear for men, with a dress for the ladies. You won't be excluded with less formal attire but may feel out of place. How can you carry the necessary clothing and still have room on your motorcycle for the necessities? Ah, the luggage van!

When I travel in Europe with my wife, we have two plans of action depending upon whether or not we're traveling with a tour. Alone, everything has to be kept on the bike with the camera equipment in the tank bag, the rain gear in a duffel on the luggage rack, and all of our clothing (including evening attire) in the saddlebags. We arrange to box and ship all souvenirs at the time of purchase, which is expensive but necessary.

I generally stay in my tent or budget motels when I travel. However, I really enjoyed staying at The Vintage (in Winter Park, Colorado) while riding with this group on BMW's "Best Test in the West" tour.

On an organized tour we carry an extra bag that goes in the luggage van with our extra clothing. Now our saddlebags are virtually empty so that we can stuff into them what we buy during the day. The gifts are then transfered to our growing bag in the luggage van each evening. We may have to pay customs duties on them when we return home, but we save the shipping costs.

When we stop to hike or eat, we can lock our rain gear and tank bag in the saddlebags for added security. One thing to keep in mind is that, under the increasing burden of those purchases, luggage vans can (and do) break down; it happened to me on one tour. As a result, we make it a practice always to carry our toiletries and a change of clothing and underwear with us on the bike—just in case.

Another advantage of tours is that the price usually includes all accommodations, most dinners, and all breakfasts. All you really need to buy is lunches, a few dinners, and gas. Thus, if you're on a budget you have a better handle on the complete cost of your tour from the beginning. If you find yourself running short of funds, well, less elaborate dinners and lunches are in order. Should you become really short, the tour guide can help you find a financial institution that can advance you funds on your credit card.

Tour Types

While many types of tours exist, I've found there are two basic types. One I call the guided tour, and the other the self-guided tour.

On the guided tour, members all leave the hotel at the same time each morning, ride as a group, eat lunch together and see the same things. The guide is always with them to order meals, help with the language, fix any mechanical problems, and show them the sights.

An organized tour provides you with a route and hotels that have been checked out, a guide, and other people with whom you can enjoy the ride.

The downside of guided tours is not being able to go off on your own. When riding in the group, you can't just pull off the road to take photos when you wish, try out that intriguing restaurant you spotted on a side street, take a different route for a few days, or visit a cousin you've never met who lives a day's ride off the route. In some cases, guided tours have a stable of motorcycles which they rent to customers, and the close supervision is a further means of safeguarding both the customers and the fleet. Sometimes, insurance considerations dictate that riders be under supervision at all times.

On the self-guided tour, you may rent the motorcycle from a dealer or manufacturer, rather than from the tour operator. Usually, a specific mileage amount will be included in the rental price that will be adequate for the tour; if you exceed that amount, you'll have to pay an additional per-mile charge. In this situation, the tour company is more likely to allow you to wander at will, and it is this type of tour I recommend.

Several weeks before you depart for your tour, you will be sent a detailed itinerary and set of maps with which you can plan your tour. Not only can you go off as you wish to ride and photograph, but, if you notify the tour guide ahead of time, you can even deviate from the route for several days and rejoin the group down the road. Because the tour company has to pay for rooms months in advance, don't expect any kind of reimbursement for rooms or meals not used.

If you say you're too timid for this type of tour—not to worry. If you want a little more security, you can have it both ways on the self-guided tour. Each night at dinner, the tour leader will announce the following day's route, plus alternates. If you'd rather, you're welcome to ride along with the tour leader for a guided, supervised tour. Of course on either type of tour, the tour leader will help if you have a mechanical problem, banking need, or whatever.

The final advantage of any organized tour can be explained by relating an experience I witnessed on a self-guided tour of Great Britain in 1986. One rider in our group, Ron, a man traveling solo, had a string of bad luck. One morning he left the parking lot of a local attraction, dutifully traveling on the left side of the road, when he encountered a family of Europeans (who had just pulled out of the hotel lot) traveling on the wrong side of the road. Ron took to the hedges, but suffered nothing more serious than a few stitches in his lip. The tour leader was able to help him file the proper papers to take advantage of Britain's free medical treatment, and minor damage to the bike was quickly set right.

Just days later, our friend was out traveling solo on the Island of Mull when he woke up in the hospital. He never did figure out what happened; the bike went down for an undetermined reason and Ron wound up with a concussion and broken arm. The tour leader rented a flatbed truck and drove 200 miles round trip to retrieve Ron and his BMW. The bike was fixable but Ron wasn't—at least in time to complete the tour. The tour leader put the bike on a train and shipped it back to the rental company, while Ron was able to complete the tour as a passenger in the luggage van. Had this occurred while he was traveling on his own without a tour, Ron's dream vacation would have been ruined. Instead, he was able to complete the route, though he was subject to much kidding and related abuse from the new friends he had made on the tour.

This story brings us back full circle. Organized tours are about friends. Motorcycling is a social activity. I know of several people who have traveled through dozens of countries alone or as a couple and had a perfectly wonderful time; my wife and I have done the same. But we find, even though we're best friends, that we prefer traveling with at least one other couple. So why not 10 or 20 others? In either case, it's all fun.

14

Foreign Travel

GOING EXOTIC

I appreciate the fact that this book will be read primarily by riders in the United States and Canada, and that we can spend a lifetime touring the North American continent without seeing all there is to see. But there's an incredibly large world out there to see beyond our experience, and many reasons for wanting to see it. My own desire to visit Europe was awakened when I was in my twenties and began reading the work of Ernest Hemingway. His romantic treatment of such places as Paris, Pamplona, Spain and the mountains of northern Italy called to me and I longed to taste a world that included grappa, chianti, cappuccino and black bread. Finally, I was able to travel in Europe on a bus tour in 1977, but every trip since then has been by motorcycle.

One option in foreign motorcycle travel, the easy one, is to take an organized tour as I described in Chapter 13. The tour company can arrange a motorcycle for you, an itinerary, accommodations, and can guide you through that part of the world. Tours will be more expensive than going on your own, but they're well worth the money for the person who doesn't have the time or knowhow to make the arrangements himself.

I recommend travelling by motorcycle in foreign countries for several reasons. Fuel tends to be more expensive overseas, so a bike's exceptional fuel mileage will save you money. Many urban areas are quite crowded, and a motorcycle can be ridden or parked there more easily. Motorcycling is widely accepted in Europe, more so than in the States, which means that riders will be welcomed wherever they go. Finally, it's best to arrive overseas with tried and tested riding gear, but in Europe the selection of motorcycle wear is so extensive that you may wish to purchase some new leathers when you arrive.

No one chapter of a book can possibly tell you all you need to know about foreign travel, but I'll give you a few basics here.

The Motorcycle

You can arrange for a motorcycle to use in a foreign land in several ways. Let's explore the pros and cons of each.

Ship Your Own

In most situations, the best motorcycle to bring on your tour is your own. It's set up for you, you're familiar with its quirks, strengths, and weaknesses, and if something goes wrong with it you're more likely to know how to fix it. On the other hand, perhaps some of those weaknesses you know about it might preclude taking your own bike.

The Alps offer a motorcyclist's paradise of jagged mountains, twisting roads, breath-taking scenery and a parade of romantic, picturesque villages.

One of the world's most challenging and invigorating rides is the Stelvio Pass, where the Alpen road is strung on the mountain like a necklace.

To bring your own bike, your best sources of information are the American tour companies that currently arrange for their customers to bring their own bikes overseas. To find these companies check *Motorcycle Touring: An International Directory,* a book published by Whitehorse Press (see the address in front of this book). The tour companies can tell you what is involved in bringing a machine to the area of your choice, and what paperwork is necessary. Of course, they're in the business of selling tours rather than dispensing free information, so you may feel you're imposing on them if you put them to the bother. However, they may also be in the business of bringing motorcycles overseas for their tours, and would welcome the opportunity to make the arrangements for you, even if you don't take the tour.

By all means contact one or more of these tour companies, as the rules and regulations concerning bringing in motorcycles are different for every country, and change constantly. At the very least you'll need overseas insurance, which is verified by a "green card," and proper registration papers. Your United States or Canadian driver's license should be adequate virtually anywhere, and the Automobile Club of America (AAA) issues an international drivers license—you do not have to be a member of AAA to obtain one.

In addition, several independent companies can help you ship your motorcycle. Depending upon your budget and schedule, air and surface shipment are both possible. Many people prefer air shipment, as surface transport can take some weeks; shipping by air, the bike flies with you.

Consider brand when renting. If you're going to Europe, especially Germany, BMWs are so plentiful that it is relatively easy to buy or rent a late-model machine.

Japanese bikes cost more in Europe than they do in the States, and Harley-Davidsons are extremely expensive, so shipping your own bike may be a more viable option than attempting to buy or rent those brands.

Buying

Another possibility is to buy a motorcycle overseas, then ship it back home with you. In the past, BMW offered a European delivery program, but it has been discontinued. Harley-Davidson currently offers such programs for its Harley Owners Group (HOG club) members.

It may be possible to make similar arrangements with Ducati and Moto Guzzi, which manufacture U.S.-specification bikes in Italy. And of course, Triumph may allow you to pick up a new machine from its facility in Hinckley, Leicestershire, England. Also, since they're all manufactured elsewhere, you won't find many U.S.-spec Japanese bikes in Europe. The starting point for any of these projects is to first contact your local dealer.

Because of stringent Environmental Protection Agency (EPA) rules, it is virtually impossible to bring a motor vehicle into the United States for personal use unless it meets the EPA's requirements regarding emissions and noise, and has equipment such as lights, horn, and MPH speedometer. Thus, if you wish to bring a bike back with you, it must be a U.S.-spec export model that meets all these requirements and has the appropriate paperwork. Yes, I have heard of "gray-market" Euro-spec vehicles brought in privately that don't meet these regulations, but this practice is questionable. Sure, it may work, but I have also heard of machines being sent to the crusher when it didn't.

Finally, there was a very entertaining story in *Cycle* magazine years ago about a U.S. rider who rode a 100cc two-stroke machine all through the States, then took it to Canada where it broke down. Because the bike was too expensive to fix, and shipping would cost more than it was worth, the owner wound up abandoning the bike in the Great White North. Likewise, I strongly recommend against planning to ship your own bike overseas and eventually selling or abandoning it there. National laws vary greatly, and it may be impossible to leave a country unless your motorcycle leaves with you. Mexico takes great care to ensure that you don't leave your vehicle behind. Research this issue meticulously before trying it.

Despite the wonderful restaurants on the continent, be sure to take the time during a European tour to pack a picnic lunch.

A passport, map, cup of cappuccino and some coins— it's all part of a European motorcycle tour. This shot was taken during a trip with Beach's Motorcycle Adventures, Ltd., of Grand Island, New York.

Rentals

It's very possible to rent a motorcycle overseas, and once again your best source of information is a motorcycle tour company or *Motorcycle Touring: An International Directory*. Renting is expensive, but recommended for shorter tours because it costs so much to ship your own machine. For longer tours, as rental costs mount, at some point it becomes less expensive to ship your own motorcycle, even considering the cost of wear and tear. Make a detailed analysis of the costs of both types of use. Don't forget to include insurance costs, and consider any additional mileage charges from the rental company. If it's a wash either way, you're probably better off with your own bike unless it's in marginal condition. My educated guess is that on trips of two months or shorter, renting will be less expensive than shipping your bike. For trips longer than two months, shipping your own bike becomes an increasingly viable way to go.

Another consideration is that if you crash your own bike, you're faced with transporting it to where it can be repaired, and waiting for it. Crash a rental bike and you may forfeit an additional deductible, but the upside is convenience. Depending upon your agreement, you may be able to pick up another bike on which to continue your trip.

Buy-Backs

On the buy-back program you arrange to buy a motorcycle from a dealer, then he buys it back from you at the end of the ride for a price that has been agreed upon in advance. The caveat for anyone involved in a rental or buy-back situation is that the agreement is only as good as the honesty of the company with which you're dealing.

There will likely be a stipulation that the bike be in good condition and undamaged when it is returned. The unscrupulous could allege that you had caused some mysterious internal malady, which means they would not repurchase the bike for the agreed-upon price, but one much lower. How effectively could you disagree or negotiate with them in a country with a language and legal system you don't understand? How effectively could you bargain, holding a non-refundable plane ticket for 10:00 the next morning? Once again, it's safer to deal through a tour company who has knowledge and experience with firms supplying motorcycles.

The Motorcycle

The best bike for your trip depends to a great extent upon the trip you plan to take. Review Chapter 2 on choosing your motorcycle. If you're going to spend your time primarily in the Alps, consider a sporting or sport-touring model. For the flat-land areas of Spain and much of the rest of Europe, more upright touring or sport-touring models are fine. For rugged terrain such as Australia, Africa, or South America, adventure tourers such as the BMW GS models, Triumph Tiger and various Japanese dual-sports were designed for this type of travel.

For more information, check the Whitehorse Press catalog and your book store for information on travel in your selected area. And have a wonderful trip!

About the Author

Born at a very young age in Three Rivers, Michigan, Bill Stermer was blessed with a father who bought his son a motor scooter before the lad was even old enough to ride it legally. But ride it he did, and once out of jail and of legal age, Bill advanced rapidly through a progression of two-wheeled machines of varying sizes and styles, from 125 to 1000cc.

Upon graduation from Western Michigan University, Bill began teaching English in a rural Michigan high school and pursued both writing and photography as hobbies. In 1977, he took a ride down the Blue Ridge Parkway on his Honda CB550; his article about that trip led to a job offer from *Cycle* magazine in California. Can you say, "dream job"?

After a couple years with *Cycle,* during which time he tested touring products and rode in Europe, Canada, Mexico and all over the United States, Bill became a freelance writer so he could pursue additional interests. In 1982 he wrote two books: *On the Perimeter* was the

as-told-to autobiography of Hazel Kolb, the "Motorcycling Grandma," and *Motorcycle Touring,* a precursor to the book you're reading now.

During the 1980s, Bill Stermer wrote feature articles and tested motorcycles for many American motorcycle magazines including *American Motorcyclist, Cycle, Cycle World, Motorcyclist, Rider, Road Rider* (now *Motorcycle Consumer News*), and many others. He also served as editor of *Motorcycle Industry,* a major trade magazine.

Bill completed the first edition of this book in 1991, and while writing it joined the staff of *Rider* magazine as editorial director. After four years there he left to continue free-lance writing. He has earned his BMW 100,000 Mile Award, currently owns a BMW R100RS and an R75/6, and plans to fill his workshop with vintage bikes. He reports he is "blissfully married" to Margery, his wife since 1982, and they are blessed with two children, Paul and Julia.

Index